TRIAL
FILMS
on Trial

TRIAL FILMS

on Trial

Law,
Justice, and
Popular Culture

Edited by
Austin Sarat,
Jessica Silbey, and
Martha Merrill Umphrey

THE UNIVERSITY OF ALABAMA PRESS
Tuscaloosa

The University of Alabama Press
Tuscaloosa, Alabama 35487-0380
uapress.ua.edu

Typeface: Caslon

Cover image: David Nees
Cover design: David Nees

Chapter 1, "Law and the Order of Popular Culture," by Carol J. Clover, is
reprinted from *Law in the Domain of Culture*, edited by Austin Sarat and
Thomas Kearns (Ann Arbor: University of Michigan Press, 1998).
© University of Michigan Press. Reprinted with permission.

Library of Congress Cataloging-in-Publication Data

Names: Sarat, Austin, editor. | Silbey, Jessica, editor. |
Umphrey, Martha Merrill, editor.
Title: Trial films on trial : law, justice, and popular culture / edited by
Austin Sarat, Jessica Silbey, and Martha Merrill Umphrey.
Description: Tuscaloosa : The University of Alabama Press, 2019. | Includes
bibliographical references and index.
Identifiers: LCCN 2018038996| ISBN 9780817320263 (cloth) |
ISBN 9780817359294 (pbk.) | ISBN 9780817392574 (ebook)
Subjects: LCSH: Trials in motion pictures. | Justice, Administration of,
in motion pictures.
Classification: LCC PN1995.9.T75 T75 2019 | DDC 791.43/6554—dc23
LC record available at https://lccn.loc.gov/2018038996

Dedication
To Ben, with pride and joy (A. S.)

To Charlotte and Harper (J. S.)

For Theo and Dash (M. M. U.)

Contents

Acknowledgments   ix

Introduction: The Pleasures and Possibilities of Trial Films
Austin Sarat, Jessica Silbey, and Martha Merrill Umphrey   1

1. Law and the Order of Popular Culture
   Carol J. Clover   17

2. Knowing It When We See It: Realism and Melodrama in American Film
   Since *The Birth of a Nation*
   Ticien Marie Sassoubre   39

3. Reasonable Doubts, Unspoken Fears: Reassessing the Trial Film's
   "Heroic Age"
   Barry Langford   81

4. Disorder in Court: Representations of Resistance to Law in Trial
   Film Dramas
   Norman W. Spaulding   111

5. "I Am Here. I Was There.": Haunted Testimony in *The Memory of Justice*
   and *The Specialist*
   Katie Model   140

6. The Appearance of Truth: Juridical Reception and Photographic Evidence
   in *Standard Operating Procedure*
   Jennifer Petersen   177

Works Cited   203

Contributors   217

Index   219

Acknowledgments

This book is the product of a conference that was held at Amherst College on November 14–15, 2014. We are grateful to the college for generous financial support and to Megan Estes for her superb work in organizing that conference.

TRIAL
FILMS
on Trial

Introduction

The Pleasures and Possibilities of Trial Films

Austin Sarat
Jessica Silbey
Martha Merrill Umphrey

In the influential 1998 essay "Law and the Order of Popular Culture," film scholar Carol Clover argues that the Anglo-American jury trial, with its adversarial form and juror orientation, constitutes a formative template for American film.[1] "So fundamental is the adversarial jury trial in the American imaginary," she writes, "that, as a ghost matrix with a life of its own above and beyond its source, it turns up in and structures even the sheerest forms of play."[2] The trial form, she asserts, has a "fantastic generativity," so much so "that the plot structures and narrative procedures (even certain visual procedures, in film and television) of a broad stripe of American popular culture are derived from the structure and procedures of the Anglo-American trial."[3] As Clover succinctly puts it, trials and films "rhyme."[4] "Real-life trials become movies . . . as easily as they do in the Anglo-American world both," she suggests, "because trials are already movielike to begin with and movies are already trial-like to begin with."[5]

In this volume, our contributors take up Clover's central insight that trials and films mutually imbricate on multiple levels, exploring connections on the level of content, in stories revolving around some sort of legal conflict; of form, in narrative structures that generate meaning through the proffering of argument and evidence; and of epistemology, in works asking their audiences to struggle with the problematics of testimony, credibility, and verifiability.[6] These scholars bring fresh eyes and a rich engagement with contemporary scholarship[7] to bear on Clover's provocative and far-reaching analysis; and in doing so, they also challenge and exceed it, looking beyond the stock repertoire of Hollywood films and complicating her schematic understanding of the trial as a legal form.

Constitutive Elements of the Trial Film

Why are trials compelling to filmmakers? One might begin to answer that question with a prior one: Why are trials a subject of public fascination as

a general matter?[8] Centrally, trials are by their very nature public performances that bring past events to life in the courtroom.[9] The adversarial trial
offers a particularly dramatic frame for the revelation of human frailty and
wrongdoing, distilling the messiness of human conflict into a two-sided
agonistic contest governed by quite specific legal constraints. The structure of trials generates competing stories and legal performances by attorneys and witnesses intended to capture and persuade their audiences.
Within the Anglo-American trial tradition, of course, the trial's most significant audience is the jury, which carries the burden of law's demand for
judgment. The jury trial has often been cast as a pedagogical space, one in
which citizens learn both the content of law and the skills necessary for
self-governance. As Alexis de Tocqueville remarked over 150 years ago, the
jury is "above all a political institution," embodying the sovereignty of the
people, and the judgments produced at trial "instill some of the habits of
the judicial mind into every citizen, . . . the very best way of preparing a
people to be free."[10]

Yet, trials compel the general public as well, drawing us in because they
offer access to the tensions and wounds of the private sphere—the trans-
gressions of social norms, the rule breakings, passions, desires, and alibis—
all framed through the camera obscura of memory and human subjectivity.
As we follow trials, we are put in the deliciously contradictory position of
the ethical peeping tom, one who can feel the thrill of subversive watching
from a sanctioned and safe position.

Of course, there are important differences between trial watching and
trial film watching, particularly on the level of form. For the sake of con-
cision and coherence, trial films edit out the tedious and confusing aspects
of trials—the delays, debates over procedure, painstakingly detailed and
repetitive testimony by expert witnesses, and so forth. Instead, trial films
concentrate on the most dramatic elements of trials: testimony and cross-
examination, courtroom strategy, surprise revelation, and uncertainty about
the truth and its relationship to justice. In doing so, they intensify spectatorial expectations about the kinds of pleasures we associate with courtroom
contest, deliberation, and judgment and, more generally, what trials can ultimately deliver. Moreover, trial film directors have formal visual strategies—
editing, flashbacks, and the like—that provide them with far more narrative
control than any lawyer could hope to obtain in a real courtroom.

And yet fundamentally, both trials and trial films engage us with the desire to see—scopophilia[11] (the pleasure from looking)—and to know, an
epistephilia generated by the truth-seeking project of the form: Who did
what? How did it happen? What was the motive? How can we be sure we
know the truth?[12] As such, films about trials (or more broadly about the

kinds of conflicts and questions trials address) capture, reiterate, and comment on the very elements that make trials themselves so compelling to the public; hence, the trial form's' "fantastic generativity" in popular culture. In doing so, they tend to transpose the position of spectator into the position of juror. As Clover suggests, "the positioning of the film audience as jury is one of the most fundamental and consistent rules of the courtroom drama."[13] Film audiences experience the immersions of a juror—the glimpse into hidden worlds, the pleasures of knitting together evidence into a story, the frisson of antagonistic performances—without the jury's ultimate responsibility to decide the outcome of a case. Moreover, we see behind the courtroom curtain, coming to know characters and context in ways prohibited to official jurors. As such, spectators watching trial films are invited to learn about and judge not only the defendant but, crucially, the law itself, its processes and ways of knowing, and ultimately its capacities for doing justice or injustice.

Positioning the audience as a jury judging both the defendant and the law, trial films deploy a set of formal conventions (opening statements, profferings of evidence, cross-examinations, verdicts) and epistemological questions (the nature of evidence, its meaning and reliability) that constitute a recognizable genre. Consider, for instance, the exemplary 1959 Otto Preminger trial film, *Anatomy of a Murder*.[14] As the story opens, we watch attorney Paul Biegler return to his office from an extended fishing trip, to be greeted by a very drunk soon-to-be-cocounsel Parnell McCarthy. Biegler, who has neglected his practice to the point that he cannot pay his secretary, Maeda, is asked by Laura Manion to defend her unpleasant and often violent husband, Frank, from murder charges. Frank has been locked up for killing Barney Quill, a bar owner who allegedly raped Laura. Biegler settles on a defense of insanity that requires the jury to believe Frank dissociated, killing Quill because of an irresistible impulse. The defense is risky partly because we as spectators are led to think Frank may be simply violent rather than insane and partly because it is an uncommon, broad way to conceive of legal insanity (compared with the more widespread, narrower inquiry into whether a defendant has the capacity to know and understand the consequences of his acts). Biegler, Frank, and his defense test our conceptions of fairness and justice: How persuaded are we by the defense? Can Biegler be the attorney-hero Frank needs? Should he be?

Much of the film's action takes place in the courtroom, and the film prominently features the jurors and large public audience listening and reacting to the attorneys as they present salacious evidence about the rape allegations, aggressively cross-examine witnesses, and posture for the judge, jury, and crowd (in Biegler's case, as "humble country lawyer" in spite of his

evident skill). As spectators taking in evidence in order to come to judgments about both Frank and the law, we often literally inhabit the physical
place of the jury or see jurors as they take in the proceedings. The oscillating trial narrative supporting and undermining the prosecution and defense stories (Clover's X-not-X narrative structure) buffets us between belief and deep suspicion: unnervingly, we cannot determine whether or not
witnesses are lying about whether or not a rape even occurred.[15] Even so,
because we follow Biegler's character outside the courtroom, the film positions us to identify with him inside, applaud his masterful handling of witnesses, and feel gratified by his ultimate (and inevitable) legal victory. By
marshaling convincing evidence of the rape at the last minute, he seems to
vindicate the legal process. And yet, we also see beyond the courtroom, being informed about Laura's propensity to drink and seduce any man around
her and Biegler's near-unethical pretrial coaching of Frank. From that point
of view, we are situated to ask: Can the formal structures and processes of
law account for and do justice in such a compromised scenario, in which no
one is fully innocent, no one fundamentally heroic? What is a good attorney, and what comprises a just verdict, under such circumstances?

 Anatomy of a Murder highlights the juror orientation, trial-like structure,
and X-not-X storylines Clover identifies as indicative of the genre precisely
because it is built around a trial. Yet other films, not so overtly dependent
on courtroom scenes, also display notable affinities with these processes and
problematics.[16] In some cases, those affinities are made visible through the
lens of particular generic conventions invested in the bifurcated logic of the
adversarial trial. In this volume, for example, Ticien Marie Sassoubre advances the argument that literary melodrama, deeply invested in the opposition of good and evil, laid the groundwork for the trial-like structure of
nontrial oriented films such as *The Birth of a Nation*.[17]

Other trial-like films emphasize problems of proof and judgment. A
number of film scholars have suggested that documentary films in particular raise trial-like epistemological questions precisely because they pur-
port to have an indexical relation to truth and reality. As Jane Gaines and
Michael Renov argue, "if the central aspect of documentary is resemblance,
the defining feature of it has been the exceptionality of its referentiality. . . .
There is thought to be a 'special indexical bond' between the photographic
image and the object in the real world to which the image refers."[18] Moreover, as Bill Nichols suggests, both trials and documentaries "create a belief
that through observing we—we the jurors, we the viewers, we the public—
can join the ranks of those who know, but simultaneously they risk engen-
dering a fraught anxiety about whether we can know at all."[19] This tension
comes into play particularly in what Nichols calls "reflexive" documenta-

ries that make the filmmaking process apparent.[20] Errol Morris's *The Thin Blue Line*[21] is an example of such a documentary, trial-like in its narrative form and focus on problems of truth production. The 1998 film effectively relitigates the capital trial of Randall Dale Adams for the murder of a Dallas police officer but in highly stylized ways that at every turn raise doubt not only about the credibility of witnesses but the very boundary between fiction and documentary film. The film begins with Adams's voice, telling the story of the night of the murder. It cuts quickly to shots of forensic evidence; then to a reenactment of his interrogation, filmed in blue light. From that point forward, the defendant in the film's retrial is not Adams but the much younger and (Morris implies) likely guilty David Harris and, more pointedly, the police who let him get away.[22] The film examines the cast of characters, impugning their motives, their actions, and their testimony; but it does so by calling attention to the constructed nature of evidence. The film discredits witness testimony by using reenactments that imagine scenes, repetitions that shift subtly in their explanatory value, and splices from fiction films and TV shows to imply that some witnesses lived in a world more fiction than fact. Morris's filmic style highlights the gap between our desire to know and our capacity to attain the truth, even as it effectively advocates for Adams's exoneration.[23]

Fundamentally, whether fiction or documentary, trial films are ideologically double voiced. On the one hand, either overtly or implicitly, they ask us to understand certain critical elements required for doing justice under liberal legal regimes. In this regard, *12 Angry Men* is exemplary. In it Juror 8 (Henry Fonda) leverages the legal requirement for a unanimous verdict into a veritable law school class on constitutional jurisprudence and procedures. What is at the root of the rule of law? An absence of prejudice and prejudgment (Juror 8 to Juror 3: "You're a sadist!"). What is required for a not guilty verdict? Not certainty but reasonable doubt ("it's possible" that the defendant is innocent). What is a principled jury's job? To think with discernment and to deliberate, question presuppositions, and focus on the evidence ("I just want to talk. . . . Let's go over it again."). What should one do with the evidence? Cross-examine it to test its probity ("Everybody sounded positive—too positive. . . . Supposing the witnesses were wrong?"). Films that are less overtly pedagogical operate on similar principles, pointing to the value of the rule of law and the pursuit of truth.

On the other hand, as Barry Langford and Norman Spaulding suggest, trial films also reveal the frailties and vulnerabilities of liberal legality, always threatening to undermine efforts to do justice. Beyond the general problem of epistemological uncertainty, sometimes human passion or prejudice corrupts law.[24] At other times, its investment in fairness and proceduralism threatens to paralyze its capacity to judge and punish.[25] Jurors may be overwhelmed by false but compelling stories, witness performances, and types of evidence.[26] In some films, the epistemological and hermeneutic space of the trial is contaminated by the past or outside events, to the point that judgment of the defendant is transmuted into judgment of a people or time or culture.[27]

Ultimately, the double voicedness of the trial film never fully delegitimizes liberal legality. It is certainly the case, as some of our contributors remind us, that trial films can be recontextualized and our identification with a given film's imagined juror disrupted.[28] We no longer, as a matter of spectatorial expectation, align ourselves with the white South in *The Birth of a Nation*. Yet, assuming a shared vision of justice as between filmmaker and audience, if the trial film succeeds in situating us as its imagined jurors, the pleasures of judging law lead not to rejection but to recuperation. Perhaps, precisely because we as spectator-jurors occupy a vantage point that allows us to witness its vulnerabilities, liberal legality is rendered approachable rather than distanced, embodied rather than abstract, and hence ultimately democratic rather than authoritarian. Justice, if not fully visible or easily achieved, is always on the near horizon.

The Chapters

The chapters in this volume both take up and challenge Clover's claims about trial films, raising questions about the aesthetic and ideological work they do in ways that are attentive to filmic form, historical context, and epistemological complexity. We begin with Clover's original essay, in which (as we have noted) she analyzes the deep resonance between trial and filmic structures. In it, she argues that the Anglo-American trial's characteristic adversarial structure and its emphasis on the oral presentation of evidence to juries generate a distinctive, "courtroom-drama-producing culture," writing that "the plot structures and narrative procedures . . . of a broad stripe of American culture are derived from the structure and procedures of the Anglo-American trial; that this structure and these procedures are so deeply embedded in our narrative tradition that they shape even plots that never step into the courtroom; and that such trial-derived forms constitute the most distinctive share of Anglo-American entertainment."[29]

In the Anglo-American jury trial, Clover notes, restrictive rules of evidence combine with an adversarial format to produce an unsettled epistemological landscape, one in which jurors are pulled rhythmically back and forth between prosecution and defense (who engage in "anxious plot-making and unmaking"[30]) and that can generate not a stable, platonic truth but only a "truth of exhausted possibilities."[31] One can find that same structure and landscape, Clover argues, in three key elements of most American films: their "relentless juror orientation," which situates film spectators as judges of evidence and argument; the trial-like tripartite structuring of films (opening arguments, presentation of evidence, closing arguments); and, out of that structure, the generation of stories that mirror the positions of prosecution and defense (guilty/not guilty or X-not-X).[32] To forward that claim, Clover offers a subtle and compelling reading of one film, *Basic Instinct*, demonstrating the ways in which even a film with no trace of a trial is trial-like, and more broadly that American film is ultimately "a shadow form of the Anglo-American trial."[33]

Our contributors use this claim, that trials and films "rhyme," as a springboard for wide-ranging analyses of the trial film, broadly defined. Ticien Marie Sassoubre explores the relationship between filmic form and meaning, taking up the relationship between film and literary genre in ways that align with Clover's general assertions. In "Knowing It When We See It: Realism and Melodrama in American Film Since *The Birth of a Nation*," Sassoubre tackles Clover's largest claim that the trial so deeply informs the American imagination that it drives the narrative structure of Anglo-American film generally, focusing in particular on D. W. Griffith's *The Birth of a Nation*. She argues that the movie is not only trial-like but it developed and made classic many of the trial-like conventions of twentieth-century cinema, which have lasted because they mirror the literary conventions of realism and melodrama. Suggesting that nineteenth-century literature relied both on "descriptive realism and social melodrama," Sassoubre takes us through a detailed history of both generic forms before moving into the cinematic. Realism in the novel made use of an omniscient narrative to create scenes carefully crafted from observation and a mutual understanding with the reader of what was believable. Cinematic realism, as such, became the successor to this narrative structure, using the camera as an invisible observer to scenes that apparently preexisted it. Melodrama emerges out of realism as a stylistic solution to the general problem that realism, left to its own devices, is frustratingly banal. In creating stark parallels and contrasts between good and bad, right and wrong, innocent and guilty, melodrama heightens and disappoints audience expectations, creating a stylistic rhythm that helps us to ascribe meaning to the otherwise uninteresting. Sassoubre sees this adversarial swing between extremes as also characteristic of the trial, where the argumentation of opposites necessarily drives us toward a narrow understanding of the truth.

The melding of these with the mechanistic indexicality of the camera resulted in the filmic realism of *Birth*, which Griffith claimed to be historical evidence while forwarding "a virulently racist, ideological argument." This work, Sassoubre writes, is an alternate trial of the antislavery north, showing black people who take advantage of the north's naïveté to advance their own imperialistic desires and honest southerners whose families and ways of life hang in the balance of postwar Reconstruction. The classic melodrama of the white-clad woman tied to the railroad tracks is reimagined in the climactic attempted rape of a young white woman by a black man, and later serves to further the trial-film notion that justice requires the intervention of private morals when he is acquitted by an all-black jury. For Sassoubre, it is melodrama that ultimately separates trial from film, if only because what each attempts to achieve in the end—justice versus satisfaction, perhaps—is not the same.

The next two chapters examine mid- to late twentieth-century trial films with a more skeptical eye, raising questions about whether, on an aesthetic and affective level, classic Hollywood trial films actually comport with easy assumptions about the ordering capacities of the courtroom. In "Reasonable Doubts, Unspoken Fears: Reassessing the Trial Film's 'Heroic Age,'" Barry Langford challenges the long-standing critical understanding of the mid- to late 1950s trial film as an idyllic portrayal of the American justice system. Pointing to classics like *12 Angry Men* and *To Kill a Mockingbird*, this narrative views the courtroom drama as highly optimistic, capturing the confidence of a postwar United States and portraying and inspiring a strong belief in legal process. While not fully overturning this view, he suggests that the onset of Cold War ideology and Hollywood's own difficulties with the government resulted in an underlying dissatisfaction that can be seen beneath a thin veneer of complacent conformity. He reads the low-key visual style of the era's films as indicative of a profound ambivalence about the promises of liberal legality.

Langford begins with *Anatomy of a Murder*, *Trial*, and *Beyond a Reasonable Doubt* to look at the trial itself. In such films, he argues, the trial process is figured in detached, uneasy ways. In *Anatomy of a Murder*, Biegler's position as the film's hero is belied by his cynically professional performance as a lawyer, charming the others in the courtroom with his folksy, down-to-earth demeanor but revealing to the audience in turn a sharply manipulative character. Judge Weaver, played by Joseph Welch, offers promise of justice, reminding viewers of the uprightness of the system that ended the abuses of the McCarthy era—but also, consequently, of the abuses themselves. Moving on to the subdued visual style of both *Anatomy* and *Trial*, critically understood as signifying a restored confidence in American jurisprudence, Langford looks to analyses of science fiction films of the same time frame. Visual restraint in science fiction projected confidence in its potential to overcome impossible threats but also suggested an uneasy unwillingness even to approach certain truths. *Beyond a Reasonable Doubt*, with its constant turns, takes this anxiety to an extreme by wresting the comfortable predictability of the trial entirely away from the viewer. Concluding with *The Young Savages, 12 Angry Men*, and *To Kill A Mockingbird*, Langford returns to the concept of the heroic trial film, pointing out that justice is achieved not only by the narrowest of margins but also entirely because of the filmic heroes' extralegal interventions. As he writes, a justice system reliant on the private virtue of such characters hardly inspires confidence.

Examining films that run into the late twentieth century in "Disorder in Court: Representations of Resistance to Law in Trial Film Dramas," Norman Spaulding is interested in the purpose and effect of disorderly behavior in courts in an era in which the jury trial has become increasingly rare. Disruption is an oft-used plot device in trial films, and yet, he argues, more often than not it serves to destabilize the adversarial X-not-X exchange that Clover sees as crucial to the climactic tension of a film narrative. Narrative disruption casts doubt on the X-not-X format itself: the outbursts, first public and then private, of Frank Galvin and the judge of *The Verdict* confirm that the judge is biased, and the exchange seen by the jury is not legitimate according to the viewers' standard of a fair trial. Disruption also generates the revelation of "epistemological remainders," information not produced in the courtroom that—as we see in *12 Angry Men*—supersedes and questions the relevance of the formal X-not-X meant to properly produce good evidence. Finally, disruption within trials—of the sort seen in *Philadelphia* when Joe Miller's outburst reveals and indicts biases against his client, Andrew Beckett—produces a kind of adversarial excess that, compounded with Beckett's final collapse following the tirade, functions as seduction: the trial itself has been overwhelmed and the audience drawn in by Beckett, so that the actual outcome takes a back seat to his death and his moral standing. This turn to sentimentality enables the seductiveness of the trial film, allowing American viewers to identify with and accept law beyond their tense, often ambivalent, approach to its institutions.

Our final two chapters analyze the epistemological dynamics and dilemmas of documentary film. In "'I Am Here. I Was There.': Haunted Testimony in *The Memory of Justice* and *The Specialist*," using two documentaries created from footage of the Nuremberg and Eichmann trials, Katie Model explores the unique contradictions embodied in documentary perpetrator testimony. "Haunted" by the past, the documentaries become temporally troubled spaces where the specific horrors of the Holocaust come into conflict with their iterability. Model compares Marcel Ophüls's *The Memory of Justice*, which juxtaposes Nuremberg footage with Nazi interviews and scenes of human rights violations committed in Algeria and Vietnam, to Eyal Sivan's *The Specialist*, put together entirely from restored footage of the Eichmann trial, in order to show the inordinately large impact that these trials have had on testimony and documentary. The trials themselves differ quite a bit in approach and intent: the prosecution at Nuremberg sought to avoid the appearance of bias by leaving out survivor testimony and using only indisputable evidence; the Eichmann court placed on trial not just the man but the atrocities he represented, putting victims at the very center of the proceedings.

The decision to film the trials themselves contributed in large part to their strange temporality. On the one hand, they became visual archives that crystallize the Holocaust into its time and place in the past; on the other, they looked with an authoritative eye toward future viewers and future trials that would tread the same paths. Ophüls makes explicit this tension by putting Nazi interviews at odds with their own testimonies, creating an agonistic space wherein their denials of wrongdoing refer backward to the trial as something finished, even as Ophüls's insertion of Nuremberg, Algeria, and Vietnam haunt the interview space with both past and future. This sort of montage reifies not only the charges against the Nazis but also accusations against the United States for having committed its own, later human rights violations. Sivan's approach grounds the viewer firmly in Eichmann's glass-delimited space, beginning with a jarring close-up of the defendant that collapses rather than opposes testimony and interview. The tension of Sivan's work is the viewers' uneasy interaction with Eichmann; the credibility we associate with documentary testimony is crushed by both his own inscrutability and our own knowledge of his guilt.

Finally, in "The Appearance of Truth: Juridical Reception and Photographic Evidence in *Standard Operating Procedure*," Jennifer Petersen makes use of a single documentary, Errol Morris's *Standard Operating Procedure*, to examine the rather uncritical approach by legal actors to photographic and filmic evidence. The documentary itself concerns the photographs that famously captured the abuses of Abu Ghraib prisoners by US soldiers. In contrast to the epistemological and pedagogical work usually done by the documentary genre, Morris uses the photographic database in conjunction with prison guard interviews and hyperreal, overtly stylized reenactments to ask unsatisfyingly open questions about the problems of photographic evidence. The photograph occupies a strange legal space as supporting evidence, becoming more substantial than its status both because it is un-cross-examinable and because it plays to our underlying assumptions about the mechanical eye of the camera. Petersen argues that the documentary form is itself reliant on visual evidence. Morris attempts an essentially impossible task in asking his audience to question its indexicality. Consequently, critics complained that he fetishizes torture and downplays the soldiers' culpability. For Petersen, these apparent misreadings of Morris's failure in turn highlight the larger legal problems raised by the underlying legal cases.

Morris attempts to make his intentions clear by foregrounding his editing and filmic techniques, providing continual reminders to viewers that someone has had a hand in creating the narrative logic before them. Yet, Petersen argues, he breaks trust with them in doing so, frustrating the expectation that the documentary camera guarantees veracity by acting as an invisible eye or observer to a preexisting scene. The detail of the reenactments works against that goal, in fact reinforcing what Morris understands (and thinks viewers *should* understand) as highly subjective. Moreover, the photographs cover up even as they expose; they show soldiers committing wrong but not the higher-ups who allowed or even gave instructions for that wrong. What this should tell us, Petersen writes, is that the bias we have toward photographic and filmic evidence is powerful—we believe what we see—and is difficult to overcome even if we are aware of it. Photographs and films must be looked at with a more critical eye in the courtroom because they are not simply captured scenes; the lawyers who present them provide narratives that give them meaning but are too easily conflated with the indexical nature of the evidence.

Taken together, these chapters explore and trouble the mimetic relationship between trials and trial films theorized by Carol Clover, specifying the ways in which films generate meaning from the trial form even as they test the values and assumptions embedded in it. Our contributors make visible the methods and modes that allow such films to situate audiences in the seats of jurors, shaping and reshaping our sense of the unstable ties between procedure and fairness, evidence and truth, and responsibility and judgment. The pleasures of the genre flow from the very process of watching, weighing, and testing characters, evidence, process, and outcome. Such films create a theater of justice and injustice; and to the extent that they interpellate us successfully as juror-spectators, they create conditions of possibility for our continuing attachment (however ambivalent) to the project of law.

Notes

1. The term *Anglo-American* refers to the American inheritance of English law.

2. Carol J. Clover, "Law and the Order of Popular Culture," in *Law in the*

Domains of Culture, edited by Austin Sarat and Thomas R. Kearns (Ann Arbor: University of Michigan Press, 1998), 102.

3. Ibid., 99–100. The analogy of the trial to other popular culture forms, and particularly theater, is not new. For example, Sir Edward Parry argued, "Even to-day when we think of a trial or a lawsuit we picture it to ourselves in terms of drama, applauding the hero or heroine, execrating the villain of the piece, chuckling at the comedian in the witness-box and expressing approval of the modest demeanour of the small-part man who walks on to the dim bench and gives the necessary cues to the great actors in the limelight. And as we read the report of a law case we recall the familiar scenery of a court house, the traditional costumes of the characters and that dramatic setting which we inwardly approve of as essential to the earliest administration of justice." Sir Edward Parry, *The Drama of the Law* (London: Ernst Benn, 1924), 7–8.

4. Clover, "Law and Order," 100.

5. Ibid., 99–100. Indeed, Clover forwards the remarkably ambitious argument that the structure and procedures of the Anglo-American trial "are so deeply embedded in our narrative tradition that they shape even plots that never step into a courtroom." She offers, as an example of a nontrial but trial-like film, *Basic Instinct* (dir. Paul Verhoeven, 1992, Santa Monica, CA: Lionsgate Entertainment, 2006), DVD. Rather than directly addressing the category problem she poses, our contributors offer analyses of film—from twentieth-century fiction films that place a trial at the center of their narratives to films, both fiction and documentary, that focus on problems of knowledge and judgment in trial-like ways—that hew relatively tightly to certain constitutive aspects of Anglo-American trials, in ways that suggest a core coherence to the trial film as a recognizable genre.

6. Well-known films addressing these attributes in sometimes overlapping ways include Stanley Kramer, dir., *Judgment at Nuremberg* (1961; Beverly Hills, CA: Metro-Goldwyn-Mayer Studios, 2004), DVD; Billy Wilder, dir., *Witness for the Prosecution* (1957; New York: Kino International, 2014), DVD, Rob Reiner, dir., *A Few Good Men* (1992; Culver City, CA: Columbia Pictures, 2007), DVD; Jonathan Lynn, dir., *My Cousin Vinny* (1992; Century City, CA: Twentieth Century Fox Home Entertainment, 2009), DVD; Otto Preminger, dir., *Anatomy of a Murder* (1959; Culver City, CA: Sony Pictures Home Entertainment, 2000), DVD; Robert Mulligan, dir., *To Kill a Mockingbird* (1962; Universal City, CA: Universal Pictures Home Entertainment, 2012), DVD; Alfred Hitchcock, dir., *North by Northwest* (1959; Burbank, CA: Warner Bros. Pictures, 2010), DVD; Errol Morris, dir., *The Thin Blue Line* (1988; Beverly Hills, CA: Metro-Goldwyn-Mayer Studios, 2005), DVD; and Andrew Jarecki, dir., *Capturing the Friedmans* (2003; New York: HBO Pictures, 2004), DVD.

7. Over the last two decades a number of scholars have explored the re-

lationship of law and film. See, for example, Nicole Rafter, *Shots in the Mirror: Crime Films and Society*, 2nd ed. (Oxford: Oxford University Press, 2006); Alison Young, *The Scene of Violence: Cinema, Crime, Affect* (London: Routledge-Cavendish, 2009); William MacNeil, *Lex Populi: The Jurisprudence of Popular Culture* (Stanford, CA: Stanford University Press, 2009); Orit Kamir, *Framed: Women in Law and Film* (Durham, NC: Duke University Press, 2006); Austin Sarat and Martha Merrill Umphrey, *Reimagining "To Kill a Mockingbird": Family, Community, and the Possibility of Equal Justice Under Law* (Amherst: University of Massachusetts Press, 2013); Naomi Mezey, "The Image Cannot Speak for Itself: Film, Summary Judgment, and Visual Literacy," *Valparaiso University Law Review* 48, no.1 (Fall 2013); Jennifer Mnookin, "The Image of Truth: Photographic Evidence and the Power of Analogy," *Yale Journal of Law and the Humanities* 10, issue 1 (1998): 1–74; Jessica Silbey, "Evidence Verité and the Law of Film," *Cardozo Law Review* 31, no. 4 (March 2010), 1257–99; "Judges as Film Critics: New Approaches to Filmic Evidence," *University of Michigan Law Review* 37, 2 (January 2004), 493–571; "Videotaped Confessions and the Genre of Documentary," *Fordham Intellectual Property, Media, and Entertainment Law Journal* 16 (2006), 789–807; and "Cross-Examining Film," *University of Maryland Law Journal of Race, Religion, Gender and Class* 8 (2008), 101–30. See also essays in Austin Sarat, ed., *Studies in Law, Politics and Society* (Bingley, UK: Emerald Group Publishing, 2009), 3–146. For thoughtful compendia of law and trial films, see Ross D. Levi, *The Celluloid Courtroom: A History of Legal Cinema* (Westport, CT: Praeger, 2005); John Denvir, ed., *Legal Reelism: Movies as Legal Texts* (Champaign: University of Illinois Press, 1996); Anthony Chase, *Movies on Trial: The Legal System on the Silver Screen* (New York: New Press, 2002); Steve Greenfield, Guy Osborn, and Peter Robson, *Film and the Law* (London: Cavendish Publishing, 2001).

8. This fascination persists, perhaps ironically, as actual trials grow increasingly rare. See Lawrence M. Friedman, "The Day before Trials Vanished," *Journal of Empirical Legal Studies* 1, no. 3 (2004), 689. In a study commissioned by the American Bar Association Section of Litigation under the rubric of "The Vanishing Trial," Marc Galanter has found that in 2002 only 1.8 percent of federal civil cases were resolved by trial, down from 11.5 percent in 1962, and only 5 percent of federal criminal cases went to trial in 2002 compared with 15 percent in 1962. Similar declines have occurred in both sorts of trials on the state level. Marc Galanter, "The Vanishing Trial: An Examination of Trials and Related Matters in Federal and State Courts," *Journal of Empirical Legal Studies* 1, no. 3 (2004), 459–570.

9. See Martha Merrill Umphrey, "Law in Drag: Trials and Legal Performativity," *Columbia Journal of Gender and Law* 21, no. 2 (2011), 114–29.

10. Alexis de Tocqueville, *Democracy in America*, ed. J. P. Mayer, trans. George Lawrence (New York: Harper Collins, 1988), 273–74. The jury is imagined as a hy-

brid of the official and the popular, the crucial link between formal institutions of legality and popular sovereignty. As such, it operates not only to check potential abuses of state power but also to educate ordinary folk into proper citizenship. Tocqueville understood the arena of jury judgment as a critical vehicle for educating people into proper citizenship, which, as he defined it in this context, consists of respect for court decisions and for the idea of right throughout all classes, a belief in equity, a tendency to take on rather than shirk responsibility, and a feeling that all have a duty toward society and a share in its government. On juries, see also Jeffrey Abramson, *We, the Jury: The Jury System and the Ideal of Democracy* (Cambridge, MA: Harvard University Press, 2000); and Stephen J. Adler, *The Jury: Disorder in the Court* (New York: Doubleday, 1994).

11. Scopophilia is a psychoanalytic concept that links the apprehension of the other with sexual desire. See Jacques Lacan, *The Four Fundamental Concepts of Psycho-Analysis* (New York: Norton, 1998), 194; and Laura Mulvey, "Visual Pleasure and Narrative Cinema," Screen 16, no. 3 (1975), 6–18.

12. On epistephilia, particularly in relation to documentary film, see Bill Nichols, *Representing Reality: Issues and Concepts in Documentary* (Bloomington: Indiana University Press, 1991), 178. Clover argues that these kinds of questions generate paranoid speculation in audiences. Clover, "Law and Order," 104–5. Hitchcock's *Rear Window* (1954; Universal City, CA: Universal Pictures Home Entertainment, 2012), DVD captures the tight relations among scopophilia, epistephilia, and elements of the trial form. L. B. Jeffries, an injured photographer, uses his camera lens not only to watch his neighbors (many of whom can be associated with discrete activities involved in making a film—music, costuming, and the like) with a self-consciously voyeuristic gaze but also to investigate a potential murder across the courtyard of his apartment complex. As Clover would recognize, Hitchcock structures the film as a trial, testing Jeffries's prosecutorial arguments and evidence against his neighbor Lars Thorwald even as his friends resist his "theory of the case" with counterarguments, constitutional limitations, and a critique of the morality of looking. See also Robert Stam, "Reflexivity in Film and Literature: from Don Quixote to Jean-Luc Godard" (Ann Arbor, MI: UMI Research Press, 1985), 43–55.

13. Clover, "Law and Order," 102n10.

14. *Anatomy of a Murder* is both widely admired and exemplary of the connections between trials and films on its face. It is on both the American Bar Association and American Film Institute's top-ten trial films lists and may be the greatest courtroom film because of the respect and accuracy with which it depicts the trial process. Its plot is tightly focused on an extended rendition of a single trial, eschewing larger social concerns of the sort present in, for example, *To Kill a Mockingbird* or *Judgment at Nuremberg*, so that the audience's attention is fully directed toward judging the trial and its participants. As such, like *12 Angry Men*,

its sole subject is the workings of the legal system; unlike *12 Angry Men*, it explicitly dramatizes actual trial processes.

15. Clover argues that these features of the trial produce "paranoid speculation" that causes spectators to indulge in fantasies of evidence cheating. Clover, "Law and Order," 104–5.

16. Our contributors engage films ranging from classics (*The Birth of a Nation*) to experimental documentaries (*Abu Ghraib*).

17. On melodrama, see Peter Brooks, *The Melodramatic Imagination: Balzac, Henry James, Melodrama, and the Mode of Excess* (New Haven, CT: Yale University Press, 1995).

18. Jane Gaines and Michael Renov, eds., *Collecting Visible Evidence* (Minneapolis: University of Minnesota Press, 1999), 4. As Jessica Silbey has remarked, "preoccupations with what it means to see and then to know, with what it means to witness and then to judge, with the role of spectatorship in forming a political community—these shaped filmmaking and the experience of film from its earliest stages. . . . And documentary film was a particularly effective tool because of its impressions of authenticity." Silbey, "Filmmaking in the Precinct House and the Genre of Documentary Film," *Columbia Journal of Law and the Arts* 29, no. 2 (2006), 155.

19. Nichols, *Representing Reality*, 31.

20. Ibid., 125. See also Silbey, "Judges as Film Critics."

21. Morris, *The Thin Blue Line*.

22. Nichols argues, "If narrative invites our engagement with the construction of a story, set in an imaginary world, documentary invites our engagement with the construction of an argument, directed toward the historical world." Nichols, *Representing Reality*, 118. That argument is, in effect, Morris's legal theory of the case: that Adams is not guilty, that Harris is guilty, and that the police pursued the wrong person out of ineptitude or perhaps even venality.

23. Indeed, because of the film, Adams's conviction was overturned, and he was released in 1989. Richard Sherwin also identifies a doubled plotline in the film, one told as a classic linear narrative that leads the viewer/juror to a verdict of not guilty and another a nonlinear narrative that "leaves a disquieting sense of inadequate resolution and residual mystery." Richard Sherwin, *When Law Goes Pop: The Vanishing Line between Law and Popular Culture* (Chicago: University of Chicago Press, 2000), 115.

24. In addition to *12 Angry Men*, see *To Kill a Mockingbird*, *The Thin Blue Line*, and *Capturing the Friedmans*.

25. Roman Polanski, dir., *Death and the Maiden* (1994; Los Angeles: New Line Home Entertainment, 2003), DVD, *Judgment at Nuremberg*, and John Ford, dir., *The Man Who Shot Liberty Valance* (1962; Hollywood, CA: Paramount Pictures, 2017), DVD.

26. See Wilder, *Witness for the Prosecution*; Preminger, *Anatomy of a Murder*; Alfred Hitchcock, dir., *I Confess* (1953; Burbank, CA: Warner Bros. Pictures, 2006), DVD; and Errol Morris, dir., *Standard Operating Procedure* (2008; Culver City, CA: Sony Pictures Home Entertainment, 2008), DVD.

27. See *Judgment at Nuremberg* and *A Few Good Men*. See also Shoshana Felman, *The Juridical Unconscious: Trials and Trauma in the Twentieth Century* (Cambridge, MA: Harvard University Press, 2002).

28. As Vivian Sobchack notes, "The film that is objectively given to the viewer may be subjectively taken up in a variety of ways, not only in its entirety, but also in its parts. The forms of our identification with specific cinematic objects may be solicited, but it is never determined a priori. Indeed, our identification is certainly as fluid, dynamic, and idiosyncratic as it is fixed and conventional." Vivian Sobchack, "Toward a Phenomenology of Nonfictional Film Experience," in Gaines and Renov, *Collecting Visible Evidence*, 252–53.

29. Clover, "Law and Order," 99–100.

30. Ibid., 107.

31. Ibid., 104–5.

32. Ibid., 102–6.

33. Ibid., 118.

I
Law and the Order of Popular Culture

Carol J. Clover

Explanations for the appeal of trials tend to focus on the crime or the punishment and run along psychosexual lines. In crime scenarios, the argument goes, we can indulge all manner of perverse fantasies, but safely, under the cloak of law and order. Following Foucault, who saw in the fascination with trials a displaced fascination with torture, we speak of our engagement with the punishment and the processes of discipline that subtend it.[1] Such explanations have a lot of force, and the last two decades have seen something of a scholarly industry along these lines. But they do not explain everything, including the obvious fact that some cultures are more, some vastly more, trial interested than others. In the West, there is a world of difference between English-speaking countries and the Continent on just this point. Especially Americans are said to be trial obsessed, and it is also the case that the courtroom drama of film and television is an overwhelmingly Anglo-American phenomenon. Robin Lakoff tells how students in a class she taught at the University of Barcelona were hard-pressed to explain how a Spanish trial worked but could describe an American one in detail.[2] A Stockholm newspaper recently began a review of a new television series by noting that "the average Swedish TV-viewer knows more about the American justice system than the Swedish one. We even know more about the British system than our own."[3] Although these stories and others like them say a lot about the hegemonic status of American media and of English-language culture more generally, they also point to a real difference. After all, Swedes and Spaniards also commit murder and mayhem and are also punished. But Swedes and Spaniards do not "trial-watch" the way Americans do, and they do not turn trials into entertainment nearly to the extent the Anglo-American world does. How to explain this cultural divide? Either the Anglo-American world has a greater investment in the deep pleasures of crime and punishment, in which case we have to wonder why, or such explanations do not tell the whole story.

The part of the story not told, the part that is culture specific, is the terrain of this chapter. The reader will notice that the line I have drawn between courtroom-drama-producing culture and if not non-, then less, courtroom-drama-producing culture coincides with the line between the two major legal systems of the West, that of the Continent and that of the Anglo-American world. It is something of a truism that the basis of the Anglo-American form in an adversary system and in oral presentation before a jury makes our trials fundamentally more dramatic than the inquisitorial and professionally judged trials of the Continent. To the extent that the Anglo-American fondness for courtroom dramas has been discussed at all—remarkably little, given the scope of the phenomenon—it has been related in a vague way to that truism. But on the whole, it is striking how little the truism has actually been investigated and how underappreciated are its implications for and in the study of popular culture. Film scholarship has not taken up the courtroom drama, no history of it has been written, and the form has no standing in the pantheon of genres.[4] There has been more interest on the law side in the so-called law-and-film movement, but even here, the focus has been not on generic issues but on individual works that are felt to rise above the pack by virtue of their legal intelligence, ethical interest, engagement with worthy issues, and quality of cinema—*12 Angry Men, Boomerang, Witness for the Prosecution, Fury, To Kill a Mockingbird*, and the like.[5]

But surely the question to be asked about the trial movie (by which term I refer to both television and film courtroom dramas) has less to do with the value of particular instances than it does with the fantastic generativity of the form in Anglo-American popular narrative. And surely that generativity devolves not on crime or punishment, at least not primarily, nor other points of content, nor law in the large sense or justice, but—as the truism would have it—something about Anglo-American procedure. I am aware that this proposition runs athwart the opinion of some academic lawyers that the differences between Anglo-American and Continental law have been overstated and indeed to a considerable extent discursively constructed, but I would argue, at the risk of circularity, that popular culture itself—above all, film and television narrative—makes a strong prima facie case for the difference of the Anglo-American system, and further, that popular culture isolates, as the source of that difference, exactly those features of the procedural structure that attend the adversarial system and the jury.

Thus, the proposition of this chapter is that real-life trials become movies (by which I mean both film and television dramas) as easily as they do in the Anglo-American world both because trials are already movie-like to begin with and movies are already trial-like to begin with. The first half of that proposition is hardly news, although the reception-oriented account that follows differs from the usual dramaturgically derived model in some crucial respects. It is the second half that concerns me here. When I say that Anglo-American movies are already trial-like to begin with, I mean to make a three-part, essentially historical claim: that the plot structures and narrative procedures (even certain visual procedures in film and television) of a broad stripe of American popular culture are derived from the structure and procedures of the Anglo-American trial; that this structure and these procedures are so deeply embedded in our narrative tradition that they shape even plots that never step into a courtroom; and that such trial-derived forms constitute the most distinctive share of Anglo American entertainment. I emphasize that I am using the term *narrative* here to mean the textual process of plot making, not as legal circles use it to refer to particular stories or plots or tale types. My interest is neither in courtroom "storytelling" nor in movie "stories" of trials. It is not in "stories" at all. It is in the extent to which the narrative substructure of so much of our cinema rhymes with the narrative substructure of our trial and in what kind of cultural conclusions can be drawn from the commonality. Needless to say, these are larger arguments than I can make here, but I hope that the case study that follows will at least suggest the direction of the larger project.

At issue in the Anglo-American trial are its two grossest features: the adversarial structure and the jury. The roots of the adversarial structure are in the illiterate, tribal, and stateless world of Germanic Europe—a world in which, in the absence of central authority, the two parties were responsible for collecting evidence, bringing suit, pleading cases, and enforcing judgments.[6] England alone retained the "adversarial" or "accusatorial" or "party-presentational" outlines of Germanic procedure, even after the emergence of a state, and to this day the Anglo-American trial retains the form of a two-sided contest, a duel, with the judge as something of a referee. The origins of the jury are disputed and depend on how one defines it. Although the trial jury proper dates to the years following 1215, protojuries of one sort or another go much further back. Looking at the earliest records, one has the sense that the primitive adversarial trial presupposed by nature some third body, agreed upon by the parties (or by a process agreed upon by the parties), charged with arriving at, if not a final verdict in the modern sense, then some significant decision that terminated the hearing. The fact that the use of juries has been curtailed in Britain (90 percent of the world's jury trials are now American) and that even in the United States many trials are bench tried should not detract from the stubbornly central position of the jury in the rhetorical architecture of the Anglo-American trial. In either case, the jury and the adversarial structure were early welded together, and from the combination proceed many other characteristics of the form, notably the degree of procedural formalism and the emergence, in later centuries, of the elaborate rules of evidence.

No one appreciated more than Tocqueville what it might mean to live in a nation of once and future jurors. First and foremost, to the institution of the jury, he ascribed the peculiar and widespread interest of Americans in lawsuits and legal logic. "The jury," he declares, "extends this habit [of legal thought] to all classes. The language of the law thus becomes, in some measure, a vulgar tongue; the spirit of the law, which is produced in the schools and courts of justice, gradually penetrates beyond their walls into the bosom of society, where it descends to the lowest class, so that at last the whole people contract the habits and tastes of the judicial magistrate." By bringing common people to the law, the jury brings the law to common people, and hence the legal habit of mind "extends over the whole community and penetrates into all the classes which compose it; it acts upon the country imperceptibly, but finally fashions it to suit its own purposes."[7] More particularly, the legal system provides a rhetorical and logical template that gives shape to all manner of social forms above and beyond the court of law. So it is, Tocqueville wrote, that "scarcely any political question arises in the United States that is not resolved, sooner or later, into a judicial question," that "all parties are obliged to borrow, in their daily controversies, the ideas, and even the language, peculiar to judicial proceedings," and that "the jury is introduced into the games of schoolboys."[8] Just what Tocqueville meant by "games of schoolboys" we do not know, but the gist is clear: so fundamental is the adversarial jury trial in the American imaginary that, as a ghost matrix with a life of its own above and beyond its source, it turns up in and structures even the sheerest forms of play. No one even vaguely acquainted with American culture can help being struck by the prescience of that observation. Not only in film and television drama but in board games, interactive software, Internet tribunals, television game shows, and radio talk shows, we enact and reenact trials, in the process positioning ourselves, as Tocqueville also appreciated, first, last, and always as triers of fact.

The relentless juror orientation (even when the ostensible point of view is that of a lawyer, judge, or police detective)[9] of Anglo-American trial-derived popular culture obliges us to ask an obvious question: What trial is it that the jury sees? Again at the risk of circularity, I want to suggest that the juror's trial differs somewhat from the official trial of lawyers, judges, and textbooks, whose accounts indeed seem so often designed to correct the lay impression; that if the juror's trial gets lots of things wrong, it gets some things, including the underlying epistemology, exactly right; and that it is these things, the things the juror's trial gets right, that have been so crucial in the production of popular culture. By way of getting at what are for popular culture the salient features of the adversarial trial as a form, let us imagine a generic instance as it might be experienced, as a strictly formal operation, by a generic jury, make it that favorite of popular fantasy, a murder trial in which the two sides are roughly balanced.[10] By *trial*, I mean the main hearing. That stretch is neatly tripartite, consisting of a long examination bookended by opening statements and closing arguments, with the verdict as a kind of coda.[11] It matches, as many have pointed out, the architecture of classic drama. It also matches the architecture of the standard screenplay.[12]

The opening statements (like the closing arguments) present us with the two positions in narrative form. Even at this early point, the story of guilt likely has the upper hand: it is more coherent, seems more explanatory of the rudimentary facts, and is braced by our prima facie assumption that the state must have a powerful case in order to bring it to court. At the end of the opening statements, there is an abrupt shift of gears, almost a change of tense, as we enter the examination phase. The highly bound, reasoned, syntactic, storytelling mode of the opening statements comes to a halt and the "text" collapses into a jumble of physical items and arrested moments: weapons, carpet fibers, testimony about drug reactions, behavior at the funeral, and so on. As if in freeze-frame close-up, these fragments now become the object of our investigation, but disarticulated and disordered, as though unrelated to one another or to any larger story. The examination is a limited case of narrative parataxis—a stretch of textual bits and pieces, without coordinating conjunctions, as causally unbound as possible. It is also, or can be, a limited case of narrative agglutination, testing our ability to register and process not just contested data but lots of them.

Two formal systems govern this extraordinary discourse: the "engine" of cross-examination (that is, the scheduled alternation between direct and cross) and the rules of evidence, the underlying assumption of which is that an event (the stabbing murder of a 7-Eleven clerk, let's say) can be broken down into particles of fact that preexist narrative and that, scrutinized singly and initially outside of the story, these fact particles will, in the mind of the beholder, assemble toward their own best explanation. The mind of the beholder posited by the "text" of the examination is thus exceptionally attentive, itself a party in the meaning-making process. "The premium on close attention is large," as Scott Turow has noted. It wants "a certain intricacy of mind."[13]

Not just one but two backstories (to borrow a film term) present themselves piecemeal for assembly. The first is the declared one, the story of the crime that we are asked to reconstruct a bit at a time. Every datum of the examination is or claims to be a piece of the puzzle, but we are also made aware—through objections, witness slips, and the like—that there are more data out there that are being kept from us, and we cannot help puzzling over what they are and what might account for their status as outtakes.[14] The other backstory is the unintended one of the trial as a performance, evoked by sidebar conferences, objections, excessive or otherwise unexpected behavior on the part of court apparatus that might prompt speculation: Does the judge favor the prosecution? Does the defense attorney really believe her client, or is she just doing her job? Are the lead attorneys on the two sides really lovers, as one juror speculates who saw them eating lunch together? Who are all those thuggish-looking people in the gallery—is the defendant mob connected and as his jurors are we in danger?[15] The rules of evidence and protocol that are designed at the point of production to maximize fairness are, at the point of reception, a veritable machine for the production of paranoid speculation far beyond the trial's official parameters.

Paranoid speculations (hidden stories that we can unlock if we remain hyperalert to the clues) are also prompted by one of the most remarkably primitive features of the adversarial trial, one that has its roots in Germanic antiquity: the separate collection and presentation of evidence. Where evidence is separately collected, it can be separately suppressed, destroyed, tainted, fabricated, delayed, planted, altered, and so on, and although official accounts of the legal system remind us that evidence meddling is illegal, the fact is that it *does* happen and it does happen to some extent because it *can* happen. No wonder we indulge fantasies (in trials both real and imaginary) of evidence cheating. At some level, we understand that the separate-collection structure provides the opportunity for it, the competitive structure of the trial provides the motive for it, the raft of rules against it admits the possibility of it, and, as in the O. J. Simpson trial, real lawyers level accusations of it. The same concerns relate to the separate presentation of evidence, which rests on the no less antique assumption that, as Macaulay puts it, the fairest decision will be reached when "two men argue as unfairly as possible on both sides" insofar as such a procedure guarantees that "no more important consideration will altogether escape notice."[16] In practice this means that the prosecution and defense create respectively the worst and the best possible versions of the incontrovertible facts. The system pays lip service to truth and justice, but the adversarial structure contemplates an odd, even cynical, notion of truth, one we might count as postmodern were it not so manifestly archaic: not the "real" or "whole" or "philosophical" truth of Platonic argument (and indeed of the Continental trial), but a truth of exhausted possibilities, what is left standing after every possible explanatory story has been tried out against it. And what kind of truth can it be that falls not to a wise professional or a trained panel, but to us?

But what unsettles us particularly about the system of arguing "as unfairly as possible" is that the two sides are not arguing *equally* unfairly. We may or may not be able to articulate the principle of different burdens (the prosecution's to prove its case beyond a reasonable doubt, the defense's merely to raise enough doubt), but we see its discursive consequences in a structure that pits a prosecution X not against a defense Y but against a defense not-X, X being a relatively fixed and coherent story with some commitment to a single account of "what really happened" and not-X being a site of proliferating scenarios, including mutually exclusive ones, of what *might* have happened. What this boils down to in practice, for the jury, is different truth statuses for X and not-X, the sense that while the prosecution is bound by the explanation it believes to be true, the defense is free to make up whatever explanations it wants. It is against the law, we are told, to suborn perjury. But we are also aware that between absolute truth and plain perjury there is a large playing field and that much of the defense lawyer's art is avoiding the end zones. Even if we did not see this idea repeatedly thematized in movies ("don't tie my hands by telling me what happened"), we would deduce it from real trials—for example, the so-called Reginald Denny beating trial, in which defense counsel for the accused argued (1) you have the wrong man and (2) the crowd made him do it. The inventive nature of the not-X position is neatly spelled out in Racehorse Haynes's oft-quoted defense against the charge that his dog bit someone last night: my dog does not bite, my dog was tied up last night, I do not believe you got bit, and I do not have a dog. Although none of these defenses is itself a story, singly and together they imply a tale of false accusation (for reasons left to the paranoid imagination).[17] In other words, jurors know that the adversarial trial is also a machine for the production of not just "versions" or "stories" or "theories of the case" (as lawyers call them) but something that looks to us an awful lot like lies.

And where there are lies, there are liars. It is no wonder, given the adversarial structure's drive toward invention and the plain fact that at least some of the people who take the oath to tell the truth will lie, that we are such hyperalert readers of demeanor, watching witnesses for the smallest twitch, shift of glance, tightening of the mouth. It is by the same token no wonder that we should be so drawn to the idea of scientific lie detection. There is something deeply unsettling about our trial's relation to truth, and in venues ranging from law school to television talk shows and fiction, we endlessly explain our legal system to each other and ourselves, as if we do not really quite get it—as if one more formulation might finally un-boggle our minds and put into focus how it is that unfairness gets us fair-ness, a widening gyre works to narrow things down, lying produces truth, and truth is nothing more or less than the best story so far. A culture with such a system might well want a truth machine, and so it is that the poly-graph has been embraced in the United States as in no other country ("as American as apple pie") and that, despite its liminal status as evidence, it hovers over the discourse of the trial ("I'll prove I'm telling the truth: give me a polygraph!") and is a commonplace in film and television forms re-lating to trials.[18]

All of this plays out on a strict schedule of turn taking—yet another pe-culiarity of the Anglo-American trial. In the early phases of the hearing, we are (for reasons suggested earlier) likely to be on the prosecution side, though apprehensively, thanks to points scored by the defense in cross-examination. But midway through the examination, when the sides have switched places in the presentation of their cases and we face defense tes-timony, we arrive at a crossroads, a time when we must choose between sturdy and familiar X and the alluring plausibility of a not-X. Textually viewed, it is the most charged moment of the proceedings, one that, once negotiated, delivers us into the most characteristic experience of the ad-versarial trial: of being pulled rhythmically back and forth, in the almost machinelike alternation of direct examination with cross-examination, be-tween the two positions. We are told to form no conclusions along the way, an instruction that seems to presume a "pure" process of data gathering that resists interim explanations. What cognitive science would say about such a model I do not know, but it is emphatically at odds with the procedure of trial movies and detective fiction, which invite us to an initial conclusion, then unsettle that conclusion with new evidence, then invite us to a new conclusion, and so on, in a succession of tentative hypotheses, one replac-ing another in a long line. Indeed, it is that process—particularly the mo-ments of textual vacuum, when a fresh piece of evidence undoes our work-ing story without quite providing us with a replacement—that is so central to our experience of this brand of hermeneutic narrative. I strongly suspect that on this point too, popular culture has it right, and that for the jurors, the process of the examination is an exercise in more or less anxious plot making and unmaking. It is in any event a process that calls not only for "close attention" and a "certain intricacy of mind" but a powerful memory and an active paranoid imagination.

With the closing arguments, the text reverts to syntactic narrative with a vengeance as each side tries to gather all the evidence into a master bundle. But all the narrative in the world cannot fully still all the prospects opened in the examination. In practice, many trials fall short of full closure (hung juries, appeals, public dissatisfaction with the verdict, lingering doubts, etc.), and even when there is a verdict and it sticks, at least the jurors may feel slightly unnerved; it is, after all, the job of the adversarial system to come up with equally plausible scenarios, and it is not easy to dump the possibilities we have come to know so well. Commonplace has it that art improves on life in this respect, that imaginary trials provide the strong ending (in the form of a Perry Mason–style confession, for example) that real trials often lack.[19] This is true of most trial movies but by no means all of them. A surprisingly large minority conclude on a tone of uncertainty or flatly with a question mark, and lest we imagine this to be a postmodern development, consider the 1916 film *By Whose Hand?*, a courtroom whodunit in which, after teasing us with two candidates between whom it has been alternating throughout, a final intertitle declares "By Whose Hand? You Are the Jury—You Decide!"[20] Different though they are, these two conclusions—firmly closed and more or less open—can be seen as responses to the same problem, that problem being a textual structure designed to produce not a full stop, but a dash or series of dots. Right down to the ending, popular culture grasps the essence of the adversarial trial.

In an often-cited 1966 article, "The Trial as One of the Performing Arts," John E. Simonett declared that trials unvarnished would never make it on television. The American experience since the reversal of the ban on cameras in the courtroom has proved him not just wrong but absolutely so. In fact, the features of the modern trial Simonett thought killed it as performance—the "advent of modern discovery procedures," the "final rehearsal of pretrial, with counsel knowing in advance who the witnesses will be and what they will say," and the law's "delay, recesses, and conferences away from the bench"—seem to bother the fans of Court TV (and its many descendants and successors) not one whit.[21] And even before the televising of trials, courtroom galleries all over the country were peopled with regular visitors known as court watchers; they too seemed, and seem, little bothered by the modern constraints and indeed grade judges and attorneys on their performances.[22] In the United States, at least, where trials are, audiences are.

And—to turn finally to movies—where audiences are, producers and directors are. If Tocqueville were among us today, he would surely not be surprised at the ways our entertainment system seizes on real trials (for example, the Menendez brothers and O. J. Simpson), how it makes up trials that should have happened but did not (the Oswald trial movies[23]), how it retries real cases, perhaps affecting their course (*The Thin Blue Line*, which led to a verdict reversal), how it turns real trials into mainstream dramas (the Scopes trial in *Inherit the Wind)*, how it re-creates trials using the transcript as script (*The Trial of Jean Harris*, for example, which never leaves the transcript *or* the courtroom), how it produces fictional trial stories (the classic courtroom drama), and, finally, how it generates fictional stories that follow the trial recipe even though they never set foot in the courtroom.

The last claim is the extreme one. But because, paradoxically, the trialness of a narrative can be most clearly seen for what it is when there is no diegetic trial involved and also because the courtroom-less courtroom drama or the trial-less trial movie is especially popular at the moment, the category is doubly interesting for our purposes, and I will devote the remainder of this chapter to it.

Let me take as my example *Basic Instinct*. Written by Joe Eszterhas and directed by Paul Verhoeven, *Basic Instinct* was marketed as a thriller or suspense drama. More generally, it fits in the detective genre, with some connections to film noir insofar as it concerns a depressed detective drawn irresistibly to a woman richer, smarter, and stronger than he is and likely fatal as well. Such generic labels (thriller, film noir, suspense drama, etc.) are based on character, setting, and manifest plot; any of them will do. What I want to propose is that the narrative machine underneath the manifest plot, whatever its label, is the trial. There may be no trial *in* the movie, but there is a trial underneath and behind it; the movie itself mimics the phases, the logic, and the narrative texture of the trial.

The promotional copy tells the plot up to a point: "Michael Douglas stars as Nick Curran, a tough but vulnerable detective. Sharon Stone costars as Catherine Tramell, a cold, calculating, and beautiful novelist with an insatiable sexual appetite. Catherine becomes a prime suspect when her boyfriend [a former rock star] is brutally murdered [with an ice pick]— a crime she had described in her latest novel. But would she be so obvious as to write about a crime she was going to commit? Or is she being set up by a jealous rival? Obsessed with cracking the case, Nick descends into San Francisco's forbidden underground where suspicions mount, bodies fall, and he finds within himself an instinct more basic than survival."[24] After Nick becomes enmeshed with Catherine, she abruptly dismisses him, saying that she has no use for him any more now that she has finished the novel she was writing about him and has killed off his character. Nick's cop friend Gus is then stabbed to death with an ice pick (by whom, we do not know, but it might be Catherine, and she might have thought Gus was Nick). Nick goes home from this unsettling incident to find Catherine waiting for him, and instead of running for his life, he goes to bed with her (thus the basic instinct of the title).

The first thing we see in *Basic Instinct* is a naked couple having wild sex, the woman on top. They pause briefly while she ties his hands to the bed (from his reaction it looks to be part of their routine). More wild sex, and when it reaches fever pitch, the woman reaches for an ice pick and then, with tremendous force, stabs him to death. At which point the scene cuts— to the next day with the cops there (in the same place) investigating the scene. Now begins the movie proper.

Standard film practice avoids putting crucial plot information in the first few moments, as though acknowledging that audiences take a while to sink into the terms. But some kinds of film, notably thrillers, routinely break the convention, opening the way *Basic Instinct* does, with an abrupt entry sequence showing a crime as it is being committed, without introduction or explanation, and often before the credits. This kind of opening jolts us into the movie, but more than that, it works as a test or a tease: we know we should pay close attention and we do as well as we can, but we do not quite get it—partly because we are not yet in full concentration (the theater lights may still be dimming) and partly because the scene does not show us everything, including, of course, the very thing that will matter most in the story to come. That thing in this case (a case of identity) is the woman's face. We see her blond hair and her body but not the one thing that will distinguish her from the other two blond, thin, like-breasted women in the movie: Roxie (Catherine's girlfriend) and Beth (Nick's ex-girlfriend), both of whom will soon become suspects as well. In other words, it is not that the gradual-entry convention just happens to be broken, here; it's that it is being precisely exploited, to catch us off guard and leave us insecure in our perception of exactly what we most need to know.

We will be reminded of our faulty apperception every time the scene is referred to throughout the film, right up to the last minute. We will be asked to recollect it each time we see Catherine naked, especially when she is having sex with Nick: Is this the same body we saw at the beginning? Are the breasts the same? Is the hair the same? Is she moving the same way and doing the same things? We will flash back again during certain sequences with Beth (Nick's former girlfriend) because, although she has dark hair, the evidence keeps building up against her, and sure enough, it emerges at some point that she is given to wearing blond wigs and impersonating Catherine. But the moment at which we most urgently recall the first scene is during the last, when Nick and Catherine go to bed together, a scene that mimics the opening sequence down to fine details. Again, wild sex, woman on top. But the question this time is not who the woman is; we know it is Catherine. It is whether Catherine is the same woman we saw in the opening sequence. So again, we work the comparison: Is the body the same? The breasts? The hair? The movements? And so on. When she reaches for the ice pick at the side of the bed, the question seems answered: yes, this woman and that woman are one and the same. Until, in the final seconds of the film, she withdraws her hand from the ice pick, letting it lie—throwing the whole thing open again.[25]

The first thing to notice here is that the overall structure of *Basic Instinct*, with its homologous first and last scenes, rhymes with the overall structure of the trial. That is, the opening scene of the movie is the functional equivalent of the opening statements (in which the crime is stated and the problem of the trial announced—in this case, identity), and the closing scene of the movie is the functional equivalent of the closing arguments, a recapitulation of the opening statement, but expanded and more knowing, and with a full context. And between these matching bookends lies a long middle, the movie proper, in which the text duplicates with remarkable intensity and fidelity the paratactic operations of the examination phase of the trial.

That phase begins, in the movie as in a trial, with an abrupt shift of gears: a dramatic cut from the dreamlike murder sequence, which seems somehow to be in the past tense even while it's happening, to the police investigation of the crime scene the day after, the movie's present tense. At this point, linear narrative shuts down and the text collapses into a concatenation of physical objects, bodily gestures, slips of tongue, random snatches of information—initially disordered and disarticulated bits and pieces whose relation to one another we will figure out only slowly and piecemeal, a process that is the sine qua non of the form and the source of much of our spectatorial pleasure.[26] In the second scene (the police investigation), we are shown in choppy sequence a number of objects close-up with a significant pause on each, a Picasso on the wall, a bloody ice pick, lines of cocaine on a mirror, semen stains the sheets (which we see in fluorescent relief through special glasses Nick puts on), and so on. In the following two scenes, when we encounter first Roxie and then Catherine, the camera treats their faces the same way it treated the objects in the earlier scene, only closer up and with even longer pauses. The camera does more than report here; it probes, almost as if it were a lie detector.[27] So the "examination" phase of the movie goes, bouncing paratactically from the close-up of an ice pick to a long shot of a speeding car to a snatch of a telephone conversation to a deliberate super-close-up of Catherine's face as she says, "No, I didn't kill him." We are in a discourse so familiar to us as late-century American filmgoers that we do not even see how odd it is as narrative—and as cinema, how constructed.

That the killer is a woman we already know: we saw her ourselves. The question is what woman. Remember that Catherine's latest novel was exactly about a woman who kills a former rock star with an ice pick. But does that fact point to Catherine's guilt? As the box cover put it (in the dueling-stories mode), "would she be so obvious as to write about a crime she was going to commit? Or is she being set up by a jealous rival?"[28] The alternatives are spelled out in dramatic detail in the sixth scene of the film, when the police consult a psychologist, Dr. Lamont.

> Dr. Lamont: I see two possibilities. One: the person who wrote this book is your murderer and acted out the killing described in ritualistic literal detail. Two: someone who wants to harm the writer read the book and enacted the killing described in the book to incriminate the author.
> Nick: What if the writer did it. Then what are we dealing with?
> Dr. Lamont: You're dealing with a devious, diabolical mind. You see, this book had to have been written at least six months, maybe even years, before it was published, which means that the writer had to have at least planned the crime in the subconscious, back then. Now, the fact that she carried it out indicates psychopathic obsessive behavior in terms not only of the killing itself, but also in terms of the applied advance defense mechanism.

One of the cops asks what that might mean, and Beth (who in addition to being Nick's ex-girlfriend is a court psychiatrist) translates:

> He means that Catherine intended the book to be her alibi. She's going to say, "Do you think I'd be dumb enough to kill anyone in the exact way I described in my book? I wouldn't do that because then I'd know I'd be the suspect."
> Nick: OK, so what if it's not the writer. What if it's someone who's *read* the book?
> Dr. Lamont: You're dealing then with someone so obsessed that he, or she, is willing to kill an irrelevant and innocent victim in order to place blame on the person who wrote that book. I'm talking about a deep-seated, obsessional hatred, and an utter lack of respect for human life.
> Gus (Nick's cop buddy): So however you cut it, we're dealing with someone very dangerous. And very ill.[29]

The "trial-ness" of *Basic Instinct* is right on the surface in this scene. We have the testimony of the expert witness (even though it is just a conversation in the police station). We have the two-story structure spelled out, and in a way that reflects the differing burdens of the adversarial system: on one hand, the known quantity of the prosecution *(the* writer: Catherine) and, on the other, the ambient alternative of the defense *(a* reader: not Catherine), an alternative that is the site of proliferating possibilities.[30]

At first the finger of suspicion points to Catherine. So systematically does the film spell out her motive (she's a man-hating lesbian of almost Nietzschean dimensions), her means (she owns ice picks and likes using them) and her opportunity (she can seduce men at will) that her guilt seems self-evident during the first third or so of the movie—the portion corresponding to the prosecution's case in the trial. But in the same way that even during the prosecution's case the defense may, in cross-examination, insinuate other possibilities, so *Basic Instinct* lodges early on the Roxie possibility and then the Beth one. Around the middle of the film, when Beth becomes a real contender in our ongoing reconstruction of the past, we have effectively moved into the trial's defense case.

It is from this point that *Basic Instinct* and films like it come into their own as the engine of the examination kicks into high gear. The bits of evidence now come thick and fast; every conversation is loaded with them. One will incriminate Roxie, the next Catherine, and then Beth, and so on, likewise all the historical data floating about the text: one bit will adhere to Catherine, the next to Roxie, the next to Nick, and so forth. The backstories we have struggled to piece together now begin to take shape. Practically every character has one in this film, but the main ones are Catherine's and Beth's, which at first seem separate but then, in one of the film's crucial revelations, turn out to be ominously linked: they were lovers in college and somehow, from the obsessive psychic bond that developed between them, murders happened (of their psychology teacher, of Catherine's parents and husband, of Beth's husband). During the last third of the film, the text becomes so saturated with possibilities that it is all but unfollowable (certainly unsummarizable) and so laden with information about the past that it seems in danger of being swamped by the particulars of its backstory. There are films in this tradition that *are* so *swamped*—*The Big Sleep* being the famous case in point. We have to wonder about the kinds of audience pleasure presumed by such a text. At the very least, we can say the exercise involves "a certain intricacy of mind," which in turn involves a certain paranoia—a paranoia played out both *in* the text (in the character of Nick) and *by* the text (engaging us in the anxious reading of clues and imagining of plots to explain them). If the particulars are new, the basic narrative recipe is deeply familiar, probably the most potent American culture has ever produced.

Finally, there is the cinematography of *Basic Instinct*, which becomes increasingly polygraphic in its close-up probe of faces, particularly the faces of Catherine and Beth, searching them for signs of lies and truth. Their performances lean heavily on their ability to appear as though they *could* be lying—not as though they *are* lying, but as though they might be lying but then again they might not be. Clearly, that skill is a prerequisite for movies of this kind, playing as they do in the terrain of aesthetic paranoia and the Freudian fetish: I know Catherine's tears *look* real, but even so . . . I suggested earlier that this is the heart of the jury experience—believing and disbelieving simultaneously, trying to hang on to a story that we also try to let go of, working to avoid narrative aporia. If that is so, then Nick is not only our surrogate inside the movie; he is also the consummate juror. That particular brand of indecision—I know Catherine did it, but even so—is the condition of his character and the condition of our spectatorship: it is what draws him into bed and us into the plot. He may be a cop in the fiction of the story, but functionally speaking, he is no better off than we are. When *Basic Instinct* ends by showing us Catherine, in bed with Nick, reaching for an ice pick only to put it back again, it joins a very long tradition of trial movies that not only play themselves out in the shadow of reasonable doubt but never leave that shadow, never quite reveal the paranoid truth, never fully resolve the fetishistic quandary. By whose hand? You are the jury; you decide.

Let me end my discussion of *Basic Instinct* with some notes on its genealogy. Eszterhas, who wrote it, also wrote *Jagged Edge*. And indeed, what is *Basic Instinct* but *Jagged Edge* with the sexes reversed? The investigator figure in *Jagged Edge* (the Nick figure) is a woman (played by Glenn Close) and the rich and scary prime suspect (the Catherine figure) is a man (played by Jeff Bridges), with whom the investigator falls in love. The plots—the proportions and the plot moves—are otherwise very much the same. It is also the case that the opening and closing scenes of *Jagged Edge* are virtually identical to the opening and closing scenes of *Basic Instinct* insofar as a sexual murder is the first thing we see and an echo murder is the last.[31] But unlike *Basic Instinct*, *Jagged Edge* is an explicit trial story: the investigator is not a cop, but a lawyer; the prime suspect is not just any rich person, but a rich client; and the site of official transactions is not a police station but a court room. *Jagged Edge* is what we might call a third-act courtroom thriller (with most of its courtroom action in the third act). But the genealogy does not end there. *Jagged Edge* is also explicitly based on another movie, Hitchcock's 1947 film *The Paradine Case*, with Gregory Peck as the barrister who falls in love with his beautiful client, the prime suspect in the murder of her very rich husband.[32] In that film, however, the trial begins early on and effectively frames the diegetic action of the film as a whole. *The Paradine Case* is a classic courtroom drama, in other words, complete with robes and wigs and courtroom grandstanding in the English manner—"the wordiest script since the death of Edmund Burke," James Agee called it.[33] We have, then, in reverse order, a full-fledged courtroom drama as the explicit model for a third-act courtroom thriller, which is in its turn the explicit prototype of a detective thriller that never goes near a court or a lawyer. (Basic *Instinct* would seem to have offspring of its own in a film like *Body of Evidence*, in which, interestingly, the courtroom has been restored.) Scratch the surface of variation, though, and you find the same basic structure and plot moves. The courtroom is optional, the sexes reversible, the investigator's profession variable; but all three films follow the same narrative blueprint, and they all play the same textual game.

My point should be clear. If *Basic Instinct* is a shadow form of the Anglo-American trial, so must be lots of other films normally classified as thrillers—by no means all of them, but a significant subset.[34] (I am convinced that the detective novel in general is back-formed from the Anglo-American trial, a proposition that has the virtue of explaining why it should be that the form originated in the United States and England and for all its Continental adaptations, remains conspicuously Anglo-American to this day.) And of course there are all the bona fide courtroom dramas—films like *Witness for the Prosecution, Anatomy of a Murder, Paths of Glory, A Cry in the Dark, Philadelphia, A Few Good Men* (my list runs to the many hundreds)—plus all those films that are counted in other genres but take the manifest form of trials: comedies like *My Cousin Vinny*, noir films like *They Won't Believe Me*, westerns like *Sergeant Rutledge*, gangster movies like *Billy Bathgate*, romantic comedies like *Defending Your Life*, documentaries like *Brother's Keeper*, melodramas like *Peyton Place*, horror movies like *Audrey Rose*, musicals like *Les Girls*, baseball movies like *Eight Men Out*, historical romances like *Sommersby*, and porn films like *In Defense of Savannah*. Add all this up and we are looking at a healthy share of Anglo-American film production.

It is also its most culturally marked share. The kind of movie narrative at issue here—fragmented, evidence-examining, forensically visualized, backstory-driven, X-not-X-structured, polygraphically photographed, intricately plotted, doubt-cultivating, and jury-directed—is, if not culturally specific, then culturally characteristic. In the 1957 classic *The Rise of the Novel*, Ian Watt proposed that certain qualities in English prose fiction—notably its formal realism and its "circumstantial view of life"—were conditioned by the English court of law.[35] The rise of Continental critical theory, in the years to follow, effectively shut down considerations of the local, like Watt's, in favor of the general. What I am suggesting here is that although much has been gained in, say, the large project of Foucault (to return to my starting point), something has also been lost, at least in areas in which the difference of Anglo-American law might matter. Watt's move toward cultural specificity via the legal system seems to me powerfully suggestive and is the context for my proposal, that a broad and distinctive streak of Anglo-American popular entertainment derives from the peculiar epistemology of the adversarial jury trial.[36]

Notes

1. "We are far removed indeed from those accounts of the life and misdeeds of the criminal in which he admitted his crimes, and which recounted in detail the tortures of his execution: we have moved from the exposition of the facts or the confession to the slow process of discovery; from the execution to the investigation; from the physical confrontation to the intellectual struggle between criminal and investigator." Michel Foucault, *Discipline and Punish: The Birth of the Prison*, trans. Alan Sheridan (New York: Vintage, 1979), 69.

2. Robin Tolmach Lakoff, *Talking Power* (New York: Basic Books, 1990), chap. 5.

3. *Dagens Nyheter*, January 21, 1995, 14 (my translation).

4. The only full-length study to date is Thomas Harris's *Courtroom Drama's Finest Hour* (Metuchen, NJ: Scarecrow, 1987), a set of appreciative readings, with little categorical attention, of *12 Angry Men, Witness for the Prosecution, I Want to Live!, Compulsion, Anatomy of a Murder, Inherit the Wind, Judgment at Nuremberg*, and *The Verdict*. For a speculation on the official nonstatus of a popularly recognized form, see Carol J. Clover, "'God Bless Juries!'" in *Refiguring American Film Genres: History and Theory*, ed. Nick Browne (Berkeley: University of California Press, 1998).

5. See especially Norman Rosenberg, "Hollywood on Trials: Courts and Films, 1930–1960," *Law and History Review* 12 (1994): 341–67. In note 8, Rosenberg suggests that by comparison with the law and literature enterprise, the law and film venture is canonless. To the extent that this is so (and I would argue that it is only somewhat so), it is surely a function of the time lag. Other recent studies of note include Richard K. Sherwin, "Law Frames: Historical Truth and Narrative Necessity in a Criminal Case," *Stanford Law Review* 47 (1994), and John Denvir, ed., *Movies as Legal Texts* (Urbana: University of Illinois Press, 1996). Not about film, but pertinent to the relation of law and narrative, is Paul Gewirtz and Peter Brooks, eds., *Law's Stories: Narrative and Rhetoric in the Law* (New Haven, CT: Yale University Press, 1996).

6. My account here is drawn from the usual sources (Pollock and Maitland, Plucknett, Millar), Thomas Green's *Verdict According to Conscience: Perspectives on the English Criminal Trial Jury, 1200-1800* (Chicago: University of Chicago Press,

1985), and my own research into the Anglo-Saxon and Old Norse primary texts. There is, in my view, some truth to the suspicion that the distinction as it has been articulated for the last century between the Anglo-American and Continental legal systems is discursively constructed, but that is not to say that there *is* no distinction. I came to this project as a medievalist with a long-standing interest in Germanic legal systems, and I am convinced that the distinction *as far as procedure is concerned* is, if anything, more deep going than the standard accounts allow and that—as this chapter should suggest—it has had profound consequences on popular narrative from the early Middle Ages on.

7. Alexis de Tocqueville, *Democracy in America*, vol. 1 (New York: Vintage, 1990), 280. Although Tocqueville was mainly interested in civil trials, his remarks apply in the main to criminal ones as well.

8. Ibid., 280, 318

9. The positioning of the film audience as jury is one of the most fundamental and consistent rules of the courtroom drama. It is surely for that reason that the jury is largely unseen in trial movies (typically glimpsed in a couple of camera pans). An exception of sorts is the subclass of thrillers in which a juror becomes involved with a lawyer (or the defendant, or whatever), but most of these films have only marginally to do with a trial or indeed with the jury experience. The real exception to the unseen-jury rule is, of course, *12 Angry Men*. In considering that film's anomalous status, it is worth remembering that it is based on a French original (the 1950 French film *Justice est faite*—though what the French were doing making a movie about a jury is another question); that it was a failure at the box office and owes its present status to a belated resuscitation on the part of art-film and law-interested viewers; that despite its jury-room framing it enacts the phases and processes of the trial (prosecution arguments, defense arguments, evidence, cross-examination, etc.) and reaches offscreen, out to us, for a verdict; and that after a couple of pale imitations, it produced no progeny. For a fuller account of *12 Angry Men's* reception history, see Clover, "'God Bless Juries!'"

10. From the privileged status of murder in trial and detective or mystery narratives, it is reasonable to conclude that an interest in criminal violence is what drives the forms. That must be largely true, but it is worth remembering that a fair share of fictional trials are about other things (slander, negligence, adoption or custody, drugs, etc.). The sine qua non of the American-style detective narrative (the basis of thrillers, including courtroom thrillers) is not murder but some sort of paranoid risk to the investigator figure, which murder nicely but not exclusively supplies.

11. For different accounts of the Anglo-American trial-as-drama, see especially John E. Simonett, "The Trial as One of the Performing Arts," *American Bar Association Journal* 62 (1966): 1145–47, and Milner S. Ball, "The Play's the Thing:

An Unscientific Reflection on Courts under the Rubric of Theater," *Stanford Law Review* 28 (1975–76): 81–115.

12. Syd Field, *Screenplay: The Foundations of Screenwriting* (New York: Dell, 1984).

13. Scott Turow, *Presumed Innocent* (New York: Farrar, Straus, and Giroux, 1987), 258. Needless to say, the sort of narrative I am describing here conforms closely to Roland Barthes's "hermeneutic code" in *S/Z* (New York: Hill and Wang, 1974); see also Peter Brooks, *Reading for the Plot: Design and Intention in Narrative* (Cambridge, MA: Harvard University Press, 1992).

14. Film metaphors permeate descriptions of trials. To judge from Court TV's live coverage, the opening statement is now characterized by the first attorney as "a preview of coming attractions" as frequently as it is the conventional "road map" or "blueprint." As for outtakes, consider Alan Dershowitz's account of a trial: "A legal case is somewhat like a long, unedited film containing thousands of frames, only a small portion of which ultimately appear on the screen as part of the finished product. The role of the legal system—police, prosecutor, defense lawyer, judge—is to edit the film for trial" (*Reversal of Fortune: Inside the von Bulow Case* [New York: Simon and Schuster, 1986], xxii–xxiii).

15. Exactly these speculations were rampant among the jurors with whom I served in a five-week criminal trial in 1990.

16. Thomas Babington Macaulay, *The History of England*, vol. 4 (Leipzig, Ger.: Bernhard Tauchnitz, 1855), 84–85.

17. Cf. Alan Dershowitz, "Life Is Not a Dramatic Narrative," in *Law's Stories: Narrative and Rhetoric in the Law*, ed. Peter Brooks and Paul Gewirtz (New Haven, CT: Yale University Press, 1996), 99–109. To propose, as Dershowitz does, that the explanatory plots that circulate in court are imported from secular narrative culture—film, television, fiction, drama—is to deny the narrative-generating nature of the adversarial structure and indeed the extent to which the "stories" of secular narrative culture originate in the courtroom.

18. "Many Europeans have never heard of the lie detector but there lurks some vague familiarity with the concept in the mind of nearly every American who can read and wears shoes. . . . Instrumental lie detection-polygraphic interrogation is a 20th century phenomenon and as American as apple pie." David Thoreson Lykken, *Tremor in the Blood: Uses and Abuses of the Lie Detector* (New York: McGraw H ill, 1981), 9, 27.

19. For example, "The trial structures disorder and thus makes it less disturbing and even enjoyable. It is the sustained process of imposing legal order on criminal violence that reaffirms that life's disorder can be controlled. One of the cultural appeals of a television series like Perry Mason, a series that all but defined law for a generation of Americans, was the patterned closure of each program.

The truth was always outed, the true criminal revealed; and the vindicated inno-cence of Perry Mason's client stood for the vindicated order that the legal process predictably imposed. The appeal of the classic detective story is similar, given its reiterated form: a puzzle of violence presented and ultimately solved (and solved through orderly reasoning). Real-life trials obviously do not have the neatness represented on *Perry Mason*, but they have some of its patterned quality—and, above all, they usually reach closure." Paul Gewirtz, "Victims and Voyeurs: Two Narrative Problems at the Criminal Trial," in *Law's Stories: Narrative and Rhetoric in the Law* (New Haven, CT: Yale University Press, 1996), 135.

20. Needless to say, this is not a plot that just happens not to close. It is con-ceived as open-ended, and it clearly means for that open-endedness to be part of its appeal. Other examples of more or less unclosed trial movies are *Reversal of Fortune, Anatomy of a Murder, Criminal Justice, A Question of Guilt, They Won't Believe Me, A Woman's Face*, and *12 Angry Men*. Many trial movies based on ac-tual cases have as their aim exactly to "unclose" the real-life trial: the various Lindbergh movies, for example, or *Brother's Keeper* or *The People v. Jean Harris* or *I Want to Live!* On *By Whose Hand?* (also known as *Who Killed Simon Baird?*), see the review in *Variety*, April 14, 1916, 26. Although I too have the impression that there has been an increase in unclosedness in movies of the last two decades, the fact that there have been unclosed trial movies in every decade of the century (including the first) indicates that the possibility inheres in the form. The adver-sarial structure is always already postmodern, in a manner of speaking. Benjamin Stoloff, dir., *By Whose Hand?* (Culver City, CA: Columbia Pictures, 1932).

21. The phrase "If Court TV were any more addictive, it would be illegal" is said to have originated as a graffito during the Menendez trial. Court TV in-cluded it in a promotional sequence that ran throughout most of 1994. Although Court TV itself has not actually existed as a media entity since 2008, its legacy is visible in the continued popularity of live or staged court proceedings on televi-sion.

22. In an article on the particularly active Chicago court watchers, Karen Dillon writes, "Courtwatching, which has been a tradition in Chicago for de-cades, is a serious business for the buffs, as they are affectionately called by law-yers and judges in the federal building. A self-dubbed shadow jury, they offer suggestions to lawyers during a trial, rate lawyers, judges and witnesses for their performances in court, and predict verdicts and sentencings with surprising ac-curacy" ("Friends of the Court," *American Lawyer*, April 1989, 130). About six regular court watchers were present every day of the five-week trial on whose jury I sat in Alameda County in 1990. Various reports (including the *American Law-yer* one just quoted) suggest that although the numbers have declined since the advent of trial television, a hard core remains committed to the live event. The *Court Watchers Newsletter* bears out the claim of Judy Spreckels, who has been at-

tending Los Angeles–area trials off and on for forty-six years, that it is "procedure, not personalities" that keeps her coming back: "I like the courtroom atmosphere, the discipline, the points of law, the brilliance of people coming up with a better lie and telling it often enough to be believed" (Amy Wallace, "Courthouse Is Clubhouse for the Menendez Watchers," *Los Angeles Times*, June 15, 1994, A33).

23. Notably *On Trial: Lee Harvey Oswald* (directed by David Greene, Charles Fries Productions, 1977) and *The Trial of Lee Harvey Oswald* (directed by Ian Hamilton, produced by Showtime, 1986). The latter film features Vincent Bugliosi as the prosecutor, Gerry Spence as the defense attorney, a real federal judge, real witnesses, and a jury of real Dallas citizens.

24. Verhoeven, Paul, dir., *Basic Instinct* (1992; Santa Monica, CA: Lionsgate Entertainment, 2007), Blu-ray.

25. That is, her putting the ice pick down indicates that Catherine elects not to kill Nick, at least not now. Does she halt because she is basically not a killer (she did not kill her boyfriend, and although she *does* want to kill Nick, she does not have it in her)? Or does she halt because she is a killer, or at least used to be, but cannot kill Nick because she has developed feelings for him? Even if this is not a halt but a hesitation, soon to be overcome, it needs explaining. My own informal survey suggests that although most viewers (maybe two-thirds) believe Catherine did it, a sizable and articulate minority vote for Beth. A second viewing brings out more clearly the elaborate system of clues implicating Beth, the larger point being that *Basic Instinct* "jurifies" its audience as surely as do the movies about Alger Hiss or Barbara Graham.

26. Like many other trial movies, *Basic Instinct* is a whodunit. This is the most popular formula, but it is by no means the only one. In other trial movies, both overt and covert, the question is not who but why or how. The fact that so many overt trial movies are based on real cases with known outcomes makes it clear that the real art and interest of these narratives is less in the answer than in the process of discovery.

27. The justice system seized upon early motion picture technology as having lie-detection potential, the idea being that because lies reveal themselves in movement over time, moving pictures (which can be replayed and run in slow motion) can capture them in a way that still photography cannot. As early as 1903, courts used motion film as a means of determining whether insurance claimants were lying or telling the truth.

28. Verhoven, *Basic Instinct*.

29. Ibid.

30. Actually, *Basic Instinct* is relatively simple in this respect. It really gives us only two suspects, Roxie and Beth, although there is a gesture toward a third in the figure of Hazel Dobkins (the older woman who is discovered to have once murdered her husband and children). In addition, the film hints throughout at

a secret and ominous society of women, lesbian and otherwise, which men (and the movie spectator) will glimpse but never know.

31. *Jagged Edge* closes more completely. In the echo crime at the end, the Jeff Bridges figure does attack the Glenn Close figure, and she does shoot him. Richard Marquand, dir., *Jagged Edge* (1985; Culver City, CA: Sony Pictures, 2000), DVD.

32. Alfred Hitchcock, dir., *The Paradine Case* (1947; Beverly Hills, CA: Anchor Bay Entertainment, 1999), DVD.

33. Verhoven, *Basic Instinct*.

34. *Basic Instinct* and *Jagged Edge* are more neatly symmetrical than most thrillers, which, instead of an echo crime at the end, have some other form of "closing argument." On the other hand, other trial-derived thrillers use the flashback (a cinematic device employed from more or less the moment of its invention by the trial form) far more than *Basic Instinct* and *Jagged Edge*, which eschew it. All in all, *Basic Instinct* is no more trial-like than most other thrillers and can be regarded as fairly typical as far as its plotting goes.

35. Ian Watt, *The Rise of the Novel: Studies in Defoe, Richardson and Fielding* (Berkeley: University of California Press, 1957), pp. 31–34. Watt's way of thinking about law and literature has been followed up with respect to the case (as exemplary precedent) by Gary E. Strankman in his "Law and the Rise of the English Novel" (manuscript provided by the author).

36. Although they are not the subject of this chapter, I might note that Continental trial movies are fewer and farther between and have a rather different shape, tending toward scenarios in which the hapless individual is borne down upon by the overwhelming apparatus of state or church authority (the Joan of Arc or Joseph K. model), hence calling upon a fundamentally different kind and level of engagement on the part of the spectator.

2

Knowing It When We See It

Realism and Melodrama in American Film Since *The Birth of a Nation*

Ticien Marie Sassoubre

Carol Clover's theory that the "narrative machine underneath the manifest plot" of most movies, whatever their genre, "is the trial," has proven enormously appealing to those of us who think about law and culture.[1] On Clover's account, Hollywood films and Anglo-American trials have the same basic structure: an examination of the facts bookended by opening and closing statements driven by the "engine" of cross-examination and governed by the rules of evidence.[2] But her account leaves a number of questions unanswered. What "rules of evidence" do movies follow? What kind of truth does the formal "engine" of cross-examination produce in film?[3] How do films affect the expectations of jurors, the practice of law, and our attitudes about law more generally? If, as Clover observes, the trial that the jury/audience sees may get "lots of things wrong" in terms of law and procedure, but "gets some things, including the underlying epistemology, exactly right," what is that underlying epistemology?[4] If American movie audiences are always in some sense jurors, who or what is on trial?[5]

Several recent documentaries suggest that the answer to the last question may be the trial itself. These documentaries—notably *The Thin Blue Line* (1988) and *The Central Park Five* (2012)—orchestrate alternate trials apparently unhindered by the procedural and institutional liabilities that led to wrongful convictions.[6] But it is not only documentaries that offer alternate trials. Law-themed films in general take up social problems with regard to which law has been unsatisfactory and try the question on different terms. Think of *Kramer vs. Kramer* (1979), which counters the "tender years" doctrine (favoring the mother) with the intimate bond forged between a father and son, or *Philadelphia* (1993), which counters the narrowness of legally provable discrimination with the experience of a loving partner and beloved son facing prejudice at every turn because he happens to be a gay man suffering from AIDS.[7]

Indeed, in the cinematic imagination, official law is indifferent, bureaucratic, and corruptible, constantly threatening to produce injustice. In contrast, "justice" is individual, unambiguous, and readily accessible. As a result, seeing justice done often requires extralegal intervention. Films offer alternate trials in which apparently realistic but emotionally charged representations of personal experience, rather than legal procedure and evidentiary standards, determine guilt or innocence.[8] And while this formula is conspicuous in law-themed films, it is also present in action movies, dramas, and thrillers. Think of Renault's decision to turn a blind eye to the Nazi Strasser's death at the end of *Casablanca* (1942), or undercover cop Brian's decision to let the criminal but morally upright Dom escape at the end of *The Fast and the Furious* (2001).[9] The fairness of the verdict in the filmic alternate trial is measured not by the standard of due process but by the viewer's moral sense.

My point is not that trials are limited by procedure in ways that films are not. Rather, as Clover suggests, in both trials and films, getting the verdict right depends on the ability of the jury/audience to know the truth when we see it. Clover attributes the "rhyme" between the "narrative substructure" of the Anglo-American trial and American film to the "fundamental" role of the jury trial in the American imagination.[10] But I argue that law and film share this narrative substructure because they share a common set of assumptions about narrative plausibility and the social world. In other words, the conventions that govern mainstream American film are also the (largely unspoken) conventions of credibility and verifiability in legal discourse. Knowing it when we see it—as jurors and as moviegoers—means accepting isolated but forensically represented pieces of evidence (a fingerprint, a close-up) to the extent that they combine to offer a plausible representation of lived experience.[11]

In this chapter, I argue that the alternate trial form in American film follows realist rules of evidence but articulates an underlying epistemology that is fundamentally melodramatic. It has done so at least since D. W. Griffith's deeply influential *The Birth of a Nation* (1915). And it continues to do so today. Indeed, American film generates melodramatic trials of our social realities. We have failed to observe this, in part, because of the reality effect of film itself.[12] But, more significantly, this narrative substructure is so familiar it has become invisible to us.

Clover correctly describes her theory as "essentially historical."[13] The adversary trial assumed its modern form in the postbellum period; early cinema borrowed much of its content and most of its personnel (actors, directors, set designers) from late nineteenth-century theater.[14] The extraordinary pressure to come up with stories for the short films that comprised early cinema (D. W. Griffith alone made four hundred) meant that much of nineteenth-century Anglo-American fiction and drama was translated into cinematic versions. And in the nineteenth century, theater and fiction were dominated by the intertwined impulses of realism and melodrama. Griffith and other early filmmakers combined these familiar representational modes with the novel resources of the camera (in terms of visualization) and film (in terms of editing). Lawyers deployed the same cultural resources as juries increasingly played a fact-finding role at trial.[15] The result is the common form that Clover describes: trials and films are both "fragmented, evidence-examining, forensically visualized, backstory-driven, X-not-X structured, polygraphically photographed, intricately plotted, doubt-cultivating, and jury-directed."[16]

There is wide consensus that *The Birth of a Nation*—as the first feature-length motion picture and the first to garner a large national audience—served as the de facto model for mainstream twentieth-century film. An estimated fifty million people saw *Birth* between 1915 and 1920, and it was rereleased in the 1930s. It is credited with overcoming class divisions in film spectatorship and forging a national film audience that would last for much of the twentieth century.[17] And in film studies, Griffith has long been hailed as the father of cinematic realism, with *The Birth of a Nation* treated as his masterpiece.[18] This critical tradition describes classical cinema in terms of realism and narrative continuity borrowed from the novel but has done so largely without interrogating the assumptions through which those effects are achieved. Counterreadings of *Birth* have insisted on the melodramatic elements in Griffith's work and argued for the ways the film registers the social anxieties of the early 1900s.[19] But even these interventions participate in a tendency to treat realism and melodrama as distinct and even mutually exclusive genres rather than overlapping representational practices.[20] This tendency has obscured not merely their interrelation but also the extent to which melodramatic elements inhere in both cinematic and legal "realism." As trial lawyers have long known, we bring the same habits as viewers to our assessment of videotaped testimony or dashboard camera footage as we do to *Downtown Abbey* or *House of Cards*.

The Evidence of Realism

Clover invokes Ian Watt's analogy of the novel-reader to the juror, but Watt does not suggest—as Clover does—that trials conditioned the expectations of eighteenth-century readers. Rather, Watt asserts that the narrative procedures employed by eighteenth-century novelists were general to investigations trained on ascertaining and reporting the truth, including trials.[21] Audiences of both novels and trials, including jurors, expected representations of the truth to conform to certain conventions. And those conventions were the conventions of realism, which rejected established forms (like the epic or pastoral) in favor of representational "fidelity to human experience."[22]

Eighteenth-century realism gave expression to a broad set of cultural and historical forces: the ascendancy of the individual in political theory, the empiricist turn in philosophy and science, the emergence of a literate middle class.[23] The realists' audience took for granted "that truth can be discovered by the individual through his senses" in a social world where individual experience was quickly supplanting the authority of traditional collective and institutional rubrics.[24] Fidelity to human experience, therefore, meant telling stories about "particular people in particular circumstances," not "general human types" against a generic background.[25] Believable, individuated characters had to be presented "in explicable relation to nature, to each other, to their social class, to their own past."[26] Physical environments were presented in exhaustive detail and the material conditions in which characters lived were treated as meaningful contexts for their beliefs and actions. Established literary style was eschewed in favor of the greater authenticity of plain language; novels became episodic, interweaving storylines, often arcing over the span of a lifetime.

In other words, features Clover attributes to the narrative structure of the trial (evidence examining, forensically visualized, intricately plotted, backstory driven, fact-finder-directed) are features of realist narratives generally. Anglo-American juries did not assume the lie-detecting function Clover emphasizes until realist conventions had come to dominate cultural understandings of authentic lived experience and the plausibility of certain narratives. In fact, a variety of rules designed to *prevent* jurors from having to determine the credibility of witnesses were in place well into the nineteenth century.[27] Sworn testimony was presumed to be truthful and competency rules ensured that juries did not hear testimony from "criminal defendants, civil parties, interested persons, felons, spouses, and nonbelievers."[28] Juries did not begin to hear the testimony of interested parties in civil suits until the 1840s or the testimony of criminal defendants until the 1860s.[29]

In practice, juries are probably no better at detecting lies than a coin toss.[30] Jurors "tend to rely on worthless clues and misread others. But while the jury does not guarantee accurate lie detecting, it does detect lies in a way that appears accurate, or at least in a way that hides the source of any inaccuracy from the public's gaze."[31] The X-not-X structure Clover identifies as the shared narrative substructure of the adversary system and the trial-like film "pits a prosecution X not against a defense Y, but against a defense not-X," "not-X being a site of proliferating scenarios, including mutually exclusive ones."[32] This structure does not produce truth, but it does produce judgments that appear accurate according to conventional expectations. As Robert Ferguson has observed, the "genre of a story, its familiar form in the telling, is a crucial factor and often the hidden ingredient in courtroom belief."[33] In the Anglo-American trial, this genre is literary realism.[34]

By the 1870s, the realism of the Victorian novel had come under attack from writers influenced by Darwinism and the emerging disciplines of psychology and sociology, on the one hand, and by the social transformations wrought by industrialization and urbanization on the other. With his 1870 call for the "experimental novel," Emile Zola emerged as the standard-bearer of a new generation of social realists. "Now science enters into the domain of us novelists," he writes, "who are to-day the analyzers of man, in his individual and social relations. We are continuing, by our observations and experiments, the work of the physiologist, who has continued that of the physicist and chemist. We are making use, in a certain way, of scientific psychology to complete scientific physiology; and to finish the series we have only to bring into our studies of nature and man the decisive tool of the experimental method.[35] "The observer," Zola insists, "relates purely and simply the phenomena which he has under his eyes. . . . He should be the photographer of phenomena."[36] The establishment of the jury's modern role as "our sole judges of credibility" in the late nineteenth century occurred precisely as this model of social realism came to dominate the American popular imagination.[37]

As Zola's analogy suggests, late nineteenth-century realism was deeply influenced by the development of photography. Photography dates to the 1830s, but photographs did not become commonplace until after the Civil War, and it was not until the mass production and distribution of photographic images became technically possible in the 1880s that they became ubiquitous.[38] Early cameras required stationary subjects and long exposures. As shutter speeds got faster, this passivity was replaced with a "new way of thinking about the camera," which included the "probing, analyzing, and active observing of scientific work."[39] Eadweard Muybridge's 1878 stop-motion photograph of a galloping horse against a grid background is the classic example.[40] Cameras also got smaller. Hand-held "detective" cameras made it possible to take photographs without a subject's consent and in previously private places.[41]

William Ivins reminds us that the camera sees very differently than the human eye and that the photographic image at first seemed more strange than familiar. But as viewers became "conditioned" to photographic images, they "gradually ceased to talk about photographic distortion [and] the photograph became the norm for the appearance of everything."[42] The camera's way of seeing became the standard for all investigation. The photograph displaced even eyewitness testimony. As Ivins observes, the "19th century began by believing that what was reasonable was true and it would end up by believing that what it saw in a photograph was true—from the finish of a horse race to the nebulae in the sky."[43]

The novelty of the photograph as a representational form is, of course, that it seems to offer an unmediated reproduction—"the scene *is there*, captured mechanically, not humanly (the mechanical here is a guarantee of objectivity)."[44] Photographs quickly replaced other forms of written and pictorial representation in the work of representing facts and experience at the end of the nineteenth century, but the "profound difference between creating something and making a statement about the quality and character of something" went largely unnoticed.[45] Unlike a drawing or a text—which are conspicuously cultural products—in the photographic image, "nature seems spontaneously to produce the scene represented."[46] Viewers treated photographic images as replicas of the real.

As replicas of the real, photographs promised to extend the empirical knowledge of the individual observer beyond the reach of her personal experience. In Oliver Wendell Holmes Sr.'s much-quoted 1859 formulation, "matter as a visible object is of no great use any longer, except as the mould on which form is shaped. Give us a few negatives of a thing worth seeing, taken from different points of view, and that is all we want of it."[47] This kind of vicarious expertise resembles the lie-detecting role extended to jurors in the postbellum period. A trial is conspicuously not a reenactment and though juries were once comprised of witnesses, the modern jury has no knowledge of the case except the trial. The juror, like the viewer of a photograph, is presumed to derive knowledge of the facts from their representation.

The list of nineteenth-century photographs claimed and treated as historical fact that were either staged or misrepresented is long: Roger Fenton's famous 1855 pictures from the Crimean War,[48] Alexander Gardner's 1866 volume of pictures from the Civil War, Jacob Riis's images of poverty in *How the Other Half Lives* (1890), and Edward Curtis's photographs of Native Americans, which he started producing in 1898.[49] In practice, nineteenth-century photographers often arranged images to conform to viewers' (and photographers') expectations of how the real would look—expectations informed by "the tourist sketch, the painted portrait, the staged tableau, even . . . the scientific illustration."[50] Photographic realism provides viewers with apparently spontaneous, authentic knowledge of objective reality. But it does so by activating preexisting, conventional understandings of the social world.

The rules of evidence observed by film combine elements of literary and photographic realism.[51] The omniscient camera replaces the novel's omniscient narrator, and the aspiration to use language as denotatively as possible translates into a seamlessness or invisibility of style.[52] The close description of physical settings becomes what we call mise-en-scène in film—the way represented objects create and inform meaning in the filmic frame. The episodic, intercut storylines provide the model for parallel editing.[53] And the emphasis on psychologically individuated characters maps onto the way bodies and faces become "focal points of attention" in the repertoire of filmic shots.[54] The realist novel's insistence on the treatment of lived experience in time finds expression in the relatively compressed medium of film in both the norm of temporal linearity and the deployment of flashbacks and other forms of intercutting to create the impression of narrative development over time. In film, "the camera seems always to include character subjectivity within a broader and definite objectivity."[55]

Literary realists themselves quickly encountered difficulties in their attempt to create an authentic report of human experience. One was at the level of language itself: however plain one's style, words do not correspond perfectly to actual things, correspond to things in various and inconsistent ways, and are never free of connotation.[56] There was also the difficulty of fashioning something interesting out of the banal stuff of everyday life.[57] Early realists solved this problem in part by writing about characters that would interest middle-class readers precisely because their stories had been untellable by previous literary convention: *Moll Flanders* (1772) is about a poor motherless girl tricked into unmarried sex, *Oliver Twist* (1838) is about an orphan criminal.[58] And late nineteenth-century social realism was just as vulnerable to charges of sensationalism in its preoccupation with "blood, sex, money, grime, garbage, immigrants, and killing snowstorms."[59]

But the challenge of authentic reporting for realists cut deeper. As Peter Brooks observes, the literary realists wanted not just to depict everyday life, but to capture the meaning implicit in lived experience."[60] Only "once the fact is ascertained and the phenomenon observed," Zola insists, does "the experimentalist comes forward to interpret the phenomenon."[61] But interpret he must. There "is always a moment in [the author's] descriptions of the world where the eye's photographic registration of objects yields to the mind's effort to pierce surfaces, to interrogate appearances."[62] In some sense, the realist is always looking for the true beneath the mask of the real.

The Epistemology of the Melodramatic Mode

By most accounts, American realists never really attempted the objective description prescribed by Zola.[63] But even among the most committed Continental realists, the "real" and the "ordinary" and "private life" were made interesting "through heightened dramatic utterance and gesture that [lay] bare the true stakes."[64] And to achieve these effects, realists borrowed from melodrama.[65]

Melodrama enacts its polarization of good and evil through a set of representational practices involving pathos (the evocation of pity through identification), the expression of intense emotion, extraordinary or implausible narrative structure, and sensationalism (violence, thrills, spectacles).[66] Gestures, rhythms, aesthetic patterns, "substitute acts," "parallel situations and metaphoric connections" inform our experience of the narrative in what Thomas Elsaesser describes as "a conscious use of style-as-meaning."[67]

Melodrama emerged as a cultural form in the late eighteenth century and suffused the nineteenth-century popular imagination. In the early melodrama of the French stage, a virtuous innocent is put in "a situation of extreme peril."[68] It appears that the threatening evil—usually a villain—will succeed until the third act, which involves "a highly physical 'acting out' of virtue's liberation from the oppressive efforts of evil."[69] A cartoon version survived well into the twentieth century: a man with a moustache wearing all black ties up an innocent girl in white and leaves her on train tracks. We watch with horror as the train approaches until the (attractive, match-appropriate) hero arrives and saves the girl.

There is broad consensus that melodrama developed in response to an experience of modernity in which "the traditional imperatives of truth and ethics have been violently thrown into question, yet where the promulgation of truth and ethics, their instauration as a way of life, is of immediate, daily, political concern."[70] In melodrama, "good and evil can be named as persons are named," and the conflict of these two forces repolarizes the moral compass of modern subjects.[71] Melodramatic forms provided a new rubric for identifying and anchoring "ethical imperatives" in a social world without transcendent values.[72]

For realists, these forms also "served as the literary equivalent of a particular, historical and socially conditioned *mode of experience*."[73] Melodramatic scenes and confrontations made renderings of lived experience feel "specific and historically real."[74] Indeed, the melodramatic was so familiar that Dickens himself proffered the argument that the apparent tension between melodrama and realism is largely a matter of perspective. The extremes and discontinuities of melodrama, he admitted, "appear absurd; but they are not so unnatural as they would seem at first sight. The transitions in real life from well-spread boards to death-beds, and from mourning-weeds to holiday garments, are not a whit less startling; only there, we are busy actors, instead of passive lookers-on."[75]

Nineteenth-century melodrama articulated Victorian anxieties about sex and class. In the enormously popular and long-running 1898 American stage play *Way Down East*, an innocent girl named Anna is tricked into a fake marriage, impregnated, and abandoned. She gives birth to a child that quickly dies, and finds refuge as a servant for the Bartlett family. But Anna is cast out into a violent snowstorm when Mr. Bartlett learns of her past. (In the famous climax of Griffith's filmic version, she floats unconscious down an icy river toward a waterfall.) At the last minute, she is rescued by the Bartlett son, who not only loves her but will marry her.

A hundred years later, even true stories are still structured as melodramatic narratives. At the beginning of the 2000 film *Erin Brockovich*, the eponymous heroine is an unemployed, twice-divorced mother of three whose courtroom outburst causes her to lose the personal injury case that is her last hope for financial stability.[76] Hired out of pity by her lawyer, she discovers that a large public utility has contaminated the water supply of a rural community with a carcinogenic chemical. She proves her virtue by working tirelessly and compassionately to help the victims. It looks like the company will succeed in avoiding responsibility and preventing the truth from coming out until the last minute, when a utility company employee—a good man, if a bad employee—in possession of documents that prove the utility knowingly contaminated the water gives those documents to Brockovich. The truth comes out. The victims are awarded $333 million. Brockovich is given $2 million of it as a gift by the benevolent lawyer.

Because melodrama's emotional stakes arise from the lived experience of (modern) social problems, the form has proved enormously protean.[77] As Linda Williams argues, when popular culture engages with moral questions, it tends to do so in the melodramatic mode.[78] The melodramatic moral binary also "sutures neatly into the courtroom, a place where opposing attorneys tend to emphasize moral clarity over nuance as they argue their cases, casting their side as heroic, the other as villainous."[79] And a wide variety of legal genres are essentially melodramatic, from victim impact statements and the description of human rights violations to day-in-the-life-of videos (showing the everyday experience of plaintiffs in personal injury cases) to testimony in custody disputes.[80]

There are good reasons for this. At a basic level, melodrama and the common law share a structural similarity: both address larger social phenomena at the level of the individual. And as Alan Dershowitz observes, "human beings must invent, not discover, laws of morality and governance to regulate human conduct so that a narrative of justice can be enforced."[81] This is precisely the set of conditions melodrama speaks to. But realist representation in the melodramatic mode has certain consequences for the construction of a compelling narrative of justice.[82]

Melodramatic narratives are variously hegemonic, subversive, escapist, political—"categories which are always relative to the given historical and social context," Elsaesser reminds us, in his description of the "radical ambiguity attached to the melodrama."[83] Nevertheless, the fundamental binary between good and evil built into melodrama, together with its expressive orchestration of meaning as much through style as plot, profoundly affect its representations of the social world in which questions of justice are raised. Perhaps most significantly, identification with the victim—and indeed the construction of a victim—is one of "the characteristic features of melodramas in general."[84] This helps account for the particular quality of "emotional involvement" on the part of the audience that characterizes Hollywood film.[85] But it also tends to conflate moral power with victimhood.

Home and family are frequently the locus of virtue in melodramatic narratives. In early melodrama, the home was threatened by the malignity of bad men. But institutions, corporations, and governments gradually supplanted individuals as the agents of evil in the melodramatic imagination (in no small part as a result of social realism). The family—and the individualized identity that springs from intimate personal experience frequently connected with the family—was increasingly imagined as isolated from and vulnerable to larger social forces.

Elsaesser draws a connection between this development and the way that most narratives circulating in American popular culture have "resolutely refused to understand social change in other than private contexts and emotional terms."[86] He observes that melodrama "seems capable of reproducing more directly than other genres patterns of domination and exploitation existing in a given society, especially the relation between psychology, morality, and class-consciousness, by emphasizing so clearly an emotional dynamic whose social correlative is a network of external forces directed oppressingly inward, and with which the characters themselves unwittingly collude to become their agents."[87] But responsibility for the "evil" suffered by the characters "is firmly placed on a social and existential level, away from the arbitrary and finally obtuse logic of private motives and individualised psychology."[88] The underlying epistemology of the melodramatic mode not only assumes a binary of good and evil at work in the social world but identifies the good with individual and familial experience threatened by larger, variously malignant or merely indifferent, social forces. The representation of this fundamental truth requires the disruption of the status quo reproduced by superficial realism. Indeed, the "dramatic tension in melodrama lies in the possibility that virtue will be masked or misrecognized through misunderstanding, disguise, or manipulation."[89] So, too, in the trial.[90] Clover's quip that "where there are lies, there are liars" manifests the melodramatic worldview perfectly: instead of innocent mistakes, inevitable slips of memory, differences of perspective, in the world of the trial there is potential (moral) meaning in every gesture and utterance.[91]

Clover draws our attention to the basic assumption inherent in the fragmented narrative structure of both film and the adversarial trial that an event "can be broken down into particles of fact that preexist narrative and that, scrutinized singly and initially outside of story, these fact particles will, in the mind of the beholder, assemble toward their own best explanation."[92] As in all melodramatic narratives, this structure invites us to an initial conclusion, unsettles it, invites us to another.[93] The dramatic tension in film works generally by "creating pressure and manipulating it."[94] Some of this pressure is generated by the plot, but there is also the pressure that "the spectator brings to the film by way of anticipation and *a priori* expectations of what he hopes to see" and it is particularly this kind of pressure that makes the discontinuities of melodrama "so effective."[95] At trial, both sides argue "as unfairly as possible," but in the end, "unfairness gets us fairness, a widening gyre works to narrow things down, lying produces truth, and truth is nothing more than the best story so far."[96] In other words, style makes meaning in the trial as well. The best story is the one that makes the best use of the expectations the audience brings to the examination of represented facts.

When we watch a film, we know it is not real but have, nevertheless, "a strange feeling of reality."[97] In 1922, sociologist Walter Lippmann observed that movies were "steadily building up imagery" that would serve as vicarious experience for viewers:[98] "Without more trouble than is needed to stay awake the result which your imagination is always aiming at is reeled off on the screen. The shadowy idea becomes vivid; your hazy notion, let us say, of the Klu [*sic*] Klux Klan, thanks to Mr. Griffiths [*sic*], takes vivid shape when you see the Birth of a Nation. Historically it may be the wrong shape, morally it may be a pernicious shape, but it is a shape, and I doubt whether anyone who has seen the film and does not know more about the Klu Klux Klan than Mr. Griffiths, will ever hear the name again without seeing those white horsemen."[99] Lippmann further noted that this is a different kind of vicarious experience than that derived from viewing a photograph.[100] As Christian Metz has since explained, the indexical quality of the photograph—its mechanical connection to a particular object in the physical world at a particular moment—fixes certain facts through their representation. In contrast, "film is able to call up our belief for long and complex dispositions of actions and characters."[101] As a result, the "initially indexical power of the cinema" often operates as "a realist guarantee for the unreal."[102]

In film, the camera operates as "an *ideal* invisible observer, freed from the contingencies of space and time."[103] On the classical account, this omniscience "discreetly" confines itself to "codified patterns for the sake of intelligibility."[104] But omniscience is also achieved through (carefully controlled) discontinuity: film tends to "render narrational omniscience through spatial *omnipresence*," "cutting within a scene and crosscutting between various locales testify to the narration's omnipresence."[105] Together with the manipulation of mise-en-scène, the narrational omniscience and spatial omnipresence of the camera present a world that "appears to have preexisted" its representation.[106] Where photographic realism offers audiences vicarious knowledge of an object or scene, cinematic realism provides audiences with vicarious knowledge of a social world.

The earliest films screened in the United States in 1895 and 1896 reproduced quotidian activities, and their appeal to viewers was precisely the representation of "the everyday world as they knew it and experienced it directly."[107] It was the indexical quality of the filmed scene, like Muybridge's galloping horses, that appealed to the audience. But very quickly, producers began to offer spectacles filmed from a fixed point of view that replicated the experience of sitting in the audience of a play or pageant, as well as simple stories told in a single scene viewed from a fixed point. The first photoplays were screened in 1902, offering "a series of situations pictorially developed not only to tell a story but so interlaced that this story became cinematically dramatic."[108] These photoplays borrowed heavily from nineteenth-century melodrama not just for stories but "for the stylistic features that allow meanings to be conveyed without words" that were already familiar to a broad popular audience.[109] From the beginning, American narrative film deployed photographic realism in the representation of a melodramatic social world.

D. W. Griffith made his first short film in 1908. Notwithstanding his relentless self-promotion, Griffith was rarely the only, or even the first, to use the many and various cinematic techniques he employed. But more than his contemporaries, "he understood that each new technique was not merely an attention-getting device but a sign, a special way of communicating, a link in a chain of cinematic discourse."[110] He is widely acknowledged as having established the conventions of cinematic realism we take for granted today.

Griffith famously rejected the industry's early insistence on continuity of shot (the studios worried that audiences would be confused by camera movement or discontinuous editing).[111] Instead, he mobilized the photographic realism made possible by film in the service of the kind of authentic report of lived experience sought by literary realism.[112] Between 1908 and 1913, he moved the camera closer to his subjects, increased the number of shots per reel, "increased the movement and variety of movements within his frame," and "gave more detailed attention to natural and artificial lighting."[113] He also "found new ways to increase the tempo and build the tension of his dramatic chase and rescue films"—innovating first parallel editing and then crosscut editing between multiple story lines.[114] He not only varied shot lengths but also shifted from "medium shots to long panorama shots to close-ups" and even to reverse shot shifts in perspective.[115]

By 1913, Griffith was using what Sergei Eisenstein would later give the name *montage*—the editing together of separate, juxtaposed shots to create an overarching idea or impression or feeling.[116] In film, montage reveals the deeper meaning of the photographic image. Montage also creates the effect of the omnipresence of the camera. Griffith's camera "seems free to rove anywhere, be everywhere at the same time. Every spot is accessible; every action knowable. All of life can come before the viewer's eye. Time and space are conquered; sitting in our theater seat, we are the unseen witness of every act, every gesture, every secret."[117] If movie audiences are always in some sense jurors and movies are trials, they are so because of the vicarious expertise created by codified patterns of montage Griffith helped establish and popularize.

Eisenstein reminds us, however, that this expertise is not rational but emotional. What makes film so powerfully affective is the vividness of emotional experience created through montage, something written language cannot capture.[118] But montage takes a particular view of the social world for granted in order to create this effect.[119] For Eisenstein, "the structure that is reflected in the concept of a Griffith montage is the structure of bourgeois society"—the binary of rich and poor.[120] But that account is too narrow. It is the fundamentally melodramatic structure of binary-ness itself that Griffith introduces and makes invisible in film form.

The Birth of a Nation as Trial

The critic Walter Benjamin worried that as "photographs become standard evidence for historical occurrences," they "acquire a hidden political significance."[121] During the 1915 promotion of *The Birth of a Nation*, D. W. Griffith predicted that film would become the standard evidence for historical occurrences. "The time will come," he claimed, "when the children in the public schools will be taught practically everything by moving pictures. Certainly, they will never be obliged to read history again. . . . There will be no opinions expressed. You will merely be present at the making of history."[122] And Griffith repeatedly insisted on the film's historical accuracy. But the form of Griffith's cinematic realism is not that of history, it is the form of the trial.

In my reading, *The Birth of a Nation* offers an alternate trial of Reconstruction and the Fourteenth and Fifteenth Amendments just as organized resistance to a solidifying Jim Crow regime was taking shape.[123] The NAACP was founded in 1909 "to eradicate caste or race prejudice among the citizens of the United States; to advance the interest of colored citizens; to secure for them impartial suffrage; and to increase their opportunities for securing justice in the courts, education for the children, employment according to their ability and complete equality before law."[124] The NAACP opposed President Wilson's segregation of the federal workforce and initiated litigation challenging a variety of Jim Crow practices, including the disenfranchisement of black voters and the segregation of neighborhoods, and began lobbying for antilynching legislation.[125]

In defense of segregation, *The Birth of a Nation* rehabilitates Chief Justice Taney's argument in *Scott v. Sandford* (1857) that persons of African descent were disqualified by their race for the privileges of citizenship and amplifies Taney's anxious invocation of the specter of miscegenation.[126] It puts flesh on the question, raised in *Plessy v. Ferguson* (1896), whether the Fourteenth Amendment "intended to abolish distinctions based upon color . . . or a commingling of the two races upon terms unsatisfactory to either."[127] And it offers a simultaneously idealized and graphically visualized representation of the "established usages, customs, and traditions of the people" of the (white) South, promoting "their comfort, and the preservation of the public peace and good order," to which the *Plessy* majority deferred.[128]

Against an account in which the evils of slavery and southern political obstinacy resulted in the Civil War and the extension of the benefits of democracy to freedman (on Clover's account, the prosecution, or X), *The Birth of a Nation* offers a series of defenses: northern hypocrisy and self-interest led to the war; slavery was not always evil; if slavery was evil, carpetbagger opportunism was worse; Reconstruction made life worse for black and white people alike; black aggression forced white southerners to defend themselves; and finally, white women were not safe with black men (not-X).[129]

The Birth of a Nation tells the fictional story of two families—the northern Stonemans and the southern Camerons—from just before the Civil War through Reconstruction. In the first half of the film, the sons of both families fight in the war while the Camerons at home suffer its effects.

In the second half of the film, Austin Stoneman enacts a policy of racial equality in the occupied South and his black protégé, Silas Lynch, rises to a position of power. Under Lynch's leadership, Stoneman's policy proves disastrous, for the South generally (represented by the Camerons) and for white women (including Stoneman's daughter, Elsie). The oldest Cameron son, Ben, founds the Ku Klux Klan, which eventually reestablishes white control. The clan's success assures a happy ending: at the end of the film, Ben marries Elsie, and Ben's sister Margaret marries Elsie's brother, Phil.

Existing prints of *The Birth of a Nation* begin with the intertitle, "If in this work we have conveyed to the mind the ravages of war to the end that *war may be held in abhorrence*, this effort will not have been in vain."[130] The next intertitle asserts that "the bringing of the African to America planted the first seed of disunion," and the first image is of manacled slaves in what appears to be a northern town square with a minister praying over them.[131] The third intertitle reads: "The abolitionists of the Nineteenth Century demanding the freeing of the slaves." It introduces the interior of what appears to be a northern congregation. A black child is walked toward the camera down the center aisle of the church, and a collection is taken while the boy looks steadily at the camera. The hands of a white man rest on his shoulders. In some versions, a woman first reaches toward and then recoils from the boy.[132] With or without that gesture, the sterility of the northern milieu and the deep pathos and isolation of the child are striking.

This scene is immediately followed by an intertitle introducing us to a "great parliamentary leader whom we shall call Austin Stoneman . . . rising to power in the National House of Representatives . . . with his young daughter, Elsie, in her apartments in Washington."[133] (Stoneman is a proxy for Thaddeus Stephens). Here again there is a sense of isolation and disconnection. Elsie wipes her father's forehead solicitously then kneels beside him as he stares forward. A wife/mother figure is conspicuously absent. So are Elsie's brothers, whom we learn will soon be traveling to Piedmont, South Carolina, to visit their friend Ben Cameron.

The scene shifts to Piedmont, "In the Southland" an intertitle tells us, at "the home of the Camerons, where life runs in a quaintly way that is to be no more."[134] The contrast between living in a "home" and "apartments" is borne out in the following scenes: the two Cameron daughters, Margaret and Flora, walk toward their mother; Margaret kisses her; they greet the passengers in a carriage, which also contains two black children; the children fall out of the wagon and are picked up in a scene that the audience is invited to read as both comic and ordinary from Ben Cameron's amused reaction.[135] Ben kisses his mother, we are introduced to Dr. Cameron, "the kindly master of Cameron Hall," and a household slave called Mammy looks on approvingly. In a scene introduced with the intertitle, "Hostilities," a kitten and a puppy play.

These scenes emphasize the intimacy and pleasure of the intact family embedded in a larger close-knit interracial community. When Stoneman's sons arrive, they are immediately accepted into this easy and light-hearted intimacy (there is playful teasing between the boys and some flirting between Margaret and Phil, the oldest Stoneman son). Then the Stonemans are taken on a tour of the Cameron plantation. Shots of slaves picking cotton are followed by a scene in which Ben falls in love with Elsie's photograph (carried by Phil), followed immediately by shots of slaves dancing during their "two-hour interval given for dinner, out of their working day from six til six." An older black man offers his chair to Ben; Ben refuses. The Stoneman sons' tour of the Cameron plantation—and the first reel of the film—ends with Ben Cameron shaking a slave's hand.[136]

Here, then, is the opening argument in the alternate trial of Reconstruction and the Reconstruction amendments. Against the Union account, *The Birth of a Nation* argues that the North, while complicit with slavery, has not understood it, and that racial hierarchy assures social stability and human flourishing. The rest of the film follows the alternating pattern that Clover identifies with the turn-taking structure of the adversarial trial. The conventions of realism establish what will count as evidence, and parallel editing provides the engine driving the interrogation of that evidence. But it is the melodramatic tension between innocent victims and malignant forces that infuses the evidence with meaning.

The "examination of the facts" in *The Birth of a Nation* begins with the southern threat to secede announced in a newspaper headline. The northern decision to go to war is represented by two scenes of political action: first, Stoneman in heated argument with Charles Sumner (at one point Stoneman pounds his fist on a table), and then, what we are told is "AN HISTORICAL FACSIMILE of the President's Executive Office on that occasion, after Nicolay and Hay in Lincoln, a History," in which Lincoln solemnly signs "The First Call for 75,000 Volunteers" and then prays.[137] Interpolated between these two scenes are the warm parting of the Stoneman sons from the happy domesticity of the Cameron household (again pictured as including slaves) contrasted with a sequence in which Stoneman's mixed-race housekeeper refuses to show a visiting Charles Sumner the subservience he expects (she drops his hat on the floor) and it is revealed that Stoneman is romantically involved with her.[138]

This melodramatic pattern of juxtaposition in which the South stands for family and community and the North stands for abstract politics compromised by questionable personal motives is repeated throughout the first half of the film. (Even the musical score alternates between instantly recognizable and regionally identified American folk music with the formal composition of Wagner.[139]) When the Cameron sons go to war, there is a ball, a crowd cheers the departing soldiers, and Ben covers his sleeping younger sister, Flora, with the Confederate flag before he leaves. In contrast, Stoneman himself apparently does not know his sons have enlisted in the Northern cause until Elsie tells him at the beginning of the third reel. An affectionate exchange of letters between Ben and Flora is followed by a raid on Piedmont by "an irregular force of guerillas" in which the Cameron household comes under attack by black and white Union soldiers. Dr. Cameron attempts to repel them with a gun but is overpowered by a white soldier as the women of the household hide in terror. Confederate troops arrive but not before the Union troops have set fire to the Cameron home. Together with Mammy, the Cameron women put out the fire. Mammy hugs one of the Confederate soldiers in gratitude.[140]

Once this pattern is established in the opening reels, the realism of the carefully staged, spectacular battle scenes lends credibility to the melodrama of the Cameron family (and the white South's) plight. The Union guerilla raid scenes are contrasted with battle scenes in which one of the Cameron sons, Wade, and Stoneman's younger son, Tod, die together after a brief moment of recognition and mercy. Sherman's march to Atlanta is depicted in unprecedentedly large scale scenes of military movement punctuated by shots of a displaced and frightened Southern mother and her three children.[141]

The fourth reel begins with the battle for a supply convoy at Petersburg in the "last grey days of the Confederacy."[142] Gradually we realize that the opposed commanders in the battle are Ben Cameron and Phil Stoneman. The Confederate soldiers are outgunned; the violence of the mortar fire is contrasted with the personal gallantry shown by Ben in helping a fallen Union soldier (the Union soldiers cheer). At the end of the battle, Phil saves Ben's life. The intertitle "The North victorious" follows shots of mangled dead bodies. The Camerons learn of the death of their second son and an intertitle tells us that loss is "The woman's part" as Margaret and Flora grieve.[143]

When the film leaves the battlefield, Griffith's "historical facsimiles," meticulously reproduced from historical descriptions and photographs, take over the work of anchoring the melodramatic narrative to apparently historical events. After the Petersburg battle, Ben convalesces in the military hospital where Elsie is a nurse. Mrs. Cameron arrives, and she and Elsie quickly form an alliance to thwart "a secret influence that has condemned

Col. Cameron to be hanged as a guerilla."[144] Elsie gets Mrs. Cameron in to see President Lincoln himself, and Mrs. Cameron persuades him to spare Ben (in the same set used for the "historical facsimile" of Lincoln signing the call for volunteers at the start of the war earlier in the film). This unofficial meeting of Lincoln and the two distraught women is quickly followed by "an historical facsimile" of Lee formally surrendering to Grant, for which the intertitle cites the authority of "Col. Horace Porter in *Campaigning with Grant*."[145] Then we see Ben return to the poverty and desolation of postwar Piedmont, where Flora makes a pathetic attempt to ornament her dress for his homecoming with raw cotton.[146]

The imbrication of the characters' experiences with representations of historical events reaches its apotheosis at the end of the first half of the film. Griffith contrasts Lincoln's benevolence toward the South ("I shall deal with them as though they had never been away") with Stoneman's ("Their leaders must be hanged and their states treated as conquered provinces").[147] And then Griffith sends us, together with Phil and Elsie, to the Ford theater to witness Lincoln's assassination in "AN HISTORICAL FACSIMILE of Ford's theatre on the night, exact in size and detail, with the recorded incidents, after Nicolay and Hay in Lincoln, a History."[148] The play is depicted on a stage with an audience (including Phil and Elsie) within the film. Scenes from the play alternate with scenes of Lincoln's arrival, John Wilkes Booth's arrival, and the assassination itself, culminating in Booth limping to the center of the stage and the intertitle, "Sic semper tyrannis."[149] This is the kind of disruption that Norman Spaulding describes elsewhere in this volume as of the highest order. The play is disrupted, the film is disrupted, history is disrupted, and Griffith uses the rupture to reset the terms and stakes of the trial.

This first half of *The Birth of a Nation* offers a defense of a paternalist white South before the war. The second half offers a defense of a white supremacist South that resisted Reconstruction. Griffith elides the difference between the two by deriving the KKK from yet another threat to the Cameron family. But in the second half of the film, the threatening evil is not an uncomprehending and self-interested North. It is a much more familiar melodramatic villain in the person of Silas Lynch. Embodying the extension of equal rights to blacks in the mixed-race Lynch and then setting in motion what is superficially a conventional plot in which the evil black-clad man imperils a white-clad innocent allows Griffith to cloak a hyperbolic and ahistorical representation of African Americans in precisely the kind of narrative structure that felt realistic to audiences steeped in a melodramatic account of the social world.

The second half of the film begins with an intertitle making the remarkable assertion, "This is an historical presentation of the Civil War and Reconstruction period, and is not meant to reflect on any race or people today."[150] The next three intertitles claim first that "the Policy of the congressional leaders wrought a veritable overthrow of civilization in the South . . . in their determination to 'put the white South under the heel of the black South'" and then that "the white men were roused by a mere instinct of self-preservation" to form the Ku Klux Klan."[151] The authority Griffith offers for these intertitles is no less than sitting president Woodrow Wilson's 1902 *History of the American People*.[152]

After these intertitles, a newspaper headline—this time reporting the assassination of the South's "best friend" in Lincoln—once again announces the coming of a war. And the second half of the film follows the same formal pattern of alternation between the personal experiences of Phil, Elsie, and the Camerons on the one hand, and apparently historical representations of general social phenomena on the other, as the first half of the film. The courtships of Phil and Margaret and Ben and Elsie play out as life in the South is transformed by Stoneman's "edict that the blacks shall be raised to full equality with the whites."[153]

But in the second half of the film, the imprimatur of historical accuracy is affixed to much more dubious representations than in the first. There are scenes in which carpetbaggers induce freedmen to stop working; Freedman's Bureau supplies are "misused to delude the ignorant"[154]; blacks participate in voter fraud and forcibly prevent whites from voting; an all-black jury presided over by a black judge acquits a black defendant to the horror of the white family that had apparently been his victim. Only one of these scenes offers documentation of its veracity. An intertitle reads: "The negro party in control in the State House of Representatives, 101 blacks against 23 whites, session of 1871. AN HISTORICAL FACSIMILE of the State House of Representatives of South Carolina as it was in 1870. After photograph by *The Columbia State*."[155] A series of shots follow in which black House members dress inappropriately, remove their shoes, drink alcohol, eat, and pass two bills: one requiring whites to salute black officers in the street and one "providing for the inter-marriage of blacks and whites."[156] It is not clear which, if any, of these acts the photograph published in the *Columbia State* depicted. Rather, the invocation of the newspaper lends the racial animus of the shots vicarious credibility.

Such "historical" scenes alternate with scenes of Ben and Elsie's courtship as the Cameron household suffers under Stoneman and Lynch's regime (including the beating of the Camerons' still-loyal black house servant Jake for voting against the "Carpetbaggers.")[157] This pattern culminates with the legislative endorsement of interracial marriage, followed immediately by an intertitle warning: "The grim reaping begins."[158] A black soldier named Gus shows too much interest in Flora, an insolence that provokes Ben to form the KKK (the Klan's costumes are inspired by an incident in which two white children frighten four black children by hiding under a sheet). But Ben is too late to save Flora.

In this notorious sequence, we first see Gus watching an unwitting Flora. Here, the natural mise-en-scène fosters the impression of reality: Flora throws a rock, draws water from a spring, sits on a log, and talks to a squirrel on a branch as it rubs its nose. Gus reveals himself and proposes to Flora. She refuses and tries to get away, but Gus pursues her into the woods. Ben finds the bucket Flora has left behind and begins his own pursuit. The following parallel-edited shots of the three characters moving separately through the woods culminate in Flora jumping from a cliff to her death. An intertitle reads: "For her who had learned the stern lesson of honor we should not grieve that she found sweeter the *opal gates of death*."[159] Gus is then pursued into a gin mill, where there is an elaborately choreographed fight before Ben finally catches Gus. An intertitle reading "The trial" introduces a montage of Gus dragged before hooded Klansmen, Flora dead in the Cameron living room, an unmasked Ben pointing at Gus, and the intertitle "Guilty."[160]

Gus's lifeless body is delivered to Lynch, who initiates an offensive against the Klan, and the Cameron home is once again invaded, this time to arrest Dr. Cameron. Phil Stoneman helps the Camerons' household slaves rescue Dr. Cameron, Phil kills a black man in the process, and he and the Camerons flee, ending up in the (oddly) homey cabin of two Union veterans and a little girl. Elsie goes to Lynch for help but quickly finds herself captive in his apartments. Lynch proposes to her. When she refuses, he first threatens to horsewhip her, then attempts to persuade her with the prospect of being a queen in his "Black Empire."[161] In the film's most overt threat of rape, an intertitle reads, "Lynch, drunk with wine and power, orders his henchmen to hurry preparations for a forced marriage."[162] Stoneman, who has endorsed the idea of Lynch marrying a white woman, reacts with outrage when he learns that Lynch wants to marry Elsie. Outside, the streets are depicted as a riot of black on white violence at Lynch's behest.

Two rides to the rescue ensue, in parallel editing. Klan spies hear Elsie screaming and bring the news to Ben; more Klansmen ride to the aid of Phil, the Camerons, and their slaves Mammy and Jake. A shoot-out at the Union veterans' cabin repels Lynch's men; Ben saves Elsie in the nick of time. The Klan restores order in the streets.

The much-celebrated realism of the Civil War battle scenes in the first half of the film confers apparent historical authenticity on the also much–

celebrated realism of these (fictional) Klan rides. The intensity of the shoot-out at the cabin, together with the intensity of the threat of rape, effectively conflate the social and political conflict between black equality and white privilege represented in the former with the formulaic melodrama of an innocent, white-clad Elsie helpless in the black hands of the villainous Lynch.[163] In other words, the parallel climaxes complete the transfer of the source of evil from northern policy to newly freed blacks themselves and of virtue from innocent girls to whites no longer sectionally divided.

The closing arguments present a new binary of violence and reconciliation. On the one hand, there is a show of force. An intertitle reads: "Parade of the Clansman." In the scenes that follow, Elsie, Ben, and Margaret return to Piedmont at the front of a column of Klan members. Blacks run in fear as whites, conspicuously women and children, cheer the Klansmen.[164] The following intertitle reads, "The next election." Klansmen with guns deter blacks from voting. On the other hand, there is the apparently happy ending. The penultimate intertitle reads: "The aftermath. At the sea's edge, the double honeymoon." The two couples, Phil and Margaret and Ben and Elsie, look out at a sunset.[165] In both couples, North and South are reconciled, but on the condition of reestablished white supremacy.

The handful of breaks in the photographic realism of *The Birth of a Nation* both reinforce the realism of the remainder and serve melodramatic ends.[166] The most striking break is the use of white actors in blackface to portray the principal black characters.[167] The blackface draws attention to the otherness of Gus in relation to Flora (Griffith also has Gus foaming at the mouth while he follows her), heightens the comedic familiarity of Jake and Mammy, and exaggerates the unnaturalness of Lynch and Lydia, the film's two mixed-race villains.

With these exceptions, *The Birth of a Nation* establishes the vocabulary of cinematic realism: the isolated close-up tells us this is an important piece of evidence; a panorama gives us perspective on the larger social forces at work; cross-cutting shows us how to interpret the relative significance of pieces of the story; parallel editing reveals the stakes of the action; montage allows us to aggregate the evidence of isolated images. And the underlying epistemology of montage thinking in *Birth* locates virtue and justice in a personal morality at odds with broader social and political forces. Through its alternate trial of Reconstruction, the film reveals the failure of official law to achieve justice.

It is no coincidence that this most impactful deployment of the new cinematic realism worked in the service of a virulently racist, ideological argument.[168] As Linda Williams argues, race has preoccupied American melodrama at least since *Uncle Tom's Cabin* (1852).[169] Race also played a significant role in the extension of lie-detecting responsibilities to American juries during Reconstruction. After Tennessee ratified the Thirteenth Amendment, "most of the South abandoned any hope of retaining slavery."[170] But while "the most radical of Northern voices called for giving newly freed slaves the vote, support for universal suffrage even in the North fell far short of a critical mass. Between these two issues lay the question of granting freedmen the right to testify in state courts of the South."[171] George Fisher reminds us that, "for a season," the question of African American competency "ranked among the most hotly contested political issues in the nation."[172] Ultimately, northern insistence that black people should be allowed to testify in legal proceedings resulted in the liberalization of competency laws generally.[173]

The postbellum convergence of questions of legal legitimacy and racialized melodrama manifests itself strikingly in the phenomenon of spectacle lynching. *The Birth of a Nation* fits squarely in a tradition of spectacle lynching that developed along with mass culture in the late nineteenth century.[174] The two trials represented in the film—the all-black trial that ends in what is portrayed as an unjust acquittal and the Klan "trial" that ends in Gus's execution—articulate the pattern repeated in American film. Official law is bureaucratic and corruptible, moral law is personal and private and, as a result, justice requires extralegal intervention. Indeed, filmic alternate trials—in which realistic but also inherently melodramatic personal experience, rather than legal procedure and evidentiary standards, determines guilt or innocence—have more in common with spectacle lynchings than their often liberal, social-justice oriented plots would suggest (or countenance).

"The Truth Came Out"

Elsewhere in this volume, Katie Model and Jennifer Petersen explore the complicated relationship between documentaries and historical trials. Documentaries are distinct from narrative films in important ways, but American documentaries—and particularly those that are seen by relatively large audiences—frequently employ realist rules of evidence in a montage style, offering melodramatic narratives in which the truth emerges from the viewer's ability to know it when she sees it.

At the end of *The Central Park Five*, Antron McCray's recorded voice tells us, "the truth came out."[175] The truth to which he refers—his innocence, along with that of Kevin Richardson, Kharey Wise, Yusef Salaam, and Raymond Santana in the 1989 beating and rape of Trisha Meili in Central Park—had, in fact, been out for eleven years when the film was released. The convictions of McCray and the others were vacated in 2002 after the confession and DNA match of serial rapist Matias Reyes. The truth at stake in the alternate trial presented by *The Central Park Five* is something different. That truth, *New York Times* reporter Jim Dwyer tells us in the film, "is almost unbearable." And it is not just that the future crimes of Matias Reyes might have been prevented if he had been correctly identified as Trisha Meili's attacker. As historian Craig Steven Wilder tells us, the truth is that "we are not very good people, and we often are not."

For all of its inversion of racial stereotypes—young black and Latino men are the innocent victims of a white legal system and white press apparently indifferent to justice—*The Central Park Five* and *The Birth of a Nation* are remarkably similar in form. An integrated, family-based community is threatened by a bureaucratic and self-serving power structure that is not only corrupt but fundamentally misunderstands the community it is destroying in the name of principles it does not really serve. Like *The Birth of a Nation*, *The Central Park Five* begins with an invocation of the ravages of war, this time a "proxy war" Jim Dwyer tells us was being fought in New York City in the late 1980s. Against an implied official narrative in which young black and Latino men were responsible for the climate of violence and crime in New York City (the X version), *The Central Park Five* offers a series of defenses: white racism and economic inequality created the conditions in which violence and crime arose; the press acted as a lynch mob; black and Latino families were victims; and finally, young men of color are not safe with white cops or female prosecutors (not-X).

The film opens with text superimposed over scenes of what we infer to be Central Park at night: the crime is briefly described, the wrongly convicted men are named, we learn that New York police and prosecutors "chose not to comment at all." Then we hear Matias Reyes's recorded voice not merely confess to the murder but guarantee that the "kids" convicted of the crime are innocent. Certain words spoken by his disembodied voice are highlighted as text on the screen. The first distinct visual image is video footage from the crime scene the day after the crime, in which a police detective describes the discovery and condition of the unclothed and severely beaten victim. For a few seconds, we see the two white women we will later learn were prosecutors at the scene. Then Jim Dwyer tells us people did not do their jobs—not reporters, not the police, not the prosecutors, not the defense lawyers. We watch a montage of rapidly juxtaposed shots of newspaper and tabloid headlines, television news reporting and interviews (including brief comments from Mayor Ed Koch and Gov. Mario Cuomo) emphasizing the racial animus in the city at the time of the crime. The background music is rap. Then, in an abrupt shift, we meet the five exonerated men as they describe their childhoods in interviews with the filmmakers, intercut with family photographs and footage of (other) black children playing in what we assume to be Harlem.

Here is the opening argument in the film's alternate trial of race in American law and culture. A psychopath on a spree committed a brutal crime, but instead of solving *that* crime, the system put five black and Latino boys from the projects, who happened to have been in Central Park the night of the crime, on trial for making white New Yorkers feel unsafe.[176] Or, in Jim Dwyer's words, "the truth and reality and justice were not part of it." The film's closing argument is that the 2002 exoneration did not right the wrong. Not only were five men's lives irreparably altered (Yusef Salaam reminds us that the time they served in prison was not vacated with their sentences, and Kharey Wise asserts that "no money could buy that time back"), but police and prosecutors refused to admit any wrongdoing. In Professor Wilder's words, the Five's "innocence never got the attention that their guilt did." They were scapegoats in 1989, and they continue to be victims in the proxy war being fought today.[177]

The rest of the film follows a familiar pattern of alternation, in montage editing, between a legal system that is self-interested (a white woman prosecutor makes her reputation, police gather at a bar to celebrate a "home run") and compromised—if not corrupted—by social and political pressure, and the plight of the five boys and their families helplessly caught up in that system. Mayor Ed Koch's assertion that it was the "crime of the century" because Central Park is "holy" to (white) New Yorkers is immediately contrasted with Kevin Richardson's sister's description of the families at the precinct trying to find out what had happened to their sons; courtroom drawings of the trials are followed by footage of Kevin Richardson's mother being taken to the hospital after passing out when the verdicts are read; news coverage of a prosecutor's refusal to accept the exonerations is juxtaposed with Raymond Santana's father saying that the day in 2002 that his son was released from prison was the best day of his life.

It is striking that *The Central Park Five* uses filmed interviews to discredit videotaped interviews without irony. But there is no irony because for all its documentary realism, *The Central Park Five* follows the same melodramatic formula as *The Birth of a Nation*. The film tells us that we cannot believe the boys' confessions because of the conditions under which they were made (and explains that jurors found them credible because it was incredible such a confession would be made if it were not true). But if the believability of testimony turns on the (invisible) context in which it was filmed, we should suspect all of the interviews in the film, including the opening confession of Matias Reyes.[178] *The Central Park Five* circumvents this problem by presenting its testimony in a melodramatic binary: the videotaped confessions are untrue because they were coerced by unscrupulous police detectives indifferent to actual guilt or innocence; the testimonial interviews with the five as adults—even though we are provided with no context for the interviews themselves, nor told about the pending civil suit that might motivate or inform their testimony until the end of the film—are truthful because they are innocent.

The representation of the way the coerced confessions themselves are obtained follows the form of Gus's pursuit of Flora in *The Birth of a Nation*. Initially, the investigators are solicitous—they say they just want information. But it quickly becomes clear that they will not take no for an answer. The boys' families realize the danger late and do not get to them in time. The investigators pursue the boys to the edge of the cliff, and the boys go over it. Angela Black describes her brother Kevin Richardson's condition when she finally sees him after twelve hours in police custody. "I walked in the room, and I could see that he was terrified. I could see him, like, shivering. I said, 'Kevin, I can't believe you saw this woman get raped.' And he looked at me. He said, 'Angie, I didn't see a rape.'" At this point it takes her almost ten seconds to fight back her emotions, then she continues: "And I said, 'Kevin, why did you say that then?' He said, 'Cause they told me to say it so I could go home.'" The film immediately cuts away from her face to footage of at least nine white police officers and detectives standing around a car. A hunched figure with a black jacket completely shrouding his head and shoulders is led out of what we assume to be the precinct by five more white police detectives and put into the back seat of a car. While we watch this, Angela Black's voice continues: "But it was like a orchestra, like they orchestrated this whole thing, and I felt so dumb for not realizing it 'til it was too late." Then we see Raymond Santana Sr. in an interview saying, "When I came back, they disappeared my son. He wasn't there no more. I said, 'Where's my son?' They say, 'They took him to another police station.'" Raymond Santana Jr. picks up the narration here: "My father did make a return, um, but when he came it was too late."[179]

The alternate trial presented in *The Central Park Five* is conspicuously one-sided.[180] As in *The Birth of a Nation*, self-interested politicians (Koch, Stoneman) and their corrupt henchmen (police officers and prosecutors, Lynch) sacrifice innocent children and destroy tight-knit familial communities. Indeed, filmic alternate trials tend to treat the X, or prosecution side of the case, as already known to the audience—its arguments are implied but only articulated as necessary to the not-X version that is the ground of the film. But even films that are apparently more evenhanded often enact a binary between moral justice and an evil working under the cover of the system. Unlike the corporate defense attorney James Mason in *The Verdict*

(1982)—who is described (appreciatively) by a plaintiff's side lawyer as "the prince of darkness"[181]—the corporate defense attorney played by Robert Duvall in *A Civil Action* (1998) is intelligent and appealing as he makes the case that the cause of a cancer cluster cannot be known.[182] Yet by the end of the film, his client is shown backlit by the river he has knowingly polluted blazing with fire. The film trial need not be impartial to be fair because we will know the truth when we see it.

Like *The Birth of a Nation* and many films between them, *The Central Park Five* relies on the news media to establish apparently accurate and representative historical context. The fact that it does so, even as it lays partial blame for the wrongful convictions on the media, testifies to the entrenched authority of published photographs and text in the realist rules of evidence. And like *Birth*, *The Central Park Five* relies heavily on the authority of experts—particularly historians and (certain, ethical) journalists—to vouch for the reality of the social world depicted by the film.

But that social world is conceived melodramatically. The victims are vulnerable children. The villains are evil to the end. With the exception of a social psychologist suggesting the likely effect of the pressures on police and prosecutors, the complexities of the case itself, and race and class politics in New York generally, are largely suppressed in favor of a racial binary repeatedly reinforced by visual imagery.[183] The film clearly intends to offer a reformist critique of the legal system. But the melodramatic formula establishes a standard of justice no institution could meet, precisely because it is established on personal, moral terms. And by reproducing this reductive structure, the film risks reinscribing the very racial binary it means to discredit.

Conclusion

Clover asserts that as jurors or moviegoers, Americans are "first last and always triers of fact."[184] And she emphasizes the fact that the Anglo-American legal trial posits an "exceptionally attentive" viewer, herself "a party in the meaning-making process."[185] But as Walter Benjamin observes, "in the movies, this position requires no attention. The public is an examiner, but an absent-minded one."[186] Our long experience as consumers of films and TV shows that follow the conventions of realism in the service of melodramatically structured narratives has taught us to think that we can know the truth when we see it. And there is no difference between the way we view video of actual events and the way we view filmic alternate trails. Both activate our personal assessments of plausibility and authenticity (realist rules of evidence) informed by our conventional understandings of the social world. The fact that we continue to view digital images as replicas of the real reveals how completely the conventional passes for the indexical in our visual culture.[187]

In 2007, the Supreme Court determined that a police officer's use of deadly force to stop a high-speed car chase was reasonable under the Fourth Amendment based solely on video recorded by a dashboard-mounted camera. The decision preempted a trial.[188] As many commentators have since noted, the Court failed to realize that they were in fact parties in the meaning-making process when they viewed the video and not passive spectators.[189] Indeed, it has been argued that *Scott v. Harris* may well have been decided differently if the Supreme Court had "watched a different video of the exact same events taken from inside the suspect's car."[190] Nevertheless, the Court again relied exclusively on dashboard camera footage to grant summary judgement in favor of a police officer accused of using excessive force in *Plumhoff v. Rickard* (2012). In *Plumhoff,* the Court viewed footage of a vehicle pursuit involving six police cars captured by three different cameras and determined that the fifteen shots fired into the vehicle after it had come to a stop were reasonable under the circumstances. No trial was necessary because the video portrayed those circumstances "conclusively."[191]

Justice Alito's description of the point at which the pursuit turns lethal in *Plumhoff* is remarkably cinematic. He constructs a single account from multiple cameras through what can only be called montage editing. It begins with an overhead long shot: Rickard "exited I–40 in Memphis, and shortly afterward he made 'a quick right turn,' causing 'contact [to] occu[r]' between his car and Evans' cruiser." Cut to medium shot of the cars: "As a result of that contact, Rickard's car spun out into a parking lot and collided with Plumhoff's cruiser." Cut to the interior of Rickard's car: "Now in danger of being cornered, Rickard put his car into reverse 'in an attempt to escape.'" Cut to wide shot of parking lot: "As he did so, Evans and Plumhoff got out of their cruisers and approached Rickard's car, and Evans, gun in hand, pounded on the passenger-side window." Cut to close-up of the back of Rickard's car in reverse: "At that point, Rickard's car 'made contact with' yet another police cruiser." Cut to side shot of Rickard's car: "Rickard's tires started spinning, and his car 'was rocking back and forth,' indicating that Rickard was using the accelerator even though his bumper was flush against a police cruiser." Cut to shot of the car from Plumhoff's point of view: "At that point, Plumhoff fired three shots into Rickard's car." Cut to view from interior of Rickard's car. "Rickard then 'reversed in a 180-degree arc' and 'maneuvered onto' another street, forcing Ellis to 'step to his right to avoid the vehicle.'" Cut to shot of the car from Ellis's point of view: "As Rickard continued 'fleeing down' that street, Gardner and Galtelli fired 12 shots toward Rickard's car, bringing the total number of shots fired during this incident to 15." Cut to overhead shot of the street: "Rickard then lost control of the car and crashed into a building." Cut to medium shot of the now stationary car: "Rickard and Allen both died from some combination of gunshot wounds and injuries suffered in the crash that ended the chase."[192]

The spectacle of the chase has long been a staple of American film. What Justice Alito describes as "outrageously reckless driving" is as much a matter of convention as of fact. The more realistic the action, the more exciting it is. But the chase is exciting because it generates uncertainty—will the bad guy be stopped in time?—in a fundamentally melodramatic narrative situation where there is a threatening peril and someone innocent (or at least virtuous) in danger. Justice Alito asserts that "under the circumstances at the moment when the shots were fired, all that a reasonable police officer could have concluded was that Rickard was intent on resuming his flight and that, if he was allowed to do so, he would once again pose a deadly threat for others on the road."[193] But if we can determine the interior states of its participants when we watch a car chase, it is only because we bring assumptions about the moral stakes of that chase with us to the viewing.

Television and online forms of entertainment have substantially eroded film's dominance of American popular culture. But realist representation in the melodramatic mode is still the norm, from reality shows to the extraordinarily popular podcast *Serial*—itself an alternate trial. In her discussion of the racialized melodrama of the O. J. Simpson trial, Linda Williams invokes Jeffrey Rosen's sense that "the Simpson trial took place in a world that had transcended facts."[194] But all trials take place in a world where representation transcends fact. And visual representation is increasingly frequent in a variety of legal settings.[195] As legal scholars and law schools address the need for training in visual literacy for lawyers, we will have to contend with the melodramatic underpinning of our polygraphic viewing.

Notes

I am grateful to Norman Spaulding and Cary McClelland for patient readings of early drafts. Rachel Kimball Wilcox and Ginny Smith provided invaluable research assistance. And I am indebted to Katie Model, Jennifer Petersen, Barry Langford, Jessica Silbey, Martha Merrill Umphrey, Austin Sarat, Matthew Smith, Bernie Meyler, Amalia Kessler, and Ari Hoffman for their thoughtful suggestions.

1. Carol Clover, "Law and the Order of Popular Culture," in *Law in the Domains of Culture*, ed. Austin Sarat and Thomas R. Kearns (Ann Arbor: University of Michigan Press, 1998), 110.

2. Ibid., 103.

3. Ibid.

4. Ibid., 102.

5. Carol Clover, "God Bless Juries!" in *Refiguring American Film Genres: Theory and History*, ed. Nick Browne (Berkeley: University of California Press, 1998), 255.

6. The success of both is dramatic. *The Thin Blue Line* prompted the exoneration of Randall Adams in the murder of a Texas police officer and identified the likely killer; *The Central Park Five* put pressure on the city of New York, eventually leading to a $41 million settlement with five men wrongly convicted in 1990, whose convictions were vacated in 2002.

7. Robert Benton, dir., *Kramer vs. Kramer* (1979; Culver City, CA: Sony Pictures Home Entertainment, 2001), DVD; Jonathan Demme, dir., *Philadelphia* (1993; Hollywood, CA: TriStar Pictures. 2002), DVD.

8. Clover does not contemplate films as "alternate trials" in "Law and Order." In another essay, she notes that in the "overwhelming majority of trial movies, from the beginning of cinema, the unofficial trial turns on an aspect of the legal system. Is the system fair across various social differences—class, race, gender? Can it be corrupted? Does money buy people off? Are lawyers human? Should the death penalty exist? Can the system really get at the truth? Can it distinguish between technical justice and real justice? Does it convict innocent people? Does it too often acquit the guilty?" Carol Clover, "Judging Audiences: The Case of the Trial Movie," in *Reinventing Film Studies*, ed. Christine Gledhill and Linda Williams (London: Hodder Arnold, 2000), 252. But Clover does not develop the observation.

9. Rob Cohen, dir., *The Fast and the Furious* (2001; Universal City, CA: Universal Studios Home Entertainment, 2002), DVD; Michael Curtiz, dir., *Casablanca* (1942; Burbank, CA: Warner Home Video, 2000), DVD.

10. Clover, "Law and Order," 100.

11. In legal discourse, the expression "I know it when I see it" evokes Justice Potter Stewart's 1964 description of hard-core pornography in Jacobellis v. Ohio, 378 U.S. 184 at 197. I mean something more general here, but the kind of melodramatic vision I use the expression to describe is not far from Justice Stewart's meaning.

12. When we watch a film, we know it is not real but have, nevertheless, "a strange feeling of reality"—this is "a classical theme of film theory." Christian Metz, "Photography and Fetish," in *The Photography Reader*, ed. Liz Wells (London: Routledge, 2003) 144.

13. Clover, "Law and Order," 99.

14. See A. Nicholas Vardac, *Stage to Screen: Theatrical Origins of Early Film: David Garrick to D. W. Griffith* (Cambridge, MA: Harvard University Press, 1949); Thomas Postlewait, "The Hieroglyphic Stage: American Theatre and So-

ciety, Post–Civil War to 1945," in *The Cambridge History of the American Theatre*, vol. 2, ed. Don B. Wilmeth and Christopher Bisby (Cambridge: Cambridge University Press, 1999), 162.

15. As Robert Ferguson has observed, lawyers "know that jurors must first recognize the developing contours of a story to accept it, and the perception makes them practical students of preexisting narrative forms." Robert A. Ferguson, "Untold Stories in the Law," in *Law's Stories*, ed. Peter Brooks and Paul Gewirtz (New Haven, CT: Yale University Press, 1996), 87.

16. Clover, "Law and Order," 118–19.

17. Robert Sklar, *Movie-Made America: A Cultural History of American Movies* (New York: Vintage Books, 1994), 58. *The Birth of a Nation* "expanded the class range of film enthusiasts in the United States. A medium that began primarily as a working-class phenomenon broadened its appeal steadily after 1915. Griffith had as much to do with that expansion of interest and patronage as anyone." Michael Kammen, American *Culture, American Tastes: Social Change in the 20th Century* (New York: Basic Books, 1999), 104.

18. See for example David Cook, *A History of Narrative Film* (New York: Norton, 1981), 59. These accounts do not so much deny the melodramatic elements of Griffith's work as assert that they do not matter or are transcended.

19. On melodrama in *Birth*, see Linda Williams, *Playing the Race Card: Melodramas of Black and White from Uncle Tom to O. J. Simpson* (Princeton, NJ: Princeton University Press, 2002); on social context, see Michael Rogin, "The Sword Became a Flashing Vision," in *Ronald Reagan, the Movie and Other Episodes in Political Demonology* (Berkeley: University of California Press, 1987).

20. Film studies has tended to treat melodrama as a genre and the melodramatic mode generally as an exception to classical cinema (see David Bordwell, Janet Staiger, and Kristin Thompson, *The Classical Hollywood Cinema* [New York: Columbia University Press, 1985]). I am following Linda Williams, Christine Gledhill, and others who have recently argued persuasively against treating melodrama as marginal and excessive, finding instead that melodrama permeates even the most apparently realist films. See, for example, Williams, *Playing the Race Card*, 16; Rick Altman, "Dickens, Griffith, and Film Theory Today," in *Silent Film*, ed. Richard Abel (New Brunswick, NJ: Rutgers University Press, 1996), 145; Christine Gledhill, "The Melodramatic Field: An Investigation" in *Home Is Where the Heart Is: Studies in Melodrama and the Woman's Film* (London: British Film Institute, 1987).

21. Ian Watt, *The Rise of the Novel: Studies in Defoe, Richardson and Fielding* (Berkeley: University of California Press, 1957), 31.

22. Ibid., 13. The result has been a diversity of implementation rendering realism itself notoriously difficult to define. For Watt, realism is "the sum of literary techniques whereby the novel's imitation of human life follows the proce-

dures adopted by philosophical realism in its attempt to ascertain and report the truth" (31). Literary realism can be loosely identified by three criteria: verisimilitude in its documentation of the observed details of the everyday world; attention to normal or representative, rather than exceptional, experience not just in choice of characters and setting but also in plot; and a dispassionate, even scientific (as opposed to subjective or idealistic) treatment of that material. George Becker, *Documents of Modern Literary Realism* (Princeton: Princeton University Press, 1963), 3–38, cited in Donald Pizer, *Realism and Naturalism in Nineteenth-Century American Literature* (Carbondale: Southern Illinois University Press, 1984), 1–2. Literary criticism juggles two temporal categorizations of realism: one encompasses the novels of the eighteenth and nineteenth centuries generally, the other applies more narrowly to "social realism" starting in the 1870s. Ian Watt's account of "formal realism" describes the former. Pizer and Becker discuss the latter.

23. In *Rise of the Novel*, Watt locates the origins of modern realism in Locke and Descartes and begins to find the theoretical formulation of the concept in the mid-eighteenth century (12). For Watt, realism reflects "that vast transformation of Western civilization since the Renaissance which has replaced the unified world picture of the Middle Ages with another very different one—one which presents us, essentially, with a developing but unplanned aggregate of particular individuals having particular experiences at particular times and at particular places" (31).

24. Ibid., 12, 14.

25. Ibid., 15. See also Richard Chase, *The American Novel and Its Tradition* (Baltimore: Johns Hopkins University Press, 1980), 12.

26. Chase, *American Novel and Its Tradition*, 12.

27. George Fisher, "The Jury's Rise as Lie Detector," *Yale Law Journal* 107 (January 1997): 575, 638, 655. Juries began to play a truth-evaluating role in the late seventeenth-century and had fully assumed the lie-detector function by the 1880s. But Fisher argues that the legal system did not "invest the jury with this new lie-detecting role because of a conviction that the jury had grown equal to the task" but rather because the gradual erosion of competency rules and the special pressure created by the argument against African American exclusion (697). Fisher concludes that the "inexorable flow of fact finding power to the jury was due, finally, to the jury's capacity to erase all blemishes"—the system's need for legitimacy. "Because it emits no light, the black box of the jury room has become the system's black hole, drawing into itself all of the questions of fact for which the system needs an unquestionable answer" (705).

28. Ibid., 657.

29. Ibid., 658–59.

30. "But most of the evidence we have suggests that juries have no particular talent for spotting lies. Not only do experimental subjects rarely perform much

better than chance at distinguishing truth from falsehood, but they think they are better lie detectors than they are," ibid., 707, citations omitted.

31. Ibid., 578–79.

32. Clover, "Law and Order," 105. On the generic structure of defense counternarratives, see Ferguson, "Untold Stories in the Law," 86.

33. Ferguson continues, "Notably, lawyers have masked the real importance of generic considerations through their appeals to the common sense of a situation. But common sense . . . is basically a culturally constructed use of experience to claim self-evidence; it is neither more nor less than 'an authoritative story' made out of the familiar." Ferguson, "Untold Stories in the Law," 87.

34. However, as Watt reminds us, "there is no reason why the report on human life which is presented by [formal realism] should be in fact any truer than those presented through the very different conventions of other literary genres." Watt, *Rise of the Novel*, 32.

35. Emile Zola, *The Experimental Novel* (New York: Haskell House, 1964), 17–18.

36. Ibid., 7 (quoting Claude Bernard).

37. Fisher, "Jury's Rise as Lie Detector," 577.

38. William Ivins Jr., *Prints and Visual Communication* (Cambridge, MA: MIT Press, 1969), 119–22.

39. Miles Orvell, *The Real Thing: Imitation and Authenticity in American Culture, 1880–1940* (Chapel Hill: University of North Carolina Press, 1989), 100.

40. See generally Eadweard Muybridge, *Animals in Motion* (London: Chapman and Hall, 1899).

41. Orvell, *Real Thing*, 101.

42. "It was not long before men began to think photographically, and thus to see for themselves things that it had previously taken the photograph to reveal to their astonished and protesting eyes." Ivins, *Prints and Visual Communication*, 138. "The photograph has been accepted as showing that impossible desideratum of the historian . . . how it actually was" (94).

43. Ibid., 94.

44. Roland Barthes, "Rhetoric of the Image," in *Image Music Text*, trans. Stephen Heath (New York: Hill and Wang, 1977), 44. Christian Metz describes this as the indexical quality of photography. The relationship between the representation and the thing represented is distinguished "by an actual contiguity or connection in the world." Metz, "Photography and Fetish," 139. Photographs "are *prints* of real objects, prints left on a special surface by a combination of light and chemical action" (139). But it is merely the "mode of production itself, the principle of the *taking*" that is indexical in the photographic image (139).

45. Ivins, *Prints and Visual Communication*, 136.

46. Barthes, "Rhetoric of the Image," 46. "This is without doubt an impor-

tant historical paradox: the more technology develops the diffusion of information (and notably of images), the more it provides the means of masking the construed meaning under the appearance of the given meaning" (46).

47. Oliver Wendell Holmes Sr. "The Age of Photography," *Atlantic Monthly*, June 1859, http://www.theatlantic.com/ideastour/technology/holmes-full.html.

48. Errol Morris gives a detailed treatment in the first chapter of *Believing Is Seeing: Observations on the Mysteries of Photography* (New York: Penguin, 2011).

49. Orvell, *Real Thing*, 95–99.

50. Ibid., 94. See generally 77–85.

51. Andre Bazin has influentially described the most realistic cinema as the most novel-like. Andre Bazin, "The Evolution of the Language of Cinema," in *Critical Visions in Film Theory*, ed. Timothy Corrigan, Patricia White, and Meta Mazaj (Boston: Bedford/St. Martin's, 2011), 324. Eisenstein asserts that "the first shoots of American film esthetic" stem from the Victorian novel. Sergei Eisenstein, "Dickens, Griffith, and the Film Today," in *Film Form: Essays in Film Theory*, ed. and trans. Jay Leyda (New York: Harcourt, 1977), 195.

52. Classical cinematic realism "depends upon the notion of the 'invisible observer'" taking in an "apparently independent" preexisting scene. David Bordwell, "Classical Hollywood Cinema," in *Narrative, Apparatus, Ideology*, ed. by Philip Rosen (New York: Columbia University Press, 1986), 24.

53. Sergei Eisenstein even finds aspects of filmic montage—the editing together of juxtaposed shots—in Dickens. Eisenstein, "Dickens, Griffith," 217.

54. Bordwell, "Classical Hollywood Cinema," 26. As in the realist novel, classical cinema's subjects are "psychologically defined individuals" "endowed with an evident, consistent batch of traits, qualities, and behaviors" (20).

55. Ibid., 25.

56. Watt, *Rise of the Novel*, 28.

57. The very forces that fostered realism—individualism, empiricism, the emergence of the middle class—created the necessity of a "new moral and aesthetic category, that of the 'interesting.'" Peter Brooks, *The Melodramatic Imagination: Balzac, Henry James, Melodrama, and the Mode of Excess* (New Haven, CT: Yale University Press, 1976), 13.

58. Much of the law and narrative movement has also gravitated to the inclusion of previously excluded narratives. Robert Weisberg, "Proclaiming Trials as Narratives: Premises and Pretenses," in *Law's Stories*, ed. Peter Brooks and Paul Gewirtz (New Haven, CT: Yale University Press, 1996), 61.

59. Orvell, *Real Thing*, 240.

60. Brooks, *Melodramatic Imagination* (1976), 1.

61. Zola, *Experimental Novel*, 7, quoting Claude Bernard.

62. Brooks, *Melodramatic Imagination* (1976), 2.

63. Donald Pizer has argued that writers like Twain, Howells, and James

"dramatize a vision of experience in which individuals achieve that which is still a goal for mankind at large"—they are, for him, "ethically idealistic." Pizer, *Realism and Naturalism*, 7. Leslie Fiedler has given a slightly different account of the persistence of Romantic idealism among American realists. Fiedler insists that "the [sentimental] novel and America did not come into existence at the same time by accident" (xxvii). "America is not exclusively the product of Reason. . . . Behind its neoclassical façade, ours is a nation sustained by a sentimental and Romantic dream" (xxxiii). Leslie Fiedler, *Love and Death in the American Novel* (New York: Meridian Books, 1960).

64. Brooks, *Melodramatic Imagination* (1976), 14.

65. The term *melodrama* is sometimes used narrowly to identify specific genres (especially in eighteenth- and nineteenth-century theater). But I am using the term broadly, as many have, to describe a set of representational structures that are not limited to specific narrative and theatrical practices. Linda Williams makes a persuasive argument for this approach in the first chapter of *Playing the Race Card*.

66. This is Ben Singer's "cluster concept" definition of melodrama. See Ben Singer, *Melodrama and Modernity* (New York: Columbia University Press, 2001), 44–49. But it is also consistent with Brooks's list of the connotations of melodrama: "Indulgence in strong emotionalism; moral polarization and schematization; extreme states of being, situations, actions; overt villainy, persecution of the good, and final reward of virtue; inflated and extravagant expression; dark plottings, suspense, breathtaking peripety," and "identification with 'monopathic' emotion." Brooks, *Melodramatic Imagination* (1976), 12.

67. Thomas Elsaesser, "Tales of Sound and Fury," in *Movies and Methods*, vol. 2, ed. Bill Nichols (Berkeley: University of California Press, 1985), 180, 175.

68. Brooks, *Melodramatic Imagination* (1976), 31

69. Ibid., 32.

70. Brooks, *Melodramatic Imagination* (1976), 14. The cause of this crisis varies by account: for Peter Brooks, it is the "final liquidation of the traditional Sacred and its representative institutions"; for Thomas Elsaesser, the French Revolution; for those in the Marxist tradition, the split between routinized work and personal identity, which is relegated to home and the family, under capitalism. Brooks, *Melodramatic Imagination* (1976), 15; Elsaesser, "Tales of Sound and Fury," 168; Chuck Kleinhans, "Notes on Melodrama and the Family under Capitalism," in *Imitations of Life*, ed. Marcia Landy (Detroit, MI: Wayne State University Press, 1991), 197–204.

71. Brooks, *Melodramatic Imagination* (1976), 17.

72. Ibid., 17.

73. Elsaesser, "Tales of Sound and Fury," 171. "Even if the situations and sentiments defied all categories of verisimilitude and were totally unlike anything in

real life," Elsaesser explains, "the structure had a truth and a life of its own, which an artist could make part of his material" (171).

74. Ibid., 172.

75. Dickens, quoted by Eisenstein in "Dickens, Griffith," 224.

76. Steven Soderbergh, dir., *Erin Brockovich* (2000; Universal Pictures Home Entertainment, 2000), DVD.

77. Gledhill, "Melodramatic Field," 38.

78. On this account, melodrama today operates as "the larger cultural mode driving the articulation of specific genres," and realism itself often articulates fundamentally melodramatic themes. Williams, *Playing the Race Card*, 17, 38.

79. Martha Merrill Umphrey, "Dialogics of Legal Meaning: Spectacular Trials, the Unwritten Law, and Narratives of Criminal Responsibility," *Law and Society Review* 33, no. 2 (1999): 413

80. See, for example, Neal R. Feigenson, *Legal Blame: How Jurors Think and Talk about Accidents* (Washington, DC: American Psychological Association, 2000), and "Accidents as Melodrama," *New York Law School Law Review* 43 (1999–2000): 741; Lenora Ledwon, "Melodrama and the Law: Feminizing the Juridical Gaze," *Harvard Women's Law Journal* 21 (Spring 1998): 141; Elayne Rapping, "Television, Melodrama, and the Rise of the Victim's Rights Movement," *New York Law School Law Review* 43, nos. 3 and 4 (1999–2000): 665; Allen Rostron, "Shooting Stories: The Creation of Narrative and Melodrama in Real and Fictional Litigation against the Gun Industry," *UMKC Law Review* 73, no. 4 (Summer 2005): 1047; Alisa Solomon, "Who Gets to Be Human on the Evening News?" *PMLA* 121, no. 5 (Oct. 2006): 1585.

81. Alan M. Dershowitz, "Life Is Not a Dramatic Narrative," in *Law's Stories*, ed. Peter Brooks and Paul Gewirtz (New Haven, CT: Yale University Press, 1996), 102.

82. Linda Williams insists that it is melodrama through which "American democratic culture has most powerfully articulated the moral structure of feeling animating its goals of justice." Williams, *Playing the Race Card*, 26.

83. Elsaesser, "Tales of Sound and Fury," 169.

84. Ibid., 185.

85. Ibid., 176.

86. "In this there is obviously a healthy distrust of intellectualisation and abstract social theory—insisting that other structures of experience (those of suffering for instance) are more in keeping with reality. But it has also meant ignorance of the properly social and political dimensions of these changes and their causality, and consequently it has encouraged increasingly escapist forms of mass entertainment" (ibid., 170).

87. Ibid., 185. It is this aspect of melodrama that may help account for the alignment of melodrama and bourgeois ideology identified by Eisenstein.

88. Ibid., 185.

89. Umphrey, "Dialogics of Legal Meaning," 413.

90. See Clover, "Law and Order," 104.

91. Ibid., 106.

92. Ibid., 103. It must be observed that Clover's description of the trial-like substructure of most American film is at odds with the long tradition of film criticism in which invisibly crafted linear narrative driven by character-motivated causality is the hallmark of Hollywood films. See Bordwell, Staiger, and Thompson, *Classical Hollywood Cinema*. Clover's description is, however, entirely consistent with a growing body of film criticism insisting on the persistence of spectacle and melodrama in mainstream American film.

93. Elsaesser, "Tales of Sound and Fury," 181; Clover, "Law and Order," 107.

94. Elsaesser, "Tales of Sound and Fury," 182.

95. Ibid.

96. Clover, "Law and Order," 105, 106. Clover also describes this as "the truth of exhausted possibilities" (105).

97. This is "a classical theme of film theory." Metz, "Photography and Fetish," 144.

98. Walter Lippmann, *Public Opinion* (New York: Harcourt, 1922), 91.

99. Ibid., 92.

100. By 1922, it was evident that film is more than a series of photographs. It is "more precisely a series with supplementary components as well, so that the unfolding as such tends to become more important than the link of each image with its referent." Metz, "Photography and Fetish," 139.

101. Ibid., 144.

102. Ibid., 139. In this way, Barthes argues, unlike photography, film as a medium is continuous with the history of fiction. Barthes, "Rhetoric of the Image," 45.

103. Bordwell, "Classical Hollywood Cinema," 24 (italics in original).

104. Ibid. Bordwell asserts that "the use of narration to make us jump to invalid conclusions" in classical cinema is "rare" (30). But even where the narration does not do so explicitly, the camera's spatial omnipresence may. Like many other early commentators on film, Benjamin argues that "the spectator's process of association" with filmic images is "interrupted by their constant, sudden change." Walter Benjamin, "The Work of Art in the Age of Mechanical Reproduction," in *Film Theory and Criticism*, ed. Leo Braudy and Marshall Cohen, 6th ed. (Oxford University Press, 2004), 808.

105. Bordwell, "Classical Hollywood Cinema," 24 (italics in original).

106. Ibid.

107. Charles Musser, *The Emergence of Cinema: The American Screen to 1907* (Berkeley: University of California Press, 1990), 118; Vardac, *Stage to Screen*, 169.

108. Vardac, *Stage to Screen*, 180.

109. Peter Brooks, "Melodrama, Body, Revolution," in *Melodrama: Stage Picture Screen*, ed. Jacky Bratton, Jim Cook, and Christine Gledhill (London: British Film Institute, 1994), 11. See also Elsaesser, "Tales of Sound and Fury," 172, on the sense in which all silent film is melodramatic.

110. Sklar, *Movie-Made America*, 54. Sklar goes on: "He [D. W. Griffith] was the first to forge them into a complete and original style of making movies."

111. Ibid., 52. Producers worried that audiences would be confused so films were composed of a few long shots in which action took place the way it would for audiences of a play watching a stage. In other words, the camera reproduced what the human eye could see in the unfilmed, everyday world.

112. Vardac argues that Griffith "worked continually to increase graphic realism. It seems that every refinement in editorial technique was associated with this desire." Vardac, *Stage to Screen*, 203. In a much-repeated story about the making of Griffith's *Enoch Arden* in 1908, Biograph Company was concerned that his use of a parallel cut-back (Arden's wife waiting for him, followed by Arden stuck on a desert island) would confuse the audience. Griffith reportedly countered with the query, "Doesn't Dickens write that way?" Eisenstein, "Dickens, Griffith," 201; Sklar, *Movie-Made America*, 51. Griffith himself was a frustrated writer.

113. Sklar, *Movie-Made America*, 54.

114. Ibid.

115. Sklar, *Movie-Made America*, 54. See generally Tom Gunning, *D. W. Griffith and the Origins of American Narrative Film* (Champaign: University of Illinois Press, 1991).

116. In an essay on Griffith, Eisenstein describes montage as "the play of *juxtaposed detail*—shots, which in themselves are immutable and unrelated, but from which is created the desired *image of the whole*." Eisenstein, "Dickens, Griffith," 232, (italics original).

117. Sklar, *Movie-Made America*, 56. In this way, Griffith redefined realism for film: in the early years, realism meant fidelity to the range of the human eye. After Griffith, filmic realism was severed from the limits of individual perception.

118. Eisenstein, "Dickens, Griffith," 249–250.

119. Ibid., 234.

120. Ibid.

121. Benjamin, "Work of Art," 798.

122. Quoted in Robert Lang, "Birth of a Nation: History, Ideology, Narrative Form," in *"The Birth of a Nation": D. W. Griffith, Director*, ed. Robert Lang (New Brunswick, NJ: Rutgers University Press, 1994), 4.

123. Compare Michael Rogin's theory that it is actually about 1915 urban class and gender conditions in "'The Sword Became a Flashing Vision,'" in *Ronald Reagan*, 200.

124. "NAACP: A Century in the Fight for Freedom," Library of Congress, accessed on October 25, 2014. http://www.loc.gov/exhibits/naacp/founding-and -early-years.html.

125. See, for example, Guinn v. United States, 238 U.S. 347 (1915); Buchanan v. Warley, 245 U.S. 60 (1917); Robert Zangrando, *The NAACP Crusade against Lynching, 1909–1950* (Philadelphia: Temple University Press, 1980).

126. Scott v. Sandford, 60 U.S. 393, 411 (1856). Justice Taney repeatedly cites state antimiscegenation laws but such laws are strange evidence of black non-citizenship, since they apply to blacks and whites alike. The repetition of the association between interracial sex and black citizenship seems rather to heighten the stakes of the question of equal rights. See 408, 413, 416.

127. Plessy v. Ferguson, 163 U.S. 537, 544 (1896).

128. *Plessy*, 551.

129. *The Birth of a Nation* is loosely based on Thomas Dixon's 1905 novel *The Clansman*, which Dixon also made into a play. Dixon was an outspoken white supremacist and both novel and play are explicitly racist.

130. John Cuniberti, *"The Birth of a Nation": A Formal Shot-by-Shot Analysis Together with Microfiche* (Ann Arbor: University of Michigan, 1979), 36 (italics in original).

131. Cuniberti argues that this scene represents the complicity of the North in the capture and selling of slaves, following Dixon's representation of northern complicity in *The Clansman* (ibid., 37). Cuniberti points to additional intertitles and an image of a Yankee slave ship, lost in existing prints but described in early reviews, as further support for this claim.

132. Ibid., 38.

133. Ibid., 39.

134. Ibid., 40.

135. Ibid., 40–41.

136. Ibid., 47.

137. Ibid., 50.

138. Ibid., 50, 48.

139. See Jane Gaines and Neil Lerner, "The Orchestration of Affect" in *The Sounds of Early Cinema*, ed. Richard Abel and Rick R. Altman (Bloomington: Indiana University Press, 2000), and Matthew Wilson Smith, "American Valkyries: Richard Wagner, D. W. Griffith and the Birth of Classical Cinema," in *Modernism/Modernity* 15, no. 2 (April 2008): 221–42.

140. Cuniberti, *"The Birth of a Nation,"* 62. In at least some copies, the shots during the fire are tinted red (63).

141. Here, the use of the iris invites the viewer to identify with the victims of "a great conqueror," ibid., 65. Another Cameron son dies as refugees flee from a burning Atlanta.

142. Ibid., 66–67.

143. Ibid., 77.

144. Ibid., 79.

145. Ibid., 82.

146. Ibid., 83.

147. Ibid., 85.

148. Ibid., 86.

149. Ibid., 90

150. Ibid., 92

151. Ibid., 92–93.

152. As a historian, before entering politics, Wilson had in fact written these words. But Wilson was critical of the KKK as an impediment to reunion. Rogin, *Ronald Reagan*, 193.

153. Cuniberti, "*The Birth of a Nation*," 94.

154. Ibid., 98.

155. Ibid., 109.

156. Ibid., 111.

157. Ibid., 108.

158. Ibid., 111.

159. Ibid., 126 (italics in original).

160. There may have been a scene in which Gus is castrated in early prints of the film. See ibid., 131, and Rogin, *Ronald Reagan*, 217 (citing Seymour Stern).

161. Cuniberti, "*The Birth of a Nation*," 146.

162. Ibid., 147.

163. Williams argues that "nothing is more sensational in American cinema than the infinite varieties of rescues, accidents, chases, and fights. . . . While usually faithful to the laws of motion and gravity, this realism of action should not fool us into thinking that the dominant mode of such films is realism. Nor should the virility of action itself fool us into thinking it's not melodrama." Williams, *Playing the Race Card*, 21.

164. Cuniberti, "*The Birth of a Nation*," 164–65.

165. Cuniberti cites evidence for an additional lost scene here of black people being deported to Liberia (ibid., 167). The (in my reading) superficial thematization of war is bookended in the final title and scenes. The title reads, "Dare we dream of a golden day when the bestial War shall rule no more. But instead—the gentle prince in the Hall of Brotherly Love in the City of Peace." And the last shots are of mangled bodies and the God of War, a Christ figure superimposed over what Cuniberti describes as "a harmonious assembly of white people," and Elsie and Ben now looking at a "vision of the heavenly city" (167).

166. A small number of frames are tinted red, marking highlights in the film's melodramatic structure: the fire in the Cameron house after the Union

guerilla raid, certain shots in the defeat of Ben's Confederate troops by Phil's Union forces, certain shots during the Klan "trial" of Gus, and shots of the Klan gathering to rescue Elsie and the Camerons. The superimpositions in the final frames—the "God of War" with a "mass and tangle of bodies," a Christ figure fading in and out of a "harmonious assembly of white people" walking and dancing "in garments of peace"—resemble nothing in the rest of the film. These descriptions are Cuniberti's, ibid., 167. But they do establish a metaphoric connection between the racialized binary of (white) justice and (black) evil in the film and of heaven and hell. They also resemble contemporary experiments in film that anticipate antirealism.

167. There was a robust tradition of blackface performance in nineteenth-century American theater but also a corps of African American actors working on the stage and in early film. Griffith could have used black actors to portray Lydia, Lynch, Gus, Jake, and Mammy but decided "to have no black blood among the principals" (Griffith in an October 1916 interview, quoted in ibid., 47–48). On the blackface tradition and nineteenth-century melodrama, see Williams, *Playing the Race Card*, 45–95.

168. This fact was treated by early film historians and critics as a different matter than the formal achievement of the film. Recently critics have begun to insist that this dissociation cannot stand. In my reading, the film's realism and its racism are inextricably and fundamentally connected.

169. Williams, *Playing the Race Card*, 5.

170. Fisher, "Jury's Rise as Lie Detector," 683.

171. Ibid.

172. Ibid.

173. Ibid., 687–88.

174. Grace Elizabeth Hale, *Making Whiteness* (New York: Vintage Books, 1999), 204–207, 221.

175. Ken Burns, Sarah Burns, and David McMahon, dirs., *The Central Park Five* (2012; Arlington, VA: PBS, 2013), DVD.

176. Annaliese Griffin, "A Profile of Matias Reyes," *New York Daily News*, April 9, 2013. http://www.nydailynews.com/services/central-park-five/profile-matias-reyes-article-1.1308560.

177. The city of New York finally settled the civil suit brought by the exonerated men for $41 million after the film was released but "denied and continues to deny that it and the individually named defendants have committed any violations of law or engaged in any wrongful acts concerning or related to any allegations that were or could have been alleged" in the settlement. Benjamin Weiser, "Settlement Is Approved in Central Park Jogger Case, but New York Deflects Blame." *New York Times*, September 5, 2014. http://www.nytimes.com/2014/09/06/nyregion/41-million-settlement-for-5-convicted-in-jogger-case-is-approved.html.

178. Indeed, Sarah Burns said of interviewing Reyes, "I do think he's a sociopath; a lot of what he said to us felt like he was telling us what we wanted to hear." Griffin, "Profile of Matias Reyes."

179. The film emphasizes the "too late" narrative, even though the parents of others were present after six hours and in some cases during the videotaped confessions themselves. The film also emphasizes the way that timing affected the outcome of the arrests. The parents of several of the boys were present at the precinct by 2:30 a.m. but the police would not release them until all of the parents were there. Raymond Santana's father did not arrive until 5:00 a.m. In the interim, the discovery of Trisha Meili and her condition were reported to the precinct, and the boys became suspects in the rape. The boys might not have been in custody at all had Santana's father arrived earlier. Sarah Burns, *The Central Park Five* (New York: Vintage Books, 2011), 31–32. Linda Williams has emphasized the role of the "in the nick of time/too late" tension in melodramatic narratives. Williams, *Playing the Race Card*, 35.

180. According to Sarah Burns, the filmmakers "tried on numerous occasions to interview the police and prosecutors who had participated in this case from the beginning—and we were unable to at every turn." Public Broadcasting Service, "Q&A with the Filmmakers," accessed December 14, 2014, http://www.pbs .org/kenburns/centralparkfive/about/filmmaker-q/.

181. Sidney Lumet, dir., *The Verdict* (1982; Century City, CA: Twentieth Century Fox Home Entertainment, 2002), DVD.

182. Steven Zaillian, *A Civil Action* (1998; Burbank, CA: Walt Disney Video, 1999), DVD.

183. This is notably not the case in Sarah Burns's book *The Central Park Five* about the same events.

184. Clover, "Law and Order," 102. Clover relies on Tocqueville here for the assertion that "the legal system provides a rhetorical and logical template that gives shape to all manner of social forms above and beyond the court of law" (101).

185. Ibid.,104.

186. Benjamin, "Work of Art," 809.

187. Digital technology eliminates the mechanical aspect of the production of photographic images. See William Mitchell, *The Reconfigured Eye: Visual Truth in the Post-Photographic Era* (Cambridge, MA: MIT Press, 1992). Lev Manovich makes a provocative observation: whereas "a traditional photograph always points to the past event, a synthetic photograph points to the future event." Lev Manovich, "The Paradoxes of Digital Photography," in *The Photography Reader*, ed. Liz Wells (London, UK: Routledge, 2003), 240–49.

188. Scott v. Harris 550 U.S. 372, at 383.

189. See, for example, Naomi Mezey, "The Image Cannot Speak for Itself: Film, Summary Judgment, and Visual Literacy," *Valparaiso University Law Review* 48 no. 1 (Fall 2013): 1. On judges responding to filmed evidence generally, see

Jessica Silbey, "Evidence Verité and the Law of Film," *Cardozo Law Review* 31, no. 4 (2010): 1257; Silbey, "Cross-Examining Film," *University of Maryland Law Journal of Race, Religion, Gender and Class* 8 (2008): 101; Silbey, "Judges as Film Critics: New Approaches to Filmic Evidence," *University of Michigan Journal of Law Reform* 37 (2004): 493.

190. Adam Benforado, "Frames of Injustice: The Bias We Overlook." *Indiana Law Journal* 85 (Fall 2010): 1333. Much has been made of the case as an example of "naïve realism." Dan Kahan, David A. Hoffman, and Donald Braman, "Whose Eyes Are You Going to Believe? *Scott v. Harris* and the Perils of Cognitive Illiberalism," Harvard Law Review 122 (2009): 837.

191. Plumhoff v. Rickard, 134 S.Ct. 2012 at 2021.

192. *Plumhoff* at 2017–18. Internal citations deleted.

193. *Plumhoff* at 2022.

194. Williams, *Playing the Race Card*, 294. See Jeffrey Rosen, "The Bloods and the Crits," *New Republic*, December 9, 1996.

195. See, for example, Elizabeth G. Porter, "Taking Images Seriously," *Columbia Law Review* 114 (2014): 1687; Richard K. Sherwin, Neil Feigenson, and Christina Spiesel, "Law in the Digital Age," *Boston University Journal of Science and Technology Law* 12, no. 2 (2006): 2.

3
Reasonable Doubts, Unspoken Fears
Reassessing the Trial Film's "Heroic Age"
Barry Langford

This chapter explores the relationship of a set of films portraying trials and courtroom practice to their social, cultural, and political contexts from the mid-1950s through the end of the Kennedy administration. Methodologically, the essay considers the trial film as a genre: genre itself functioning as a tool whereby (as a "vertical" axis of interpretation) large and diffuse structures of context can be focalized, expressed, and mapped in local and determinate ways onto individual texts that are also (as a "horizontal" axis) related reciprocally and dialogically to one another and to the larger generic corpus of which they are a part and to whose evolving nature by their production they contribute. Genre criticism of American legal cinema (trial and courtroom films) has proceeded, broadly, along two lines: the more conventional process of defining, demarcating, and interpreting the films that might constitute the courtroom genre (as mapped out, for example, by Nicole Rafter)[1]; and the theoretically and philosophically ambitious project mooted by Carol Clover, to conceive the adversarial and forensic procedures of the trial itself as a or perhaps even *the* genre undergirding the epistemological (pragmatic and fact-based) structures of most mainstream American film narratives, regardless of genre. This is what Clover characterizes as "the fantastic generativity of the [trial] form in Anglo-American popular culture".[2] At the same time, however, these readings are also informed by the principle that the jury trial on film, as Clover (following Tocqueville) has argued elsewhere, offers an idealized, formalized distillation of the process and promise of American democracy itself: that exploring and enacting this, indeed, is the genre's fundamental "offer" to its audience.[3] On such an account, the trial film speaks to questions of American national identity and self-perception in ways that extend beyond the immediate contexts of cinematic spectatorship. If therefore the *trial* as "genre" indeed subtends the very question of genericity as the essential "ground" on and from which generic questions are themselves posed, do discernible modifications or adjustments in enactments of the *trial film*'s generic procedures[4] accordingly indicate shifts and shocks (superficial or tectonic) in that "ground"? Further, if, upon closer inspection, trial films in a given period seem to question or even subvert the goal-oriented, fact-determining procedures on which Clover insists, should we attribute this primarily to the impact of contemporary epiphenomena, or might it indicate a need more fundamentally to reassess the premises of Clover's forensic ontology?

To answer these questions, this essay will reexamine (paying close and specific attention to details of narrative, mise-en-scène, performance, and film style) a brief period in the history of the trial film. This period has been chosen because a substantial body of writing on the trial film considers these years to mark a heroic high point in the onscreen representation of American jurisprudence—in particular, commentary by lawyers and legal scholars discussing movies (perhaps less so film scholars and cultural historians, who tend to be wary of very sharp and uninflected demarcations and characterizations of historical periods). In the films of this period, it is claimed, the courtroom and its participants—preeminently the principled and determined individual trial lawyer, his apotheosis of course Gregory Peck as Atticus Finch—can be understood, following Clover, as actors in a stylized and idealized drama of fundamental American values in which constitutional-democratic principles are tested and ultimately reaffirmed. During this "heroic" phase, as Rafter describes it, bracketed roughly by *12 Angry Men* and *To Kill a Mockingbird*, law films promoted a broadly positive vision of a prosocial legal system grounded in, and in its turn sustaining and improving, a far-from-flawless yet essentially robust and functional civil society.[5] David Ray Papke writes of a "golden age" of the Hollywood law film, "golden in terms of not only the quality of their screenwriting, directing, and acting but also their presentations of lawyers, trials, and law in general. The films endorse the rule of-law; they inspire belief in that rule of law."[6] These films' lawyer-protagonists such as Finch, Paul "Polly" Biegler (James Stewart in Otto Preminger's *Anatomy of a Murder*), or Judge Dan Haywood (Spencer Tracy in Stanley Kramer's *Judgment at Nuremberg*) are characterized with slightly absurd hyperbole by Michael Asimow as "honest, competent professionals—sometimes even heroes . . . wonderful role models for everyone in the profession from law students up to grizzled veterans."[7]

The broadly optimistic tenor of this passage of the Hollywood law film is typically understood in an expressive relationship to sociohistorical contexts including, broadly, national self-confidence born of postwar US domestic prosperity and economic and strategic hegemony, and with specific reference to the law, the Warren Court's role in advancing progressive social change within constitutional frameworks. According to Nevins, most of the law-related films of this era "reflected" the "idealism of the Warren Court and early civil rights era" and their protagonists are lineal descendants of Lincoln himself—if not the historical Lincoln, then at least his onscreen embodiment by Henry Fonda in John Ford's *Young Mr. Lincoln*.[8] The ensuing social and political upheavals of the 1960s—so this conventional narrative continues—ensured that when the law film revived in the early 1980s, it did so in a new mode of skepticism if not outright cynicism that chimed with the era's radical disenchantment with the American Dream generally, and crucially with the capacity of key institutions such as the legal system to deliver truth, justice, and social progress.[9] The trial film's "heroic" era, therefore, takes on an Edenic quality, suffused with the bittersweet nostalgic glow of prelapsarian lost content before faith in the integrity of legal, judicial, law-enforcement, and governmental process alike was ineradicably corrupted by (take your pick) the Warren Commission, the Pentagon Papers, COINTELPRO, Watergate, and the manifold other shocks to the American system of the later 1960s and 1970s.

This chapter will put this version of American legal/legal-film history "on trial" by posing two obvious questions. The first, and though clearly necessary perhaps the less interesting if only because it *is* so obvious, is how far is this version accurate or indeed tenable, whether as a snapshot of the Eisenhower/Kennedy years generally, as a characterization of Americans' attitude toward law and lawyers in those years, or as an account of the films depicting the legal process produced at that time. I will argue that, although there is no need to overturn or discard wholesale this historiography—which has proven robust enough to become the most widely accepted narrative of the trial film in the 1950s and early 1960s—the historical and the cinematic records alike indicate the need for its significant reappraisal and adjustment.

My second question—harder to answer definitively, but with potentially more far-reaching implications—asks not "is it *accurate?*" but rather "what is its *motive?*" That is, what purposes might the construction of a "heroic" era of American trial movies serve, either in retrospect or—more interestingly still—at the time? Particularly when, viewed from the perspective of a disenchanted posterity, it is contrasted to subsequent periods whose difficulties and complexities are explicitly or implicitly rebuked, the narrative possesses a distinctly conservative cast, a nostalgia for an era when heroic (white, male) lawyers could stand tall and defend (or dictate?) justice without compromise or self-doubt. For all that the values of this hallowed era might be conceived as broadly liberal, the valorization of a halcyon pre-1960s epoch has a distinctly conservative, even Reaganite, tinge.[10] At the same time, moreover, numerous social and cultural histories of the Eisenhower years have suggested that beneath the received image of conformity, consensus, and indeed complacency in the America 1950s lurked subterranean—and often not so subterranean—currents of dissent, anxiety, and profound ideological difference.

One does not in fact have to scratch the chrome-and-Bakelite 1950s surface very deeply to find these hidden seams of sociocultural difference and dissensus. They were openly on display in the period itself. By middecade strong voices were already arguing that the price of all the material comforts that typified the postwar suburban American dream was a marked erosion of American traditions of individualism and personal liberty. As early as 1950, sociologist David Riesman suggested that the pioneering, entrepreneurial, self-motivated "inner-directed" American character was being supplanted by an "outer-directed" personality who sought approval and direction from others: a (best-selling) analysis that in important ways foreshadowed the American New Left critique of consumer capitalism in the 1960s.[11] William Whyte famously characterized the white-collar worker as a faceless "organisation man" dominated by "groupthink," oriented less to his ostensible professional task than to mastering the intricacies of the modern bureaucratic environment in pursuit of self-advancement.[12] The more-radical C. Wright Mills pointed to the growing domination of the US economy by a few gigantic enterprises like General Motors, AT&T, and IBM and the emergence of a "power elite" detached from traditional structures of democratic accountability.[13] For all of these writers, whose bestselling books spread their ideas far beyond academic circles, suburbia—natural habitat of the "organization man"—embodied these trends, with its artificial communities, frantic consumption, highly conformist lifestyles, and rigid policing of sex and gender roles.[14]

Cultural criticism of the 1950s has found rich material in the novels, poetry, drama—and films—of the period for counter-readings of Eisenhowerera conformism. The leading Hollywood genres of the period—such as the Western, the science fiction film, the social problem film, the melodrama, and even the musical—have all been effectively mined for evidence of the ambivalences and uncertainties of this ostensibly confident period by close textual analyses, whose findings often belie the affirmative positions such films "officially" adopt.[15] The courtroom drama, however—a minor genre in purely numerical terms that has received less sustained attention than others (it "has no standing in the pantheon of genres," as Clover puts it)[16]— seems to have been largely bypassed by such critical interventions. This chapter, therefore, in line with historical accounts that challenge the received view of the Eisenhower era's alleged complacent uniformity, and with film scholarship that explores films as complex cultural productions implicated in the ideological contests of their times will propose a reevaluation of the representations of law and jurisprudence in the "heroic" era of American trial movies at the turn of the 1960s. Looking at both genre classics and lower-profile films (which for such readings can be just as significant), the chapter will examine how narrative content interacts with visual style in a range of trial films of the "heroic" era to instantiate complex and sometimes conflicted attitudes toward the legal process.[17] These will include as well as the classic movies already cited and such other notable contemporaries as *Anatomy of a Murder*, Fritz Lang's *Beyond a Reasonable Doubt* (RKO 1955), lesser-known and/or less extensively discussed genre entries such as *Trial* (Mark Robson, dir.) and *The Young Savages* (John Frankenheimer, dir.). Following Jessica Silbey, the chapter pays close attention to the ways in which trial films interpellate the viewing subject.[18] Drawing parallels between law films and other key genres of the period (notably science fiction), I argue that the generally undemonstrative visual style of most law films in this period can be read symptomatically, as the textual assertion of a confidence in conventional procedures repeatedly belied by narratives that depict questionable legal practices and outcomes. A deep textual reading of these films suggests a profound ambivalence about the law in an era struggling to come to terms with the still-raw memory of legal/procedural abuses by McCarthy, Cohn et al. on the one hand—to say nothing of Hollywood's own postwar difficulties at the hands of the courts—and the uncertain future being plotted by the judicial activism of the Warren Court on the other. Moreover, the emphasis almost all of these films place on the heroic trial attorney himself—typically a figure of somewhat solitary if beleaguered integrity who in his palpable humanity combines natural justice and the legal code and who is opposed or contrasted to more impersonal, mechanistic, dehumanized, or even corrupt juridical and/or political structures—begs the question of whether this overstated heroism may not bespeak a hidden anxiety that it is precisely *only* heroic action that can deliver American justice: that is, that without exceptional measures/the measures of the exceptional individual, the system may not in fact deliver justice at all. As we will see, this is in fact a recurrent motif even in some of the period's most ostensibly affirmative legal screen fictions.

In fact, there are grounds for arguing that during the 1950s concerns emerged around the place and role of the law in American society that in some ways paralleled the critiques of bureaucratic and corporate culture offered by Riesman et al. If the trial has indeed historically offered a symbolic reaffirmation of democratic republican principles, the 1950s marked a point of crisis for the adversarial system and hence implicitly the values it subtended. On the one hand, the New Deal, now effectively institutionalized by twenty years of Democratic administrations and the consensus policies subsequently adopted by Eisenhower, offered an alternative to government by and through courts and trials, in favor of rule by bureaucracy, government regulation, and the administrative state.

Trials offered an alternative to what by the mid-1950s many were starting to perceive as the stifling constraints of a heavily managed society. This alternative was rooted in the concreteness, tangibility, and relative transparency of legal process (in its adversarial forms). Perhaps more surprisingly, as actualizations of the legal process trials—though de facto rational procedures—also offered sites of potential resistance or countervailing possibility to the hypertrophic rationality of Cold War America. For while working within tightly defined abstract structures, (trial) lawyers are nonetheless embodied in ways that rationality suppresses. The trial lawyer's voice, facial expression, posture, and body language all define a locus wherein the appeal to abstract legal principles is worked through the irreducibly human individual. By performing the mediation of the abstract and bureaucratic by the human and individual, trials thus balance the drive on the part of the bureaucratized state for rules that supersede the human. Nowhere is this more visible than in movies, which necessarily trade in the concrete, specific, and individual rather than the abstract and general. In this respect, the "vernacular authenticity" of the law—the performance of everydayness, as undertaken by Ford's Lincoln or Paul Biegler in *Anatomy of a Murder*—has an acute topical relevance and may indeed be considered to be undertaking important cultural "work." At other points—see, for example, my discussion of visual style in *The Young Savages*—emphasis on the embodiment of law (and lawyering) can be interpreted as reacting to the tendency within the law itself to abstractions that counter "common sense" perceptions of "natural" justice.

Movies do not, of course, straightforwardly "reflect" society—especially when that society is itself (as all open societies are) a multidimensional polity marked by difference and debate. (Nor is there a clear linear progression to be charted from one film to the next. The "evolution" of genres, if it happens at all, can only be plotted across a longer arc than the short span discussed here.[19] Hence, films will not be discussed in strictly chronological sequence.) Rather, films are here understood as ideological artifacts—"ideology" taken in an Althusserian sense to denote representational structures allowing the individual subject to conceive his or her lived relationship to transpersonal social realities.[20] To avoid reductively reflectionist interpretations, the chapter's critical methodology applies a model of "expressive causality" to film genre: understanding genres as a crucial means of mediating complex large-scale social and political phenomena and their articulation in and through cultural practice; as, in Fredric Jameson's enduringly influential formulation, "socially symbolic acts."[21]

Film Genre as a Socially Symbolic Act

Genre provides scholars with a historically grounded method of establishing "family resemblances" between films produced and released under widely differing circumstances and of mediating the relationship between the mythologies of popular culture and social, political, and economic contexts. Much genre theory and criticism, in fact, has been motivated by the conviction that genre offers a privileged insight into "how to understand the life of films in the social."[22] As Fredric Jameson observes, (literary) genres "are essentially . . . *institutions*, or social contracts between a writer and a specific public, whose function is to specify the proper use of a particular cultural artifact" (emphasis in original).[23] Genre films, similarly, are by definition institutionalized, in significant measure collective rather than singular objects: their meanings are comprised relationally rather than in isolation. Thus, whereas to attempt to "read off" social or political debates in the broader culture onto individual films is likely to prove reductive and speculative, the sheer number of films in a given genre means that changes in generic directions and attitudes across time may reasonably be understood as responses and/or contributions to the shifting concerns of their mass public. Genre films solicit audience approval through both continuity and variation; audience responses encourage genre filmmakers to pursue existing generic directions or to change them. Film genres have frequently been characterized as popular (or mass) "myths"—"myth" here broadly designating the ways in which genres rehearse and work through these shared cultural values and concerns by rendering them in symbolic narratives. The regular consumption of genre films by a mass audience may or may not be taken to indicate endorsement of the values and positions "sedimented" (Jameson's term) in these fictions—if, indeed, these positions are in fact readily legible. But equally, in the context of a commercial film industry the repeated production of narratives each engaging in similar (never identical) fashion with common thematic material may reasonably be held to betoken a degree of acceptance or at the very least ongoing interest in that material. To the extent that genres present a consistent "worldview," their ongoing popularity suggests in turn that worldview has some purchase on the audience's sympathies and interests.[24]

Jameson argues that these essential characteristics of a genre be regarded as "ideologemes": "a historically determinate conceptual or semic complex which can project itself" in the form of a specific set of attitudes, political or philosophical positions, or narrative structures. The ideologeme itself, however, Jameson adds, must be grasped as "a form of social praxis, that is, as a symbolic resolution to a concrete historical situation."[25] Jameson uses the "magical narratives" of romance and fantasy (contrasted to the dominant literary traditions of nineteenth-century realism) as the test case for his immanent critique, arguing that the harmoniousness toward which romance narratives drive (and upon which they are generically predicated) can be understood as a symbolic response to the actually irreconcilable oppositions of premodern and modern forms of social life, whose conflict in the transitional phases of history out of which romance emerged had not yet found clear articulation in outright class conflict and thus become amenable to (and perhaps only to and in) such "magical" resolutions.

Trial films by their very nature also possess a strong drive toward narrative resolution: the delivery of the verdict is invariably the climactic and often the culminating element in the film (for example, one of the films I discuss, *The Young Savages*, ends within an onscreen minute of the jury's verdict). Yet, the stark and incontestable fact of the narrative and (absent the appeals process, which more rarely forms part of the universe of the trial film—though it is invoked as a tragically unrealized opportunity for justice in *To Kill a Mockingbird*) legal closure through the verdict does not invariably bring resolution to the complex human and social problems that, in trial films, the trial process typically brings to light. This is true even of *12 Angry Men*, the best-known and also the most obviously didactic narrative of any of the films considered in this chapter—in whose meeting of narrative form and content constitutional democracy may be considered to have passed its examination in the trial film successfully, if not with flying colors, yet which still leaves conspicuously unresolved (among other things) the racial prejudice of Juror 10 (Ed Begley), the indifference and disengagement of Juror 7 (Jack Warden), the vapidity of Juror 12 (Robert Webber), and the overwhelming sense of personal grievance of Juror 3 (Lee J. Cobb).[26] In other films discussed here, where there is a discrepancy between the jury's verdict and the audience's sense of natural justice—or where legal protocols impose themselves on or interpose themselves between the human actors in the legal drama in an overstated or unexpected way, as may also be the case—the ensuing mismatch of form and content, experienced simultaneously as a crux in narrative and in narration, may be interpreted as symptomatic of the trial film's difficulty in carrying through its essential ideological work in the specific historical circumstances of its production and consumption.

Equally, however, it can be argued that a degree of irresolution in the trial film is less anomalous than it might at first seem. Trials themselves can be seen not as vehicles to deliver definitive answers but as acts of rhetoric whose overriding purpose is repeatedly to perform an *idea* (or ideal) of fixity grounded in the needs of the social imaginary for such closure: an idea or ideal, however, that inevitably fails. The very procedures of the adversarial trial—the alternation of statement and counterstatement, direct and cross-examination—that notionally arrive forensically and by a process of logical exclusion at a singular truth, in fact almost invariably produce the opposite: revealing the processes where by what we (legally and colloquially) call "truth" is not discovered so much as discursively *produced*. The trial, in other words, is inherently a space where the very project of eliminating doubt in fact produces indeterminacy. The presence of negativity in familiar court locutions—"beyond a reasonable doubt," or in Scottish law "not proven"—can be read as the rhetorical return of this procedural repressed. The trial—and the trial film too—are thus far from closed or definitive as some scholars maintain. Rather, they might be said always already to possess an uncanny potentiality in the form of the revelation of ultimate undecidability that haunts the verdict's rhetoric of clarity.

This is not however to say that all trial films, or all trial films at all times, admit or confess this uncanny element to an equal degree or openly. On the contrary, it may be precisely in the valences of its suppression/confession of indeterminacy in and through the legal process that the ideological labor of the trial film becomes visible. In the late 1950s, this ideological work is naturally inextricable from the inescapable context of the escalating Cold War. David Ray Papke notes the growing importance of official American self-definition as a law-governed society over the Communist bloc, perceived as reliant on force and coercion (including Eisenhower's 1958 promulgation of May 1 as "Law Day"—"for the cultivation of the respect for law that is so vital to the democratic way of life," more vital evidently than respect for the rights of organized labor internationally celebrated on the same day).[27] Hollywood, meanwhile, still prostrated by the aftereffects of the House Un-American Activities Committee (HUAC) witch hunts at the start of the decade, was only too eager to produce pictures whose "Americanism" could not reasonably be faulted. Films celebrating the new American-democratic sacrament of the law offered an ideal opportunity to do so. Yet, not only was this investment in law as a transcendent value driven, all too obviously, by the strident and ubiquitous anti-Communism of the time: the Red Scare itself had in the first half of the decade given rise to serious abuses of power and process—most notably Sen. Joseph McCarthy's crusades against alleged Communist infiltration of the US government and military but also the kangaroo-court style of the HUAC hearings and the prison sentences handed down to the "Hollywood Ten," and—in the eyes of much of the outside word at least—the trial and execution of the "atom spies" Julius and Ethel Rosenberg. The film industry's abject response to HUAC's assault on constitutional freedoms, and the ongoing scandal of the blacklist, ensured a significant measure of bad faith would attend its championing of the rule of law. Meanwhile, the major Hollywood studios of course also had their own parochial reasons for ambivalence toward the law: in 1948, the Supreme Court's *Paramount* decision compelled them into a traumatic rearrangement of their business model requiring divestment of their theatrical exhibition arms and associated restrictive practices; and four years later, the Court's decision in *Burstyn v. Wilson* ("the *Miracle* decision"), while ostensibly benefiting the industry by restoring the First Amendment protections denied it four decades earlier in *Mutual v. Ohio*, equally started to unpick the (self-)regulatory apparatus that had since the 1930s guided and underpinned classic Hollywood's generic and representational conventions.[28]

One might say therefore that Hollywood's "legal turn" in the late 1950s was classically overdetermined. At the same time, given this complex and ambiguous context, it would hardly be surprising if upon inspection the received image of the era's legal films as unequivocal celebrations of American law and its lawyers turned out to need some qualification. And indeed, the two most celebrated trial films of this period, Otto Preminger's *Anatomy of a Murder* and Robert Mulligan's *To Kill a Mockingbird*, illustrate very well the subterranean stresses operative upon the genre in these years—revealing a striking gap between their subsequent reputations as touchstones of the "heroic" lawyer film and their considerably more ambivalent actual portrayals of the justice system and those who work within it. In other films, such as *Trial*, *The Young Savages*, and even to a certain extent *12 Angry Men*, the extravagant adaptations or outright breaches of due process necessitated of the protagonists to deliver a semblance of justice from trial situations seem to testify to a partly disavowed unease at the adequacy of a system rooted in the good faith of the Lincolnian vernacular to the complexities of a modern society. Fritz Lang's unclassifiable *Beyond a Reasonable Doubt*, meanwhile, revels in disorienting secure, normative assumptions about narrative orientation and spectatorial identification to a degree that throws into question due process of any kind at all—legal or cinematic.[29]

Due Process and Its Discontents: *Anatomy of a Murder*, *Trial*, and *Beyond a Reasonable Doubt*

Of all trial films, *Anatomy of a Murder* is the most closely focused on the trial itself. The actual trial proceedings (including conferences in chambers and brief exchanges in the courtroom during recesses, etc.) consume well over half the film's lengthy 154-minute running time and 109 of the final draft screenplay's 204 pages, an exceptionally high proportion among trial films generally.[30] Although personal details of defense attorney Paul Biegler (James Stewart) are economically sketched in at the start of the film—for instance, the economic exigencies faced by his practice owing to his lacka-daisical attitude toward his practice, from which the Manion case prom-ises (though it will ultimately fail) to deliver him—compared to many trial films (for example, Sidney Lumet's *The Verdict*) Biegler's personal conflicts and struggles play relatively little part in proceedings. His role for the au-dience is to all intents and purposes defined, as it is for his client, by his professional duties.

As a defense attorney, Biegler's constitutional and legal duties are self-evident: to defend his client against the charge of first-degree murder lev-eled against him by the state. The case is an unusual one in proceeding from the acceptance on both sides that Lieutenant Manion did indeed kill Barney Quill. Thus, the standard reversals of the trial film, with the real killer being dramatically revealed Agatha Christie-style in the final reel, are never on offer here. The film invites us to consider instead the details and ultimately the ethics of criminal justice. As has been frequently observed, Preminger's film offers not so much an anatomy of a murder as an anatomy of a murder *trial*.[31]

Whether prosecutor or (as in the majority of trial films) defender, on-screen attorneys tend toward a high and perhaps implausible degree of ide-alism: that is, idealism of a truth-based natural justice in which the spirit of the law may have to be realized by adapting or superseding its letter. Their ideals, indeed, may even motivate them to radically reinterpret their duty toward their clients or their employers in the process of delivering this jus-tice. As we shall see in due course, this construction of the "heroic" lawyer begets, or reveals, its own important difficulties and contradictions. In any case, however, Paul "Polly" Biegler does not belong in this company of ide-alists. That he has ever been conscripted to the ranks of "heroic lawyers" tes-tifies to the successful and altogether intentional confusion of performance and reality, at both diegetic and extra-diegetic levels. During the film's fic-tional trial, Biegler repeatedly represents himself as a "little guy" in the great tradition, David fighting the well-resourced Goliaths of both local district attorney Mitch Lodwick and more importantly his big-city colleague from the attorney general's office in Lansing, the pallid and sharklike Dancer (George C. Scott), who quickly supersedes Lodwick as Biegler's real op-ponent. In so many words, at one pivotal moment in the trial, Biegler de-claims—with one hand on the witness stand and in close proximity to the jury—that he is "just a humble country lawyer trying to do the best I can against this brilliant prosecutor from the big city of Lansing."[32] But this is transparently a *performance*—a brilliant one—and recognized and admired, reluctantly or otherwise, as such by Biegler's professional colleagues. As Biegler's team await the jury's verdict, his whiskey-soused sidekick Parnell applauds "that humble country lawyer bit"—cheerfully punning that it "had Mr. Dancer dancing" (with rage or because Biegler was pulling his strings).[33] Biegler's affectation of Lincolnesque prairie authenticity is a "bit"—a turn, a number—and one he carries off with aplomb. When, while indicating to Judge Weaver (Joseph Welch) during a crucial conference in chambers the obscure 1886 precedent on which his entire defense will rest, Biegler simultaneously woos and charms Weaver with his account of fashioning fishing lures to hook bullfrogs, the two prosecutors exchange glances confessing their grudging admiration of his skill as a "fisher of men" (tellingly, it is the more accomplished and sophisticated Dancer who appears the less annoyed and more appreciative of what he recognizes as a legitimate dimension of Biegler's work).

Equally critical to this—in effect helping to win over the audience just as Polly wins over Judge Weaver—is the casting of James Stewart as Biegler. Stewart's performance delves deeply into his repertoire of gangly aw-shucks mannerisms—the homespun little-guy guilelessness that became such an integral part of his screen persona in such classics as Frank Capra's *Mr. Smith Goes to Washington*, *Harvey*, and, of course, Capra's *It's a Wonderful Life*. As the *New York Times'* 1989 obituary noted, Stewart's "portrayals of decent, idealistic and naive small-town Americans made him a beloved national icon."[34] But as the *Times* also noted, after his return from active service in World War II, directors such as Alfred Hitchcock and Anthony Mann frequently cross-cast Stewart in a different, darker vein of roles, where his amiable received image could be intelligently set off by unexpected streaks of cruelty, obsession, and neurosis. *Anatomy of a Murder's* distinctively narrow focus on Biegler's professional duties to the exclusion of most of his personal life precludes his becoming as rich or compelling a character study as Scotty in Hitchcock's *Vertigo*, Howie Kemp in Mann's *The Naked Spur*—or, indeed, the hysterical, suicidal George Bailey in *It's a Wonderful Life*. In fact, compared to these roles "Polly" Biegler is granted a pronounced, and surely intentional, lack of interpretable interiority. While nothing Biegler does outside the courtroom (his dealings with Laura Manion and Mary Pilant, for example) directly contradicts his bearing within it as a plainspoken if worldly and capable man, at the same time we, like his courtroom opponents, are held at a remove from the inner man—whose private motivations and feelings are, of course, ultimately irrelevant in his discharges of his duty to his client. Biegler's amateur jazz piano playing underscores both this performative dimension to his character and—in the "cool" quality of the music, which Parnell compares unflatteringly to the more evocative standards of the previous generation—his quality of self-containment and reserve.

This withholding of Biegler's personality endows the film, similarly, with a striking quality of detachment, a forensic approach—an anatomy, indeed—to the judicial process wherein Stewart's homey persona effectively masks Biegler's clear-eyed, borderline cynical approach to his task just as Biegler's folksiness is an effective delivery mechanism for his legal skill. One question the film scrupulously forebears to ask is whether Biegler *believes* in his client's innocence under the law—that is, in the diagnosis of "irresistible impulse" on which the defense relies and, ultimately, triumphs. In the key scene where the defense strategy is decided, Biegler all but directs Manion to his plea of temporary insanity—while carefully avoiding actually doing so: telling Manion, "I'm not *telling* you to do anything. I want you to understand the letter of the law."[35] Later in the scene, as Manion struggles toward "his" discovery of a "*legal excuse*" (emphasis in the original) for the killing, Wendell Mayes's script describes Biegler watching him "poker-faced, eyes hooded": directions aptly carried through to Stewart's performance of the scene. The tiny half-grin that curls Biegler's lips when Manion arrives at the line "I must have been mad" is readable—barely—as his relief at coming up with a plausible defense, but more readily as Biegler's gratification that his cynical deployment of "the letter of the law"—not, tellingly, its spirit—has paid dividends.[36]

A close viewing of *Anatomy of a Murder* in my view makes somewhat problematic—for example—Orit Kamir's ascription of Biegler to the tradition of the "hero-lawyer" derived in part from models of heroic masculinity familiar from the western: boasting "extraordinary, professional fighting skills and 'true manhood', which entails a commitment to justice and natural law, as well as inherent honour."[37] In the first place, as noted previously, this fails to discriminate between those attributes of Biegler, and his approach to law, that are proper to the character and those he consciously adopts as part of his *performance* of lawyering—to the extent that the film allows us to make the distinction. Nothing of the relatively little that we see of Polly outside the courtroom and interactions with his client and witnesses directly contradicts his persona within it; but this is merely to suggest that the refinement of his persona is thoroughgoing enough and sufficiently grounded (as all good performances are) in his essential character to be seamlessly maintainable through all circumstances. Kamir's observations on the western hero also bear further scrutiny: insofar as they appear to identify the screen attorney with the *professional gunfighter* (rather than the cattleman or homesteader, for example), these comments tend to overlook (as generalized comments about westerns often do) that in precisely the period under consideration the gunfighter was (a) a relatively novel figure in Hollywood westerns and (b) far from unequivocally heroic or admirable in most of his screen appearances. In fact, in a series of prestigious classic westerns from the early postwar period through the 1960s such as *The Gunfighter*, *Shane*, *Vera Cruz*, and *The Magnificent Seven*, the ethics, morality, and, perhaps above all, the social (dis-)location of the gun-for-hire were subjected to sustained and often critical scrutiny. (It is perhaps worth noting that, in this same period, in Ford's autumnal western *The Man Who Shot Liberty Valance*, he directly contrasted the nation- and culture-building properties of the gun and the lawbook and the *different* models of masculinity they respectively subtended.[38]) There may be a good argument for identifying Paul Biegler—first seen, significantly like Shane, as *outside* the community he notionally serves (driving, rather than riding, back into town from a fishing trip)—with the gunfighter whose skills are available for a price. Like most screen gunfighters (and many screen lawyers), Biegler is socially semidetached, most notably—in the domesticated Eisenhower era—in his bachelorhood. This detachment is a professional advantage but is certainly rather different from the firm integration of the lawyer and his community exemplified by Atticus Finch or Ford's Lincoln. Contrary to Nicole Rafter's claim, Biegler is some way removed from a plausibly "Lincolnesque" figure.[39]

In *Anatomy of a Murder*'s ambivalent account of law-as-performance, Biegler is counterbalanced by Judge Weaver, as personified by Joseph Welch, who directs the Manion trial with its lurid open-court discussion of sexual climaxes and panties with impeccable discretion and evenhandedness, his avuncular yet firm and astute presence on the bench the very model of American judiciary, embodying the gravity of the law yet at the same time overseeing justice with matter-of-fact directness, not Olympian detachment. Like Stewart/Biegler, Welch/Weaver engages inter- and extratextual elements in the service of *Anatomy*'s exploration of authenticity in the trial process. Yet, whereas Biegler's knowing deployment of the tropes of James Stewart's familiar screen persona serves ultimately to deconstruct that persona for the spectator even as it works its magic upon the screen jury, Welch's presence arguably works in the opposite direction: readily recognizable (to an American audience in 1959, with the memory of his nationally televised 1954 confrontation with McCarthy during the Army-Navy hearings still relatively fresh) as an avatar of legal integrity and restraint in the face of a politicized quasi-judicial process, Welch/Weaver reassures us of the identity and continuity of (courtroom) performance and performer, and by extension of profession and principle. Provided, that is, that what Welch's presence called to mind was indeed McCarthy's eventual containment by due process and common "decency" (in Welch's words)—rather than his four-year reign of terror during which constitutional protections were impotent and ignored. But the line is a disturbingly fine one, and there is little elsewhere in *Anatomy of a Murder* to suggest where, in the event of any future McCarthy's assault on the integrity of constitutional process, we might expect to find comparable reserves of principle to defy it.

The encounter of legal principle and practice is dramatized in a more direct, and considerably less subtle, manner in a far less-celebrated court-room drama of the period, Mark Robson's *Trial*.[40] Though generally well-received critically (*Film Daily* voted it the seventh-best film of the year) and opening strongly enough to merit MGM placing a double-page spread in *Box Office* trumpeting the film's prospects, it ultimately placed a modest fifty-sixth in *Variety's* year-end box-office listings, with estimated rentals of $2 million, and has since largely disappeared from view.[41] The case in the film is in itself a simple enough affair: Angel Chavez, a Mexican American youth, is accused of the murder of a young white woman at the beach in a small southern Californian town, San Juno. His defense attorney is law professor Blake (Glenn Ford). New regulations at the state university require faculty to have courtroom experience: Blake has none, meaning he will lose his job unless he can secure the necessary credentials over the summer vacation. He lucks into a small law firm run by Castle (Arthur Kennedy) who has taken on the Chavez case and seizes on Blake as a lawyer who will argue his client's case with passion and determination because he is actually (unlike Castle, it is implied) convinced of the youth's innocence. This rather contrived premise seems geared to underscore *Trial's* principal concern as an exploration of the bruising clash between legal theory and professional practice in the bearpit of contemporary American democracy: Can Blake's abstract conceptions of justice and legal process survive the encounter with raw reality? MGM clearly hoped that its picture (scripted by Don Mankiewicz from his own novel) would indeed gain some traction as a serious contribution to legal debates, taking out a full-page ad for the film in the *American Bar Association Journal* and organizing special screenings for the legal community.[42]

In fact, Blake proves a hard-edged and (barring a few false starts composing an overly academic opening address) competent advocate: he is sufficiently unintimidated by his new role and surroundings to tell the African American presiding judge (Juano Hernandez) to his face that he has concerns over his objectivity (he fears the judge has been assigned the case in the expectation he will favor the prosecution to avoid being seen to overly sympathize with the minority defendant). And Glenn Ford is as ever a somewhat unlikely candidate for ivory-tower neophyte (though there are resonances between his role here and as the newly qualified teacher in *The Blackboard Jungle* the same year). Consequently, the dramatic crux of the film concerns less the conflict of abstract and actual than the stresses in a judicial system open to exploitation and abuse from the political extremes of both left and right as the Chavez case becomes a litmus test for racial prejudice, political opportunism, and ideological manipulation.

Toward the start of the film, it is the racist Right who pose the greatest threat to the administration of justice: having hijacked the funeral of Chavez's alleged victim, local white supremacist factions lead a lynch mob to the county jail where Chavez awaits trial. At this stage, Castle takes the leading role in protecting his client, using the threat of bad civic publicity to induce the local sheriff to face down the mob (whose prejudices he mostly shares). Once the trial is underway, however, Castle's true motivations are revealed, and the film's political critique veers sharply rightward: when Blake is called to attend a fundraising event in New York—the Chavez case having become a liberal cause célèbre—it quickly becomes apparent that Castle, a Communist, is using the case to establish a Communist front organization. (From this point on, the racist campaign against Chavez ceases to figure in the film, which becomes stridently anti-Communist.) As the trial nears its climax, Castle reasserts control over the defense tactics, insisting over Blake's objections on putting the intimidated and inarticulate youth on the stand—in the expectation that a disastrous cross-examination will deliver a guilty verdict, a death sentence, and thus a martyr. Chavez is more valuable to the Communist cause on the gallows than if he walks free.

Though Castle succeeds in sidelining Blake and engineering the guilty verdict he desires, Blake ultimately saves Chavez's life by drawing the judge's attention to his power to send Chavez, as a minor, to the State Industrial School to be "reformed" rather than executed: thus putting his scholarly knowledge of legal technicalities to urgent real-world use. In a final irony, Castle—whose progressive racial views, even, have been exposed as a sham when he race-baits the African American judge in an attempt to provoke him into pronouncing a death sentence—is condemned to thirty days in jail for contempt of court (a salutary yet restrained sentence that denies him too any claim on political martyrdom).

As in most of the films under discussion here, in *Trial* the legal system ultimately delivers a reasonable measure of justice—but only by the thinnest and most reversible margins. The jury record a guilty verdict against Chavez when the film has left us in little doubt of his innocence (the dead girl suffered from a hereditary heart condition). As in *To Kill a Mockingbird*, prejudice ultimately trumps duty to the law—without, as in the latter, the contextual excuse of period distance. Legal ethics are vulnerable to malicious abuse by counsel, who deliberately acts against his client's best interests for ideological reasons. Chavez's life is only saved through the quick-wittedness and lawbook savvy of a novice advocate: hardly resounding grounds for confidence in the system as a whole.

One aspect of *Trial* that strikes the modern viewer is its adoption of an extremely understated, not to say downright uninteresting, visual style. Nicole Rafter notes that this quality marks many courtroom movies of the "heroic era," whose "less dramatic . . . less radical—one might almost say more respectful" camerawork differentiates them from their noirish predecessors of the 1940s like William Wyler's *The Letter* and Boris Ingster's *Stranger on the Third Floor*, films whose expressionistic stylings she follows Norman Rosenberg in reading as textual registers of doubts about the fallibility of the legal system—visual opacity expressing disturbed legal and moral perspectives.[43] *Trial*, by contrast, aside from its moody nighttime opening sequence at the beach, unfolds—like *Anatomy of a Murder* and the courtroom (rather than the childhood) scenes of *To Kill a Mockingbird*—in rather unadventurous, even stolid, fashion, relying on a highly conventional visual lexicon of medium shots (the famous *"plan Américain"*), an eye-level camera in mostly fixed positions, and even, "high-key" lighting. Together with the occasionally impoverished production design (notably underdressed interiors), that is a feature of other films of the decade, the overall look of the film is "square" in a way that we readily associate with the blandness and conformity of the Eisenhower era.

Nonetheless, Preminger's stylistic reserve in *Anatomy of a Murder* seems to bespeak a more conscious and motivated directorial strategy than Robson's approach in *Trial*. Preminger's camera identifies itself with Paul Biegler in adopting a similar stance of scrupulously professional but ultimately noncommittal interest in its subject. Generally abjuring close-ups in favor of medium shots, singles for two-shots and groups, and undemonstrative interiors for exteriors, as Foster Hirsch observes "Preminger typically places the camera in the position of an observant spectator who knows the value of discretion and of maintaining a certain distance."[44] This culminates in the deliberate withholding of one of the genre's "money shots"—the expected close-up of Lieutenant Manion's face as he hears the jury deliver his acquittal (compare this to the extravagant crane shot that accompanies Frank Galvin's moment of redemption in Lumet's *The Verdict*). By denying us our expected privilege of emotional intimacy with a major character at the decisive moment in his story, Preminger reaffirms his film's concern with procedure and outcomes rather than emotion and reversals of fortune. *Trial* does not give the viewer the impression of a similarly considered visual style—which may make its "degree-zero" style more all the more suggestive.

The implication of Rafter's characterization of this kind of visual restraint in the decade's trial films as "respectful"—that the uncertainties of the 1940s have been assuaged in the balmy certainty of the prosperous 1950s—seems reasonable enough. If noir's disturbance of the stable visual field of classical Hollywood cinema is held, as it widely is, as expressive of a measure of disquiet besetting American culture in the wartime and immediate postwar years, then by the same token noir's displacement by the four-square filmmaking of the 1950s could reasonably be argued to reflect the ebbing of those currents of anxiety.[45] Yet in truth the social symptomatization of film style is an inexact science. To the extent that noir is seen as a cinematic "return of the repressed," its own marginalization could be seen either as a reflection of recovered sociocultural health and confidence—*or* a "secondary repression" whose very sobriety (those workmanlike features, shot following conventional shot) bespeaks its actually acute anxiety.

This may strike some readers as speculative at best, tortuous at worst. However, it is worth pointing out that another emblematic genre of the 1950s, which shares with courtroom dramas a dramatic and thematic focus on the marshaling of civic institutions and competences to face down threats from within and without—science fiction—also shares this propensity for a highly normative visual register. Vivien Sobchack has suggested that the oft-lamented flatness and lack of directorial signature that afflicts much 1950s science fiction cinema—so different from the Expressionistic stylings of prewar horror in the hands of James Whales and Jacques Tourneur at Universal and RKO, to which 1950s SF is often compared unfavorably—may operate as a way of naturalizing (by understating) fantastic narrative content. The stolid framing, four-square blocking, even lighting, and lockjaw acting vigorously reassert a confidence in the ultimate transparency and explicability of the physical world mirrored in the technocratic alliance of science and the military that typically brings the films of the decade to a satisfactory, if fiery, conclusion.[46]

Yet, few would argue against the view that, regardless of the decade's SF films' resolutely affirmative tenor, the mere fact of the genre's move in the 1950s from the margins to the center of Hollywood's genre economy itself testifies to deep-seated and pervasive anxieties in the culture, perhaps so profound that they could only find expression in the displaced mode of the fantastic. These sources of such anxieties in the Cold War and nuclear panic are equally clear. In which case the stylistic matter-of-factness of these films may be seen as working to recontain the destabilizing energies acknowledged and partly released (if, of course, only to be finally overcome) by the films' narratives. Stylistic sobriety is at once a restatement of SF's confidence in its ability to defeat the threats posed by the atomic mutations and alien invaders that beset the genre in the 1950s *and* a symptomatic reaction to them in the form of an anxious, overcompensatory repression of truths the text dare not confess too openly.

Applying this argument to the trial film would suggest that the general abandonment of the noir tropes of the 1940s registers not so much the sunlit confidence of the accepted version of the genre in the 1950s as the tensions within it, between the view of the law these films so earnestly propound and the concerns discernible in the interstices of their narrative and stylistic vectors. This is seen to an extreme degree in Fritz Lang's *Beyond a Reasonable Doubt*, a film that begs to be read—is indeed almost incomprehensible unless it *is* read—as an index of incipient crisis in the representational and juridical codes alike on which it ostensibly relies. In the film's climactic reversal, journalist Tom Garrett (Dana Andrews), has seemingly been convicted on the basis of evidence he has himself fabricated to prove the fallibility of the evidential process but is exonerated by the traditional deus ex machina of a hitherto-undiscovered letter, only for it then to be revealed that he was in fact guilty all along. The reversal reveals an order of things wholly invisible to the narration as it has been unsuspected by the judicial process—a sensational twist all the more startling for the emphatically quotidian tenor of the film's visual style.[47] In this "subversive" film, in Dennis White's words, "a perverse atmosphere of subliminal uncertainty prevails over the established surface reality."[48] This is a film, in fact, in which protocols of procedure and evidence (always objects of suspicion for Lang from as far back as *M*) merely mask abysses of unguessable conspiracy and bad faith they have no capacity to render visible. There is no point "beyond reasonable doubt": in fact, the only reasonable stance in a condition of radical indeterminacy is to doubt everything, especially the processes that would seek to persuade us otherwise.

"Unhappy the Land That Needs a Hero": *The Young Savages*, *12 Angry Men*, and *To Kill a Mockingbird*

The films discussed in the previous section of this chapter explored with various degrees of ambivalence the structures, processes, and outcomes of criminal law. It may not be coincidental that two of these films were directed by European expatriates in whose homelands the rule of law had recently been dismantled in favor of institutionalized criminality. More typically, however, the Hollywood trial film is identified with the struggle of the steadfast, often isolated, individual to uphold and deliver justice in adverse circumstances. The heroism of the "heroic" is most firmly located in, and identified with, these characters—typically trial attorneys. Here too, however, a careful consideration of the films of the period indicates a sense of the limits of individual capability and the pitfalls of a system that relies so largely upon it. Ultimately, rather than validating the lawyer- (or juror-) hero, these films echo Brecht's observation about the misfortune of the society that needs heroes to sustain itself in the first place.[49]

Of all the films under discussion here, arguably *The Young Savages* most unequivocally delivers the "heroic lawyer" protagonist regarded as the era's hallmark.[50] *The Young Savages* is the first and least well-known of the four 1961–1964 collaborations between Frankenheimer and star/producer Burt Lancaster. (The others were *Birdman of Alcatraz*, *Seven Days in May*, and *The Train*). In *The Young Savages*, Lancaster's assistant district attorney Hank Bell variously performs the roles of prosecutor, investigator, surrogate parent, social worker, tough guy, defender of the weak, heroic maverick, and ultimately redeemer. His personal conflicts and mixed (and changing) motives drive the film in a way quite unlike *Anatomy of a Murder* (and, in the view of *New York Times* reviewer Bosley Crowther, threatened to "nullify" the film's attempt at a realistic portrayal of gang warfare in early-1960s Harlem).[51]

Like *Trial*, *The Young Savages* depicts the criminal jury trial as a crucible in which justice runs the gauntlet of racialized politics. The film—whose treatment of Italian American and Hispanic gang strife has always been overshadowed by *West Side Story*—is loosely based on a notorious real-life racially aggravated crime, the 1959 "Capeman" murders of two white youths in a New York park by a sixteen-year-old Puerto Rican gang member.[52] (Edward Anhalt and J. P. Miller's screenplay—from Evan Hunter's novel— reverses the ethnicity of the crime, making the defendants members of an Italian American gang, the Thunderbirds, and their victim a blind Puerto Rican teenager.) Since the three youths are shown committing the murder behind the opening credits, as in *Trial*, the facts of the case are not fundamentally at issue. What prosecuting attorney Hank Bell has to determine is whether each of the three Thunderbirds shares the same degree of culpability or whether, as it increasingly comes to appear, a complex combination of contexts—social pathologies, the exploitation of a gang member with profound learning disabilities, and peer pressure—have impelled the youths to commit the crime; and if so, whether the administration of criminal justice is sufficiently flexible and insightful to deliver penalties that truly fit the crime.

Again, as in *Trial*, due process is threatened by political interference—

in this case, by the impending gubernatorial campaign of Bell's boss, New York district attorney Dan Cole (Edward Andrews). Running on a law-and-order ticket, he instructs Bell to deliver on a charge of first-degree murder. Initially enthusiastic and determined (to his liberal wife's horror) to send all three youths to the chair, over the course of the film Bell—born Bellini, himself a child of the slums whose own success disinclines him to go "soft" on the next generation—has to grapple with the emerging facts of an intractable social reality that renders otiose his drive for a simple "guilty" verdict. Having determined that defendants and victim alike were trapped and their actions largely determined by circumstances far beyond their personal control, in the film's climactic courtroom sequences Bell effectively reverses (or, one might say, ignores) his prosecutorial obligations and uses his cross-examinations to ensure different sentences for all three, fitting his new conception of the crime, that avoid the death penalty. The defense is rendered little more than a bystander before Bell's heroic if wildly unconventional interpretation of his role as agent of a transpartisan truth rather than one side of an adversarial process.

Stylistically, the film reflects the new energy that started to become visible in Hollywood cinema in the early 1960s, in the wake of Hitchcock's radical formal and narrative experiments in *Psycho* and the emergence of a generation of younger directors, many of them with backgrounds in television drama and/or news and journalism, including both Lumet and Frankenheimer. Making extensive use of location shooting in slum areas of east Harlem (and prominently featuring the "clearance" of ethnic districts as part of the massive municipal construction projects of master builder Robert Moses), in the trial scenes especially, Frankenheimer abjures the restrained, noncommittal style of Mark Robson or Preminger in favor of searching close-ups in Lionel Lindon's wide-angle cinematography. The courtroom here is not the tonally neutral, transparent, and readily negotiable space proffered (however disingenuously) by *Trial* or *Anatomy of a Murder* but a manifestly fraught, intense crucible of emotions in which the personalities of witnesses and lawyers alike are put on naked display.

It is tempting to read *The Young Savages'* adjustments of the Eisenhower-era trial film template in the context of the Kennedy era. Lancaster's energetic, proactive, fearless crusading public servant maps appealingly onto a New Frontier ethos of individualism in the service of a greater good. His refusal either to defer to the requirements of machine politics or to be bound by the protocols of his assigned role as prosecutor equally endows him with idealized Kennedyesque attributes. Again, however, upon closer inspection, the film both questions the viability of the heroic lawyer and asks troubling questions about the flaws of a system that requires such heroes to fulfil its basic function of delivering impartial justice. Bell's eye-opening reconception of his juridical responsibilities—taking it upon himself to act as a supplementary (in fact, as far as the film is concerned, principal) defender rather than prosecutor—seems to imply a system whose binary logic no longer adequately addresses the bafflingly complex and contradictory social environments it serves. Across the duration of the trial, in traditional generic fashion, a series of revelations unfold that significantly alter Bell's, and our, understanding of the case. Roberto, the unarmed harmonica-playing blind teenage murder victim, proves on investigation to have been not only a bagman for the Puerto Rican gang the Horsemen but his underage sister's pimp. One of his Italian American assailants is revealed to be mentally incompetent; another, the youngest, turns out not to have actually knifed Roberto at all, but simply to have mimed a stabbing action to impress his more hardened associates. Breaking with generic convention, however, none of these accomplishes the traditional reversal of fortune. Roberto may not have been the saint it is politically expedient for his community to maintain him to have been: he remains for all that a victim of cold-blooded, premeditated murder. The youngest defendant may not have been individually guilty of murder in the first degree: under the principle of joint enterprise, he is still guilty of murder. What Bell's discoveries indicate, therefore, is not, as in the traditional trial film, a new narrative that is as satisfyingly, though differently, clear and cogent as the original (say, of innocence rather than guilt), but rather an intractably complex and multivalent social reality that resists the law's (and also politicians') attempts to render it in starkly adversarial, clean-edged terms.

The desperate measures Bell undertakes to rectify the anomalies through this, as the film suggests, self-evidently maladjusted system amplify his heroic stature. They also, however, confirm the extreme dysfunctionality of a legal system that requires a prosecutor to do double duty as a public defender in order to deliver a measure of justice. The film's heightened visual style, contrasting as we have noted with the stylistic conservatism of its Eisenhower-era forerunners, adds to the viewer's sense of a process operating at the edge of its capabilities, and suggests both/either a greater willingness to acknowledge, rather than to mask, the flaws in the system and/or a weakened confidence in the system's capacity to overcome or adjust for such flaws. Again, if stylistic excess is indeed a textual "symptom" of ideological stress—the expression on the textual body of contradictions beyond narrative resolution but also beyond open discussion—*The Young Savages'* heightened visual rhetoric, taken alongside the film's critique of the heroic lawyer myth, all in the context of a case where race is a key issue, might be read as the acknowledgment of race as an issue where the law's capacity to offer remedy reaches its limits in the face of historical and social experiences beyond the reach even of judicial activism in the era post–*Brown v. Board of Education*.[53]

Nor, ultimately, does *The Young Savages* securely validate Bell's heroic actions. Early in the film, at Roberto's funeral Bell encounters his grieving mother, who declares her conviction that justice will only be done when her son's attackers are stabbed to death as he was. This confusion of justice and revenge (racially coded as an expression of a "primitive" and inadequately assimilated Hispanic culture) is set up in classic opposition to the "civilized" practice of criminal justice and proportional retribution that it is Bell's duty to discharge. It also casts in an ironic light Bell's own initial determination to secure the death penalty for the defendants, which his appalled wife sees as both atavistic and (because politically motivated) cynical. Bell in due course recants his sanguinary attitude and through his courtroom heroics compels verdicts and sentences that more-or-less adequately address the specifics of the crime, the requirements of society, and the needs, as well as the guilt, of the individual defendants. Exiting the courtroom at the end of the film, however, the victim's bereaved mother confronts Bell again, asking him if she has received the justice he promised her earlier. A deflated Bell can only respond that "many people bear a share of the responsibility" for her son's death; and on this muted and unsatisfactory note, the film concludes. Taken together, the legal contortions Bell needs to perform in order to secure a truly just—rather than simply a legally justifiable—outcome; and the much larger questions his investigations have opened up, but which neither the criminal justice system nor, it appears, any other governmental agency, program, or social movement can begin to address, suggest strongly that courtroom heroics are, at best, cosmetic remedies to systemic problems in American society—but that without them anything approaching justice is even less likely to be secured.

There are no on-screen lawyers at all in *12 Angry Men*, a movie that stands alongside *To Kill a Mockingbird* as one of the most fondly remembered of the "heroic" era of American trial films and also as the film that, from the moment of its release, has been recognized as a self-conscious lesson in the (necessarily laborious) processes, pitfalls, and ultimate triumph of American democracy. Instead, as has often enough been noted, the jurors themselves take on the burden of working through forensic procedure and cross-examination, "putting the audience through the steps and processes of the trial itself" that, it is implied from the little we see (a bored judge delivering his instruction to the jury at the start of the film) and hear (references to an underprepared defense counsel), failed to occur in the trial proper.[54] In this very fact, however, like *The Young Savages*, the film gestures to flaws in the system it strives so mightily to validate. It is not simply that (as has often been noted), absent the cussed heroics of Juror 8 (Henry Fonda), the youthful (presumably Puerto Rican, though it is never stated outright in the film) defendant would be quickly, even cursorily, convicted by the other variously indifferent, ignorant, neglectful, or prejudiced jurors. Part of the film's vision of the American settlement is that a sufficiency of Fonda-like men of principle and integrity (not to say the class privileges of education and self-confidence), though inevitably a minority, act as a yeast prompting their peers to rise to the challenge of their democratic responsibilities. Rather, it is that in order for this to come about, the very legal procedures in which American democracy is vested, and which the film so robustly validates, must be not only stretched but violated, and not negligibly.

As Norman Spaulding smartly points out elsewhere in this collection, in the process of driving his colleagues to reverse their original positions Juror 8 and the allies he accumulates along the way flagrantly violate their assigned role and legal procedure in ways that—if anyone bar the audience knew about it[55]—would provide certain grounds for a mistrial: most notably, by purchasing a switchblade (an illegal act in itself, as Juror 8 acknowledges: "I broke the law") and still more by taking upon himself the role of defense investigator and visiting the crime scene, not to mention introducing new evidence (the eyewitness' missing eyeglasses). It is not of course that we doubt the rightness of the conclusion to which the jurors are thus led—as Lincolnian avatar, Fonda's judgment commands our trust from the outset—but that we are implicitly required to accept that legal protocols have become sufficiently dysfunctional that they can only be salvaged by para- or extralegal means. *12 Angry Men* is of course a far cry from the virtual endorsement of vigilantism in movies of the crisis-ridden early 1970s such as *Dirty Harry* or *Death Wish* films that explicitly dismiss legal constraints and the rule of (written, rather than natural) law generally as mere legalism (*Dirty Harry* features a Berkeley law professor whose effete regard for constitutional procedures ensures the serial killer Scorpio is freed to kill again). But in its reliance on the efforts of a heroic, rule-bending if not outright rule-breaking, individual to ensure justice is done despite, as much as through, the law, it qualifies or even threatens to revoke the very reassurance in legal and constitutional procedures its narrative—like those of other films of the period—explicitly intends to proffer.

No screen lawyer of the "heroic" era has a firmer claim to embody the idealized legal virtues of wisdom, decency, erudition, gravity, and exceptional humanity than Atticus Finch in *To Kill a Mockingbird*—even to the extent that subsequent, more ambiguous or outright negative cinematic portrayals of the legal profession might, it has been suggested, be discussed under the rubric "what has happened to Atticus Finch?"[56] There exists a small industry of Atticus Finch hagiographies in the (often not-very) critical literature, summed up, perhaps, in Ross Levi's flat declaration that Finch is "surely the most flattering portrayal of a lawyer (and perhaps of a human being) in all of legal cinema."[57] Alongside Fonda's Lincoln, Atticus Finch— "crowned with the white fedora of truth"[58]—is *the* unimpeachable personification of legal virtue: or so it seems.

There are nonetheless dissenting voices to this worshipful reception of the character, whose number has grown in recent scholarship. Criticisms are generally framed in one of two critical perspectives. The first forms part of a broader critique of the limitations of the racial and social attitudes of the film, and of Harper Lee's original 1960 novel, whose range and scope and continuing relevance as a vehicle for promoting tolerance in a contemporary multiracial society have all been questioned. (For example, Mark Holcomb dryly notes that after the narrowly averted lynching of Tom Robinson at the Maycomb jail, Atticus's commendation of his children for making "'Walter Cunningham stand in my shoes for a minute' temporarily disregards the rather more vulnerable position of the man standing in Tom's."[59]) The second, and more relevant for our current purposes, focuses more narrowly on *Mockingbird*'s depiction of the law, and Atticus's practice of it. Here, the questions to be answered—and which are difficult to reconcile with the film's supposedly wholehearted endorsement of republican virtue guaranteed to prevail in the hands of such men as Atticus Finch— concern the administration of justice in the novel and film and the conundrum of its ultimate failure.

The argument can be succinctly summarized: for all of Atticus Finch's nobility, justice does not prevail in *To Kill a Mockingbird*—and ultimately Atticus himself, rather than abiding by a legal code that has ceased to serve civic or individual needs, chooses a subjective version of justice (accepting the rough justice that sees his children's assailant dead and his killer, Boo Radley, escape further investigation) that while undoubtedly delivering the "right" outcome in the audience's mind is equally clearly at odds with the commitment to legal process Atticus has maintained throughout the film. It may be Boo's whiteness that allows, or compels, Atticus into an identification with his position before the law (as object, not subject), which for all his sympathy he never quite achieves with Tom Robinson. In any case, what Atticus confesses, without ever saying as much, in this moment of outsider identification and the act of extralegal pragmatic ethics that follows from it, are the limits, rather than the absolute integrity, of the law and of the obligation on the individual to defend an abstract notion of due process in the face of palpable injustice—however legal. In Mark Holcomb's words, "[Boo Radley] is firmly outside [the] system, and Sheriff Tate and Atticus's ultimate reliance on his act of rough justice proves how impotent they and the system have become."[60]

Conclusion

According to Kathy Laster, "courtroom films of all persuasions mostly manage to reestablish the legitimacy of the prevailing system or at least belief in the rule of law."[61] The films of the later Eisenhower and Kennedy eras discussed here all stay within these broad outlines. But whereas the received image of the period would suggest an unequivocal, even monotonous, celebration of the American legal system and its practitioners, close examination reveals a group of films that express a considerably more nuanced, and often ambivalent, view of lawyers and the law. There are in fact fewer outright heroes than expected in this "heroic" era of the trial film, and the validity of legal "heroism" itself is held up for skeptical scrutiny. To the extent that film genres frame, and are framed by, the prevailing discourses of their times, the dominant tenor of these films is more an anxious interrogation of legal practices and principles than their unproblematic restatement and reaffirmation.

Space has prohibited consideration of another important trial film of the period, Stanley Kramer's earnest *Judgment at Nuremberg*. This is a film that at first sight appears to give the lie to the arguments advanced here: the film is stolidly lacking in any evident anxiety about the robustness of American democratic legal principles. Its faith in this robustness is embodied in the craggy integrity of the aging Spencer Tracy, whose universal validity the Nazi jurists on trial, led by Burt Lancaster, ultimately concede. It could however reasonably be pointed out that validating American justice by comparing it favorably to Nazi jurisprudence is setting the bar fairly low. Is it in fact only extraterritorially, and in direct opposition to its antithesis, that the system regains the self-confidence that once seemed so manifest in the truly heroic days of Ford's *Young Mr. Lincoln*?

These films betray a pervasive concern about the sustainability of fundamental principles of American jurisprudence in a context where both over-politicization and over-professionalization threaten those principles—the one making it increasingly hard to ensure equal treatment before the law, the other abstracting the justice *system* (an increasingly loaded word by the early 1960s) from the human experiences and sufferings it litigates and mediates. Far from embodying a prelapsarian moment of legal-cultural confidence, in fact, upon closer inspection—and like other texts and film genres of the same period—the Eisenhower/Kennedy-era trial films manifest still-inchoate stresses that nonetheless clearly foreshadow the full-blown crisis of legitimation of the later 1960s and 1970s.

Notes

1. Nicole Rafter, "American Trial Films: An Overview of Their Development, 1930–2000," in *Law and Film*, ed. Stefan Machura and Peter Robson, 9–25 (Oxford: Blackwell, 2001), and *Shots in the Mirror: Crime Films and Society*, 2nd ed. (Oxford: Oxford University Press, 2006), 135–62.

2. Carol J. Clover, "Law and the Order of Popular Culture," in *Law in the Domains of Culture*, ed. Austin Sarat and Thomas R. Kearns, 97–119 (Ann Arbor: University of Michigan Press, 1998).

3. Carol Clover, "God Bless Juries!" in *Refiguring American Film Genres: Theory and History*, ed. Nick Browne, 255–77 (Berkeley: University of California Press, 1998).

4. In Clover's much-cited summary, the "fragmented, evidence-examining, forensically visualized, backstory-driven, X-not-X-structured, polygraphically photographed, intricately plotted, doubt cultivating, and jury-directed" narratives that are shared by trials and movies alike: Clover, "Law and Order," 118.

5. Rafter, "American Trial Films," 14–17.

6. David Ray Papke, "Law, Cinema and Ideology: Hollywood Legal Films of the 1950s,", *UCLA Law Review* 48 (2001), 1473–93; online at http://scholarship.law.marquette.edu/cgi/viewcontent.cgi?article=1275&context=facpub.

7. Michael Asimow, "Bad Lawyers in the Movies," *Nova Law Review* 24 (2000), 531–49.

8. Francis M. Nevins, "Reconnoitring Juriscinema's First Golden Age and Lawyers in Film 1928–34," *Vermont Law Review* 28 (2004).

9. Asimow, "Bad Lawyers in the Movies," 535. See also Rafter, "American Trial Films," and Nevins, "Reconnoitring Juriscinema's First Golden Age."

10. On the nostalgic construction of the social imaginary of the early 1960s in film, see Barry Langford, "*American Graffiti*," in *America First: Naming the Nation in US Film*, ed. Mandy Merck, 157–76 (London: Routledge, 2007). On the Reaganite imaginary, see among many others Garry Wills, *Reagan's America*, 2nd ed. (London: Penguin, 2000); more recently, Rick Perlstein, *The Invisible Bridge: The Fall of Nixon and the Rise of Reagan* (New York: Simon & Schuster, 2014).

11. David Riesman, *The Lonely Crowd: A Study of the Changing American Character*, 2nd ed. (New Haven, CT: Yale University Press, 1961); see also Daniel

Geary, "Children of *The Lonely Crowd*: David Riesman, the Young Radicals, and the Splitting of Liberalism in the 1960s," *Modern Intellectual History*, 10.3 (2013), 603–33.

12. William H. Whyte, *The Organisation Man* (New York: Simon and Schuster, 1956).

13. C. Wright Mills, *The Power Elite* [1956] (New York: Oxford University Press, 1999).

14. See Martin Halliwell, *American Culture in the 1950s* (Edinburgh: Edinburgh University Press, 2007).

15. See for example Jackie Byars, *All That Hollywood Allows: Re-Reading Gender in 1950s Melodrama* (Chapel Hill: University of North Carolina Press, 1991); Peter Biskind, *Seeing Is Believing: or, How Hollywood Taught Us to Stop Worrying and Love the Fifties* (New York: Pantheon, 1983); Mark Jancovich, *Rational Fears: American Horror in the 1950s* (Manchester, UK: Manchester University Press, 1996).

16. Clover, "Law and the Order of Popular Culture," 98.

17. Barry Langford, *Film Genre: Hollywood and Beyond* (Edinburgh University Press, 2005), Chapter 1.

18. Jessica Silbey, "Patterns of Courtroom Justice," in Machura and Robson, eds., *Law and Film*, 97–116.

19. On the "life cycle" of genres, see John Cawelti, "*Chinatown* and Generic Transformation in Recent American Films," in *Film Genre Reader II*, ed. Barry Keith Grant, 227–46 (Austin: University of Texas Press, 1995); on generic "evolution," see Thomas Schatz, *Hollywood Genres: Formulas, Filmmaking, and the Studio System* (New York: Random House, 1981), 36–41. See also Langford, *Film Genre*, 23–28.

20. Louis Althusser, *Essays on Ideology*, trans. Ben Brewster (London: Verso, 1984).

21. Fredric Jameson, *The Political Unconscious: Narrative as a Socially Symbolic Act* (Ithaca, NY: Cornell University Press, 1981), 106.

22. Christine Gledhill and Linda Williams, eds., *Reinventing Film Studies* (London: Arnold, 2000), 221.

23. Jameson, *Political Unconscious*, 115.

24. For a discussion of film genre as myth and social practice, see Langford, *Film Genre*, 17–22.

25. Jameson, *Political Unconscious*, 117.

26. Sidney Lumet, dir., *12 Angry Men* (1957; Century City, CA: Twentieth Century Fox Home Entertainment, 2008), DVD.

27. Papke, "Law, Cinema and Ideology," 1490. 36 U.S. C. § 113 at http://www .law.cornell.edu/uscode/text/36/113.

28. For the (Foucauldian) argument that the Production Code of America functioned as an engine of discursive productive as much as, or more than, a re-

pressive apparatus, see Leonard J. Leff, "The Breening of America," *PMLA* 106.3 (1991): 432–45.

29. Fritz Lang, dir., *Beyond a Reasonable Doubt* (1956; New York: RKO Pictures, 2011), DVD.

30. Wendell Hayes, *Anatomy of a Murder*, screenplay, February 25, 1959, available at http://www.dailyscript.com/scripts/anatomy_of_a_murder.pdf.

31. Otto Preminger, dir., *Anatomy of a Murder* (1959; Culver City, CA: Sony Pictures Home Entertainment, 2000), DVD.

32. Hayes, *Anatomy of a Murder* (screenplay), 190.

33. Ibid., 198.

34. http://www.nytimes.com/1997/07/03/movies/james-stewart-the-hesitant -hero-dies-at-89.html?module=Search&mabReward=relbias%3As.

35. Hayes, *Anatomy of a Murder* (screenplay), 27.

36. Ibid., 28–29

37. Orit Kamir, "Anatomy of Hollywood's Hero-Lawyer: A Law-and-Film Study of the Western Motifs, Honor-Based Values and Gender Politics Underlying *Anatomy of a Murder*'s Construction of the Lawyer Image," *Studies in Law, Politics and Society* 35 (2005): 39.

38. Although *The Man Who Shot Liberty Valance* is without doubt one of the most important legal films of this period, it is not discussed further here both from considerations of length and also because it is not a *trial* film. For an excellent exploration of the "valences" of liberty and law in the film, see Tag Gallagher, *John Ford: The Man and His Films* (Berkeley: University of California Press, 1986), 383–413.

39. Rafter, "American Trial Films," 17.

40. Mark Robson, dir., *Trial*, (1955; Beverly Hills, CA: MGM, 2014), DVD.

41. *Variety*, January 25, 1956.

42. According to MGM's advertisement in *Box Office*, October 15, 1955, 2–3.

43. Rafter, "American Trial Films," 15. See also Norman Rosenberg, "Law Noir," in *Legal Realism: Movies as Legal Texts*, ed. J. Denvir, 280–302 (Urbana: University of Illinois Press, 1996).

44. Foster Hirsch, *Otto Preminger: The Man Who Would Be King* (New York: Alfred A. Knopf, 2007), 319.

45. The literature on film noir is vast and endlessly expanding. On noir's visual style(s), however, as good a place to start as any is James Naremore, *More Than Night: Film Noir in Its Contexts*, 2nd ed. (Berkeley: University of California Press, 2008); on the relationship to postwar American economics and culture, see Mike Chopra-Gant, *Hollywood Genres and Postwar America: Masculinity, Family and Nation in Popular Movies and Film Noir* (London: I. B. Tauris, 2006).

46. Vivian Sobchack, *Screening Space: The American Science Fiction Film*, 2nd ed. (New Brunswick, NJ: Rutgers University Press, 1987), 143–45.

47. Lang, *Beyond a Reasonable Doubt*.

48. Dennis L. White, "*Beyond a Reasonable Doubt*," in *Film Noir: An Encyclopedic Reference to the American Style*, ed. Alain Silver and Elizabeth Ward, 21–22 (Woodstock, NY: Overlook Press, 1992).

49. Bertolt Brecht, *Life of Galileo*, trans. John Willett (London: Methuen, 1980), 98.

50. John Frankenheimer, dir., *The Young Savages* (1961; New York: Kino International, 2014), DVD.

51. Bosley Crowther, "Lancaster Stars in 'Young Savages': Plays Prosecutor of Juvenile Toughs," *New York Times*, May 25, 1961, http://www.nytimes.com/movie/review?res=9900E6DF123BE13ABC4D51DFB366838A679EDE&partner=Rotten%2520Tomatoes.

52. See Rachel Rubin and Jeffrey Paul Melnick, *Immigration and American Popular Culture: An Introduction* (New York: New York University Press, 2007), 108–13.

53. On stylistic excess and ideology, see D. N. Rodowick, "Madness, Authority and Ideology: The Domestic Melodrama of the 1950s," *Velvet Light Trap* 19 (1982): 40–46; Barbara Klinger, *Melodrama and Meaning: History, Culture and the Films of Douglas Sirk* (Bloomington: Indiana University Press, 1994).

54. Clover, "God Bless Juries!," 267.

55. Or if Juror 3, the final holdout, knew enough law to draw it to the court's attention.

56. Steve Greenfield, Guy Osborn, and Peter Robson, *Film and the Law*, 2nd ed. (Oxford: Hart Publishing, 2010), 95.

57. Ross D. Levi, *The Celluloid Courtroom: A History of Legal Cinema* (Westport, CT: Praeger, 2005), 101.

58. T. Appelo, "Atticus Doesn't Live Here Anymore," quoted in Greenfield, Osborn, and Robson, *Film and the Law*, 95.

59. Mark Holcomb, "*To Kill a Mockingbird*," *Film Quarterly* 55, no. 4 (Summer 2002), 34–40.

60. Ibid., 39.

61. Kathy Laster, with Krista Breckweg and John King, *The Drama of the Courtroom* (Sydney: Federation Press, 2000), 12.

4
Disorder in Court

Representations of Resistance to Law in Trial Film Dramas

Norman W. Spaulding

"Your Honor, do we have to sit here and listen to this?"

—Juror in Alfred Hitchcock's *The Wrong Man* (1956)

The denouement comes late in *The Wrong Man*, Hitchcock's 1956 film drawn from a true story of mistaken identification.[1] Only after Henry Fonda's wrongly accused character, Manny Balestrero, has prayed, after the right man is caught in a new robbery, does the "look-alike" robber happen to pass Manny in the hall of the police station as the robber is brought in and positively identified. Although otherwise implacable, the robber cannot hold Manny's stare, and he shuffles off with two police officers when Manny attempts to rebuke him. Manny also sees two of the insurance employees who falsely identified him in a police lineup and at trial. They scurry past him after having identified the right man, too ashamed by their errors to address him. Even in the penultimate scene, Hitchcock prolongs the irresolution. We learn that Manny's wife, Rose, remains unwell—driven mad by Manny's false arrest and trial, unable to leave the mental institution where she was placed just before the trial. When the movie finally cuts to the closing intertitle and a shot of a family of four strolling along a sunny, palm-lined boulevard, it is the first shot of clear weather and one of the only exterior daylight shots in the entire film. The intertitle explains that Rose was "completely cured" in two years and "lives happily in Florida with Manny" and their two boys.[2]

The condition of this denouement is of course the strange outburst during Manny's trial quoted above, made by a member of the jury as Manny's lawyer clumsily cross-examines an employee of the insurance company where the robbery occurred. The identification of Manny on direct is unambiguous, and it is the third positive identification made on the witness stand by employees of the insurance company. This leaves Manny's lawyer grasping at straws, straining to establish a possibility of misidentification by testing the employee's memory of other suspects in the lineup at the police station when she picked out Manny. As importantly, Manny's lawyer strains to hold the attention of everyone but his client.

Suddenly, a well-dressed, elderly man rises from his chair in frustration from the back row of the jury box and poses a question: "Your Honor, do we have to sit here and listen to this?"

Without the mistrial caused by this disruption revealing the jury's tedium and its certainty that Manny has no defense, Manny would surely have been convicted. And, crucially, the conviction would have occurred before the right man is caught in the commission of a new robbery. Manny might have challenged the guilty verdict, but Hitchcock has already primed the viewer to accept that the system would not likely rectify the error. Manny's lawyer is totally inexperienced in criminal matters, he has foisted all of the pretrial investigation onto Rose and Manny, alibi witnesses have disappeared or died, and the evidence identifying Manny appears overwhelming (not just multiple eyewitness identifications but a handwriting sample).

Indeed, just before the juror's outburst, Manny has been surveying the courtroom, coming to the terrible realization that nearly everyone there in an official capacity is bored, distracted, and either convinced of his guilt or indifferent to the possibility of his innocence. Hitchcock has taken care not to suggest official corruption—a common theme in trial dramas. Instead, Manny's terrifying realization is that grave mistakes can be produced by the ordinary operation of law and bureaucratic rationality. The law can innocently convict the wrong man. This makes the seemingly irrational claims made by Rose when she loses hope and goes mad before the trial ("It doesn't do any good to try," "How do I know *you're* not crazy," "How do I know you're not guilty, You could be, You could be," "You can't win") appear not only prescient and lucid as Manny scans the courtroom, but eerily true. Maybe Manny *is* crazy to think he is innocent or that his innocence matters. The way the scene is shot as Manny scans the courtroom—alternations between close-ups of Manny's face and different parts of the courtroom while witness examination, objections, rulings on the objections, and testimony drone in the background—reinforces the vertiginous feeling we see in Manny's face.

Hitchcock adds a final contingency to make clear that Manny would not have escaped conviction absent the outburst of the juror: the right man is not immediately recognized as the perpetrator of the other robberies when he is arrested. One of the detectives on Manny's case just happens to see the robber being brought in for booking as he leaves for the day. Even he almost misses the man's similarity to Manny, passing him in the hall and getting all the way to the sidewalk outside the police building before recognizing the possible similarity and turning around to investigate. The detective might have missed this altogether if Manny had already been convicted of the prior robberies—in his mind those crimes already would have been "solved." As Jean-Luc Godard observes, the film exposes "the primordial role . . . played by chance. . . . The only suspense in *The Wrong Man* is that of chance itself."[3]

Manny has been complaining about his bad luck all along. And it is just like Hitchcock to situate a bit of good luck in an event that initially seems to *extend* the suffering of his protagonist. Here, the outburst of the juror prolongs Manny's torturous run-in with the law by ensuring that he will face yet another trial—a process he tells his mother feels like "being put through a meat grinder." But it is in fact the condition of his exoneration. The juror's outburst is thus crucial to the film. This is obviously so at the level of form. Hitchcock's alternation between medium shots of the courtroom from Manny's viewpoint at the defense table and reaction shots of Manny's distressed face leading up to the outburst force identification with and interrogation of Manny just as the film's central question of identification is being adjudicated and revealed as a foregone conclusion. The viewer has already been made to experience the first witness's chilling positive identification of Manny via a close-up of her laying a shaking hand on Manny's shoulder at the prosecutor's invitation—a shot that mirrors the "terrible immediacy" of the earlier close-up of Manny's fingerprints being taken.[4] These physical "mark[s] of shame" and conditional guilt are given explicit, verbal ratification by the juror's outburst—itself a premature verdict.[5] The outburst is equally crucial at the level of narrative (providing the plot twist that leads to resolution) and at the level of legal process (interrupting the adjudication—ending it, in fact—and providing the occasion for extrajudicial disposition of Manny's case).

Disorder in court of this kind is always possible, but it is fairly rare in actual trials.[6] Civil and criminal pretrial discovery rules, which expanded in the twentieth century, are designed precisely to diminish the risk of surprise at trial, if not to avoid trial altogether, by making the evidence available to each side beforehand.[7] For this and other reasons (most prominently a dramatic shift in the division of decisional labor between judges and juries over the twentieth century), civil and criminal jury trials are now *exceedingly* rare events.[8] This is true even though overall criminal and civil filings have continued to increase.[9] Moreover, even in cases that do reach trial, the judge's power to hold participants in contempt, to grant new trials, to instruct the jury, and to review jury awards diminish incentives to deviate from the rational presentation of and deliberation upon evidence. So actual trials are not only rare but often relatively dull affairs.

The case should not be overstated. The structure of viva voce adversarial exchange permits, if it does not invite, strategic and unplanned outbursts.[10] As I have elsewhere argued, this seemingly aberrant conduct—more precisely, the possibility of it—is an element of the democratic legitimacy of trials: "Resistance, disruption, surprise, adversarial excess, deception, nullification, and passion are neither endorsed nor invited, but they are always possible. There is room then for unexpected reversals—room for the embarrassment of reason to be displayed in the very space in which we expect and hope to see reasoned argument prevail. And there is public space in and about the courthouse for satyr play—space in which the local practice of justice can be mocked, satirized, defied, called to account, or ignored altogether while court is in session and the community is present. The organization of [adversarial] space thus concedes, if it does not celebrate, that justice is not a set of fixed principles to be applied, but a set of relations to be mediated."[11] Trials, simply put, cannot be both meaningfully participatory and free of the risk of outburst, interruption, passionate display, and other forms of disorder in court. The opportunity to be heard is the essence of due process of law.[12]

While actual trials are rare and moments of disruption are possible but relatively infrequent, disorder in court is a staple feature of the trial drama. *Fury* (1936), *Young Mr. Lincoln* (1939), *12 Angry Men* (1957), *The Verdict* (1982), *A Few Good Men* (1992), and *Philadelphia* (1993) all include prominent scenes of disorderly conduct.[13] Why should this be so? Do trial dramas provide a kind of imaginary space for passionate courtroom display to compensate for the tedium of actual trials and make trial films worth sitting through? Or are outbursts in trial dramas a hyperbolized, nostalgic borrowing from the (vanishing) adversarial traditions of actual trial? If Carol Clover is right that movies are "trial-like" in their "plot structures and narrative procedures" and that trials are "movielike,"[14] what exactly are we to make of these spectacular moments when the rules of trial process are violated? And how do these moments of disorder relate to what Clover calls the "underlying epistemolog[ical]" identity between film and adversarial trial process (i.e., the "fragmented, evidence-examining, forensically visualized, backstory-driven, X-not-X-structured, polygraphically photographed, intricately plotted, doubt cultivating, and jury-directed" mechanics of movies and trials)?[15]

In what follows, I argue that scenes of disorder in court are crucial not only to "plot structure and narrative procedures"—the condition of reaching a denouement, if not a verdict—but also to the "underlying epistemology" and distinctive melodramatic appeal of trial dramas. In Clover's account, by far the best to date on the epistemological issue, the crucial element is the X-not-X structure of adversarial exchange—the "strict schedule of turn taking" in the presentation of proof, regulated by the rules of evidence.[16] The "most charged moment" in trial films (including films that are trial-like even if there is no trial in them) occurs "midway through the examination, when the sides have switched places in the presentation of their cases and . . . we arrive at a crossroads, a time when we must choose between sturdy and familiar X [e.g., the prosecution narrative in a criminal case] and the alluring possibility of not-X."[17] The moment is charged, Clover argues, not only because of the introduction of epistemological doubt, but because of the oscillating nature of the way doubt is introduced. The viewer is "pulled rhythmically back and forth, in the almost machinelike alternation of direct examination with cross-examination, between the two positions."[18] The process becomes "an exercise in more-or-less anxious plot making and unmaking."[19]

Notice however, that this account fits *The Wrong Man* awkwardly. The outburst comes from a juror—the participant whom Clover contends is nearly invisible in most trial films in order to support the substitution of the viewer as juror.[20] Moreover, the juror's outburst disrupts the X-not-X oscillation just as Manny's lawyer is rather tediously trying to establish it. The not-X alternative (of the trial, anyway) never gets off the ground. Finally, well before the trial begins, almost everything we learn about Manny is designed to establish his innocence even as the film oscillates back and forth on the question of how he might prove it.[21] Simply put, the viewer knows he is the wrong man. The scene that leads to the outburst of the juror is so poignant and vertiginous precisely because we have no reason to doubt this knowledge and because Hitchcock has already given us the palpable feeling that the legal system is but "a machine grinding inexorably on," *not* because X-not-X oscillation has made some kind of suspenseful speculation necessary.[22]

To be sure, Clover is not indifferent to "unexpected behavior on the part of court apparatus" or to "objections, witness slips, and the like."[23] On her account, they give edge to backstories by implying the existence of "more data out there that are being kept from us"—where "us" means the juror/viewer.[24] But because Clover sees the X-not-X structure of adversarial exchange as epistemologically fundamental, these events are salient primarily for what they contribute to "the production of paranoid speculation far beyond the trial's official parameters."[25] Indeed, she repeatedly and provocatively links the energy and intrigue of the epistemological oscillation in the X-not-X structure with paranoia.[26]

I shall argue instead in what follows that while scenes of disorder in court can certainly appear within the X-not-X structure—ratifying one side's narrative over another by providing the most decisive X-not-X clash in the film—they also typically rupture the X-not-X structure. They do so in at least three ways: (a) by vividly exposing crucial epistemological remainders ("backstories," in Clover's account), (b) by drawing the validity of the X-not-X trial process itself into doubt, effectively putting the trial "on trial" even as one side's narrative is ratified, and, as importantly, (c) by moving beyond data or facts rationally classifiable as evidence of the past event that is the subject of adjudication, quite often to a transformative emotional register saturated in form and content with melodramatic elements. Paranoia about the truth may be part of what animates engagement with backstories and the formal X-not-X structure of adversarial exchange, but not all kinds of doubt, or even curiosity for that matter, have their foundation in paranoia.[27] In scenes of disorder in court there is a more basic epistemological and normative operation: an oscillation in and out of court, in and out of compliance with the rules of law, and in and out of confidence in the distinctions between facts and values, past and present, and passion and reason. These distinctions ostensibly define the formal X-not-X structure of adversarial exchange and the rule of law—and yet they are constantly at risk of being dissolved by the resistance that very structure provokes. The transformative potential of this dissolution is, I conclude, a standard object of ambivalent attachment in a culture riven by competing conceptions of the good.

One-Sided Ratification

One of the most basic epistemological and plot functions of the courtroom outburst in trial dramas is to decisively confirm one side's view of the case. This is certainly an effect of the pitched arguments during the trial in *The Verdict* between the Frank Galvin character, played by Paul Newman, and the judge. Galvin's client has suffered severe, debilitating injuries and lost the baby she was carrying as a result of improperly administered anesthetics at a prominent Boston hospital. The film depicts the transition between Galvin's initially incompetent and eventually heroic efforts to mount a case against the hospital and its elite defense lawyers. During the presentation of direct testimony by the plaintiff's medical expert, the judge stands up at the bench and interrupts the testimony in order to pose his own questions. Galvin objects:

Galvin: Your Honor . . .
Judge: Yes, Mr. Galvin.
Galvin: If I may be permitted to [*stuttering*] question my witness in
   my own way . . .

Judge: I'd just like to get to the point, Mr. Galvin.

Galvin: I'm getting to the . . .

Judge: [*Yelling*] Mr. Galvin, I believe I have the right to ask the witness a direct question! Now, let's not waste these people's time.

When Galvin relents, the judge corners the plaintiff's expert into admitting that the defendant doctors would not be legally negligent under the circumstances posed in the judge's hypothetical. The judge then dramatically expands the effect of the concession and promptly excuses the witness from the stand:

Judge: Then you are saying there is no negligence, based on my question?

Witness: Given the limits of your question, that's correct.

Judge: The doctors were *not* negligent?

Witness: [*indicates assent and is excused*]

Galvin complains that he has not finished questioning the witness and then offers the famous retort "Your Honor, with all due respect, if you are going to try my case, I wish you wouldn't lose it."

The judge immediately calls a recess and orders counsel to chambers where he threatens to report Galvin to the bar disciplinary authorities. Galvin then turns aggressor:

Galvin: You open your mouth, you're losing my case for me.

Judge: You listen to me . . .

Galvin: No, you listen to me. All I wanted out of this trial was a fair shake. Okay. Push me into court five days early; I lose my star witness and I can't get a continuance; and I don't care. . . . You know, they told me about you, said you're a hard ass, you're a defendant's judge. I don't care. I said to hell with it, to hell with it! [*Banging fist on judge's desk*]. . . . Don't give me that shit about you being a lawyer too. I know about you. You couldn't *hack* it as a lawyer, you were a bag man for the boys downtown and you still are. I know about you.

Galvin then insists that he wants a mistrial, he asks the judge to disqualify himself, and he threatens to seek the judge's impeachment before the board of judicial misconduct. The judge rejects the motions out of hand and says the trial will go forward. "We are going back there, . . . and we're gonna try this case to the end. Now you get out of here before I call the bailiff and have you thrown in jail!"

There are three outbursts here. One by the judge in court, two in chambers as the judge and Galvin spar over what happened in court. The first fits most comfortably in the X-not-X structure, though it is the judge doing the work of ratifying the defendants' case not the defense lawyers (indeed, the lead defense counsel looks on, silent and bemused, throughout the entire scene). The fireworks in chambers then shift the epistemological valence of the incident rather decisively toward the plaintiff's case. The suggestion of the judge's bias, which jury and viewer see together in court, is ratified conclusively for the viewer by the judge's conduct in chambers (adversarial space the jurors and public never see in actual trials) as well as the backstory about the judge's corruption from Galvin's outburst in chambers.

At the level of plot, the moment is pivotal precisely because of this division between what the jury knows and what the viewer knows by virtue of the camera's penetration into private adversarial space. The viewer is left to wonder if the jury senses that the judge is truly biased and if it will adjust its assessment of the evidence accordingly. The scene also foregrounds the climactic outburst by the admitting nurse whom Galvin spends most of the trial trying to locate and whose testimony exposing the doctors' malpractice and cover-up is suspiciously excluded on a technicality. Finally, the scene establishes Galvin's desire to fight for his client—a question both viewer and juror might have doubted given his desultory opening statement, his alcoholism, and his listlessness in much of the first half of the film. His stammering, meek objection when the judge first intervenes in court becomes a volcanic display of adversarial zeal in chambers. The viewer, if not the jury, learns that he is finally committed to the case.

At the level of epistemology, however, the primary effects of the incident are not in the X-not-X framework. Rather, the scene operates to dispel any lingering doubt about whether the trial will be fair. The viewer now knows it will not be, just as certainly as she knows from other out-of-court scenes of the doctors' guilt. There is, in fact, no meaningful speculation about the guilt of the doctors from the very beginning. Mickey Morrissey, Galvin's mentor, tells him that the case is a "good case," a "money-maker," as long as he handles it "right." The first medical expert he consults is even more certain, telling Galvin emphatically that "her doctors killed her. They gave her the wrong anesthetic and she wound up drowning in her own vomit. Her doctors murdered her. . . . I have an interest in hospitals and I don't want those bozos working in the same profession as me."

Other tantalizing X-not-X plot oscillations center on whether Galvin will botch the case, whether the jury will follow the cramped admissible evidence, and who is spying on Galvin for the defense. But the judge's strange intervention and the outbursts that follow are most significant because they *remove* doubt about the legitimacy of the formal adversarial X-not-X exchanges the jury will see. To frame this as just another layer of X-not-X oscillation is to miss the respects in which it ratifies a broadly shared cultural suspicion of the adversary system and normatively situates the viewer on the side of Galvin and his client as the underdogs.[28] The extralegal excesses of the judge and defense counsel also prime the viewer to cheer for Galvin when he breaks into a mailbox in order to locate the elusive admitting nurse and invite the viewer to forgive him for striking Laura Fisher when he learns she is the defendants' mole. What's on offer here is moral certainty regarding legal corruption and failure, not doubt.

The prototypical trial drama that employs outbursts to remove rather than feed doubt is of course *Young Mr. Lincoln*, a fictional account of the early life of Abraham Lincoln featuring a murder trial in which he agrees to defend two accused brothers. In court, Lincoln repeatedly interrupts the proceedings to mock opposing counsel and witnesses, he kicks his feet up on the counsel's table and leans back in his chair, he advises the mother of his clients not to answer the prosecutor's question that would implicate one of her sons regardless of the judge's instructions, and, having just protected his clients' mother from a tough cross-examination, he harangues the prosecution's key witness into making a confession after he has left the stand. Over and over, the orderly arrangement of participants in the courtroom is upset and the orderly flow of evidence is disrupted—not by orderly objections and court rulings but rather by jokes, slips, outbursts, and other flagrantly disorderly conduct. Some function as "outtakes" or information that forces the viewer to speculate about what part of the story is missing from the formal evidence.[29] But the standard effect of the outbursts is to strip the anxiety away from uncertainty created by the X-not-X oscillation of proof about who murdered Deputy White and, as with Lincoln's harangue of the prosecution witness, to reveal decisive facts that eliminate the uncertainty altogether. The film is unusually reliant on outbursts (perhaps a reflection of its attempt to depict frontier justice), but strikingly few trial dramas even attempt to adhere to the formalities of adversarial exchange in their trial scenes.

There are of course many narrative and filmic techniques for removing doubt, focusing speculation, and triggering or taming forensic curiosity. Jennifer Petersen's contribution to this volume provocatively explores Errol Morris's attempt to introduce skepticism about the meaning of photographic evidence of the torture of prisoners at Abu Ghraib prison. In the trial drama, however, the outburst has become a standard device. To appreciate why action that is not just outside but quite often in defiance of the standard oscillation of proof should play such an important role in these films, it is necessary to examine how representations of movement outside the ordinary forensic exchange of trial express resistance to law.

Epistemological Remainders

"Breakage . . . is the postulate of interpretation."
—Michel de Certeau, *The Writing of History*

A powerful source of the dramatic appeal of trial films is precisely their resistance to the strict X-not-X structure of direct and cross-examination. At the epistemological level, resistance is a feature of all systems of representation regarding past events. All such systems create what Michel de Certeau calls "remainders": "Whatever this new understanding of the past holds to be irrelevant—shards created by the selection of materials, remainders left aside by an explication—comes back, despite everything, on the edges of discourse or in its rifts and crannies: 'resistances,' 'survivals,' or delays discretely perturb the pretty order of a line of 'progress' or a system of interpretation."[30] In *12 Angry Men*, for instance, the turning points of the film are all shaped by disorderly conduct that has the effect of introducing evidence and arguments not produced in court. Most significantly, Juror 8, played by Henry Fonda, convinces the jury to deliberate fully on the merits of the case when it has no interest in doing so. He accomplishes this by suddenly brandishing a switchblade identical to the murder weapon and stabbing it into the center of the table just as another juror has emphasized testimony that the murder weapon was unique. The incident begins with a shot of Juror 8 from the level of the table with the murder weapon standing upright in the foreground.

> Juror 4: Take a look at this knife. [*Gesturing to the murder weapon.*] It's a very unusual knife. I've never seen one like it. Neither had the store-keeper who sold it to the boy. Aren't you asking us to accept a pretty incredible coincidence?
> Juror 8: I'm just saying a coincidence is possible.
> Juror 5: And I say it's not possible.
> Juror 8: [*Stands, reaches into his jacket pocket, removes an identical knife, opens it, and stabs it into the table next to the murder weapon. Jurors jump up from their seats to look at it.*]

All of this is rank illicit conduct on the part of a juror, and the movie signals this at least in part. A switchblade, another juror says, is illegal to buy or sell in the jurisdiction. Juror 8 flatly responds, "That's right, I broke the law." As importantly, visiting a crime scene and conducting other forms of outside research on a case are clear grounds for exclusion of the juror and mistrial.[31] But it is just this conduct that sways one juror to side with Juror 8 in the secret ballot vote that follows. And Juror 8 has already gotten everyone to agree in advance of the vote that unless the secret voting is unanimous (excluding his own vote) they will "stay and talk it out." Stay and talk it out they do. Two other major turning points in the jury's deliberation center on disorderly conduct as well: Juror 8's accusation that Juror 3 is a "sadist," designed to provoke him to make a death threat and thus prove that the defendant's death threat made against his father in the heat of argument is not unequivocal evidence of intent; and Juror 10's vituperative soliloquy revealing his class and ethnic prejudice against the defendant (this is the scene when nearly all the jurors leave the table in disgust as Juror 10 rants—the scene that initiates the collapse of the remaining holdouts).

The conventional view is that that *12 Angry Men* "enacts the phases and processes of the trial" with Juror 8 acting as defense counsel and the holdouts for a guilty verdict playing the role of the prosecution.[32] But even if that is so, we are again confronted with the fact that the formal X-not-X back and forth regarding the relevant evidence is structurally superficial compared to the disorderly conduct taking both the jury and viewers out of the sphere of relevant evidence. The effect of the disorderly conduct is neither to set aside the evidence adduced at trial nor precisely to see it from the defendant's perspective (though Juror 8 provides a constant reminder of the principle of reasonable doubt). It is rather to position the jury as a genuine *finder* of fact, not relying on the X-not-X presentation of proof at trial as much as its own standards of relevance and its own (slow, messy, almost ungovernable) collective judgment. Recall, for instance, that the most articulate, evidence-focused, and persuasive holdout, Juror 4, is finally turned (along with two others) when Juror 9 spots the marks from glasses on the side of Juror 4's nose and decides that the prosecution's key witness may not have seen the murder at all because she could not have been wearing glasses when she rose from her bed to look out the window at the commotion she heard. Neither side's counsel addressed this possibility at trial. It is instead a possibility wholly constructed from the jury's deliberation. We could certainly say, with Clover, that the jury has learned to think in X-not-X terms, but it has also learned to reject the formal constraints of X-not-X, and not as a result of paranoid speculation but because Juror 8's disorderly conduct piqued its curiosity. The film thus draws participation, disorderly conduct, and democratic legitimacy into a generative relationship by making outbursts and illegal conduct the sparks that lead to genuine deliberation on the part of the jury.

Putting the Trial on Trial

Another important function of the outburst in trial dramas is to put the trial itself on trial. Frank Galvin does this for the viewer in _The Verdict_ by exposing the judge's bias in the colloquy in chambers; so too the scene of the juror's outburst in _The Wrong Man_ and the volcanic monologue on national security imperatives in _A Few Good Men_ interjected by base commander Col. Nathan Jessup, played by Jack Nicholson, when Tom Cruise's character, JAG lawyer Lt. Daniel Kaffee, incites Jessup to admit on the witness stand that he had ordered the physical abuse of an underperforming and disliked marine private.[33] And in _Fury_, a series of courtroom outbursts by spectators, who argue that the trial of the accused participants of a lynch mob is a joke and "a shame against the good name of our town," lead to a homily on national lynching statistics and the introduction of news reel footage of the lynching of Joe Wilson. The film shows that defendants and witnesses, such as the sheriff who claimed the lynchers "must have been men from out of town," have themselves been making a mockery of the trial by their own perjury.[34]

Lincoln also puts the trial on trial in _Young Mr. Lincoln_ when he refuses to allow the prosecution to ask the defendants' mother which one of them committed the murder. As the prosecuting attorney threatens to see to it that the mother is held in contempt, Lincoln intervenes,

> Prosecutor: Don't you know that under the law they are equally guilty of murder? That under the law they may both be hanged for it?
>
> Witness: But I can't tell you [_tearing up_]. And you can't make me!
>
> Prosecutor: Don't you understand I am offering you the life of one son? Take it and tell us which boy killed Scrub White.
>
> Witness: No. No! No!
>
> Prosecutor: Don't you know this court can make you answer this question? Don't you know that you can be sent to jail yourself? That shielding a criminal makes you an accessory to that crime? . . . Don't you know?!
>
> Lincoln: That's enough of that. Your Honor, I protest against the prosecution's attempt to force this woman to decide which of her two sons shall live and which shall die. In her eyes these boys hold an equal place.
>
> Prosecutor: Perhaps if my learned friend knew more of the law . . .
>
> Lincoln: [_Facing the prosecutor with his arms crossed in front of his chest as the prosecutor turns away_] I may not know so much of law, Mr.

Felder, but I know what's right and what's wrong. And I know what you're asking is *wrong.* [*Standing before the judge's bench and addressing the judge directly*] Put yourself in this woman's place, your Honor. Can you truthfully say you'd do differently? Look at her. She's, she's just a simple ordinary country woman. . . . Yet, has she no feelings, no heart? [*Turning to approach the jury*] I've seen Abigail Clay exactly three times in my life, gentlemen, and yet, I know everything there is to know about her. I know her because I've seen hundreds of women just like her. . . . Women who say little but do much, who ask for nothing and give all. And I tell you that such a woman will never answer the question that's been put to her here. Never. [*Turning to the witness*] I'd rather Mrs. Clay see you lose both your boys than to see you break your heart trying to save one at the expense of the other. So don't tell 'em.

The prosecutor then withdraws the question before the judge rules on the evidentiary objection.

Notice that there is no not-X here—the fact-finding function of the trial is suspended and rendered subordinate to the mother's honor, to Lincoln's noble desire to protect that honor, to the community's traditional family values, and, of course, to Lincoln's sense of right and wrong.[35] The X-not-X structure is also dissolved in Lincoln's haranguing of the only other eyewitness, Palmer Cass, after he leaves the stand. Lincoln shifts from questions about why Cass lied about the degree of visibility on the night of the murder, to a flat accusation that Cass is the murderer. Lincoln then offers a stream of facts that have nowhere appeared in evidence as he bears down on Cass until he breaks and confesses. The prosecutor offers no objections to protect his witness even when a man wraps Cass's arms behind his back and the scene takes on the appearance of an extrajudicial, compulsory interrogation. The contrast with Lincoln's jealous protection of the defendants' mother is acute—unlike the mother, Cass is a *proper* target of adversarial excess.

To be sure, one purpose of these scenes is to depict frontier trial procedure as relatively informal and primitive. But another function is to reveal the adversary system as illegitimate and unworthy of respect in its pretenses of formality if the formalities demand that injustice (or anything dishonorable) be tolerated. The most dynamic oscillation is accordingly less between the evidence presented for each side regarding the guilt or innocence of the defendants than between justice and the formalities of adversarial exchange—between natural justice and the administration of justice. Lincoln's character and values are represented as simultaneously above the law (entitling him to seize control of the trial process and deviate from its formalities at will) and a condition of trusting the law (recall that the trial occurs only because Lincoln uses a combination of humor, courage, and shaming to avert a lynching, and it concludes with exoneration only because Lincoln steadfastly refuses the judge's ex parte advice to enter a guilty plea).

The same justice-law oscillation is triggered in *Philadelphia* when the plaintiff's counsel, Joe Miller (played by Denzel Washington), converts a response to a simple evidentiary objection he has deliberately provoked into a homily on discrimination against gays. In direct examination of an associate at the firm where Andrew Beckett (Tom Hanks) worked before he was fired, Miller asks, out of the blue:

Miller: Are you a homosexual?

Witness: What?

Miller: Are you a homosexual? Answer the question. Are you a homo? Are you a faggot? You know, a punk, a queen, pillow biter, fairy, booty snatcher, rump roaster? *Are you gay?*! [*Gavel bangs several times*]

Judge: Order!

Defense Counsel Conine: Objection. Where did this come from? Suddenly counsel is attacking his own witness! Mr. Collins's sexual orientation has nothing to do with this case.

Judge: Please have a seat, Ms. Conine. Would you approach the bench, Mr. Miller? [*Miller approaches; judge speaks with voice lowered*] Could you kindly share with me what's going on inside your head because, at this moment I don't have a clue.

Miller: [*Stepping back from the bench*] Your Honor, [*turns away from the judge toward the spectators and the camera as it pans slowly in from a long shot of the courtroom to center in on Miller*] everybody in this courtroom is thinking about sexual orientation, you know, sexual preference, whatever you want to call it. Who does what to whom, and how they do it. I mean they're looking at Andrew Beckett, and they're thinking about it. They're looking at Mr. Wheeler, Ms. Conine, [*gesturing to the defense table*] even you, your Honor, [*turning back to the judge*] they're wondering about it. [*Chortling*] Trust me, I know that they are looking at me and thinking about it. [*Turning to the spectators and camera, spreading his hands open*] So let's just get it out in the open, let's get it out of the closet because this case is not just about AIDS, is it? So let's talk about what this case is really all about—the general public's hatred, our loathing, our fear of homosexuals. And how that climate of hatred and fear translated into the firing of this particular homosexual, my client, Andrew Beckett. [*Turning back to face the judge*].

Miller is neither cautioned nor punished for his use of explicit language, nor is he questioned about whether he intends to treat Mr. Collins as a hostile witness, and defense counsel makes no motion for a mistrial or objection to Miller's homily. The judge simply says, "Please have a seat, Mr. Miller." Beckett, who is initially surprised when Miller turns on the witness, congratulates him when he sits shoulder to shoulder next to him.[36] Then the judge continues, again addressing Miller rather than the jury:

> Judge: In this courtroom, Mr. Miller, justice is blind to matters of race, creed, color, religion, and sexual orientation.
> Miller: With all due respect, your Honor, we don't live in this courtroom though, do we?
> Judge: No, we don't. However, as regards this witness, I'm going to sustain the defense's objection.

The power of the scene lies precisely in its radical disruption of the orderly X-not-X presentation of evidence—the plaintiff's counsel turns on his own witness using language designed to shock the conscience and then converts adjudication of the defendant's objection into an occasion to put the homophobia that surrounds the trial on trial.[37] When Miller turns to face the spectators and the camera, he has figuratively displaced the judge, who sits mute in the background as the homily proceeds uninterrupted. That displacement continues even after Miller sits down in the form of his retort: "We don't live in this courtroom though, do we?" The judge limply responds by sustaining the defendant's objection without addressing any of the other elements of the incident that might have tainted the jury's ability to impartially deliberate on the admissible evidence. As in *Young Mr. Lincoln*, Miller's resistance to the formalities of adversarial exchange places his advocacy above the law (indeed, responding to the call that law be made meaningful out of court, "where we live") and as a condition of the viewer's faith in the rest of the trial. The move above the law is all the more powerful in *Philadelphia*, however, because the viewer has watched Miller struggle out of court to recognize homophobia as an injustice.

Passionate Display: Beyond Justice as Rectification

Thus far, I have argued that outbursts can ratify one side of a case, draw attention to evidence that rests outside the X-not-X structure of proof, and put the formality and validity of adversarial exchange itself on trial—displacing and cabining the X-not-X rhythm in a more basic oscillation between the desire to see justice done, on the one hand, and respect for the constraints of a rationally ordered and deliberative legal process, on the other. Outbursts also frequently rupture the very epistemological distinctions upon which the rational application of law to fact is supposed to turn (distinctions between fact and value, past and present, and reason and passion). In *Philadelphia*, most strikingly, Beckett collapses to the courtroom floor as Miller is in the midst of cross-examining Charles Wheeler, Beckett's former boss and mentor. Beckett is taken to the hospital and the next scene at trial begins with an image of Beckett's empty chair as Miller cross-examines another partner of the law firm that fired Beckett. The viewer learns the jury's verdict just before learning that Beckett is dying.

The scene in which Beckett collapses initially turns disorderly when Miller breaks into sarcastic applause at the end of Wheeler's direct testimony and asks Wheeler if he is gay—disruptive conduct that explicitly recalls the earlier scene in which he turns on his own witness and delivers his homily. The rest of the cross-examination is shot in a way that deftly conflates the progression of Beckett's illness and delirium (he imagines the jury bursting out in laughter at him) with the increasing hostility of Wheeler's responses to Miller. In the moment that precedes Beckett's collapse, Wheeler turns to look Beckett in the eye as he criticizes Beckett's performance at the firm. The camera takes up Wheeler's menacing gaze from a low angle and zooms in so close that his face fills the screen. The viewer is thus made to assume Beckett's subject position during this long-deferred and climactic confrontation. The camera then cuts to a reaction shot of Beckett, eyes wide, recoiling in his chair and reaching feebly for his cane before he attempts to rise and collapses, first striking the table in front of him and then, with the camera shifting to a bird's-eye view, falling, twisting, and violently striking the courtroom floor below the jury box.

At the level of plot, one can certainly read the scene in X-not-X terms—a classic cross-examination in which Miller goads Wheeler into showing his hostility toward Beckett without forcing Wheeler to explicitly admit that he is a bigot. Moreover, the scene is, in Clover's terms, "fragmented, forensically visualized, and polygraphically photographed"—most particularly as the camera alternates between shots of Wheeler's face and Beckett's.[38] But the conflation of Beckett's mortal illness with Wheeler's hostility produced by this alternation has deeper implications. First, it overrides the discrete legal question of whether Wheeler fired Beckett because he found out he had AIDS. Neither the jury nor the viewer ever learns what happened to the complaint that went missing from Beckett's desk on the day it had to be filed in court—the supposedly neutral reason given for Beckett's termination. Second, the melodramatic display of Beckett's suffering—quite literally, the beginning of his death throes—overwhelms the X-not-X structure of the trial altogether. If the result is not a foregone conclusion, the viewer's feelings about how the case should be resolved are definitively settled.

Finally, the incident overwhelms the oscillation between justice and the formalities of law triggered by Miller's homily—at least insofar as justice is concerned with the rectification of discrete prior violations of rights, rather than brute suffering arising from mere misfortune.[39] From the beginning of the film, the viewer has repeatedly been asked, advised, and implored to identify with Beckett—not just with the injustice he has suffered at the law firm and his determination to see the case through but with his basic humanity and his suffering from AIDS. Cinematically, this is achieved via direct, often lingering, shots establishing eye contact between the viewer and Beckett and shots that repeatedly show how Beckett is seen by others. But in the courtroom scene in which he loses consciousness (right before our eyes, in front of the jury box, with one of the most important witnesses on the stand), the passionate display of his current suffering and mortality *demands* identification.[40] The camera places the viewer squarely in Beckett's gaze as his eyes widen and he falls.

All the other elements of courtroom outbursts discussed above are present in this scene: Beckett's values and his present suffering, highlighted by the seething hostility of Wheeler's account of his work at the firm, are decisively ratified; the jury is invited to infer dispositive facts regarding Beckett's termination from Wheeler's demeanor; and the formalities of trial are ruptured on terms that force recognition of the suffering associated with AIDS, suffering in the closet, and suffering caused by homophobia. Not only is the trial put on trial, the community in which the court and theater audience sits is put on trial. There are no closing arguments because Miller's homily and Beckett's collapse have sealed the case. The jury finds for Beckett, but even if it had entered a defense verdict, that would merely have confirmed a further injustice and the failure of the jury to meet its duty. There is no deliberate act of resistance here, certainly no strategic outburst like Miller's, but it is all the more poignant for just that reason, viscerally triggering the viewer's resistance to the rational, dispassionate, retrospectively focused forensic stance supposedly demanded by the practice of justice in court.

This shift from the mechanics of adversarial exchange into a deeply sentimental, melodramatic register in scenes of disorder is central to the appeal of trial dramas.[41] The distinctive appeal of the melodramatic can perhaps be drawn into sharper relief by recalling the power of analogous ruptures in nonlaw dramas.[42] Paradigmatically, there is the scene in *Metropolis* (1927) when Freder loses consciousness at the sight of his father standing beside Maria/The Machine Man.[43] The clash here is not between X-not-X but rather the classic melodramatic clash between a known good and a known evil (X and Y), between narratives of fall and redemption. Freder has been torn between his life as the son of the beautiful city's most powerful figure and the plight of the laboring masses he has discovered underground. Freder's attempts to find Maria (the prophet who first exposes him to the impoverished children of the laborers) draw him into deeper appreciation of the plight of the laborers and farther away from his father. Thus, when he thinks he sees Maria with his father (not realizing that she has been cloned by his father and the Inventor), he loses consciousness. The scene is crucial to Freder's development into the Mediator who ultimately reconciles the laborers and his father after the city has descended into revolutionary violence. The other word Lang uses for the Mediator is the Heart, emphasizing the ethical value of compassion and its somatic distance from the seat of reason in the mind. Beckett's death throes in court similarly complete his (and Miller's) transformation into the status of "mediator" regarding homophobia, and the transformation is made most powerfully at the sentimental level, at the level of the heart.

The scene in which Beckett collapses also parallels the climactic melodramatic outbursts in contemporary nonlaw dramas. Consider the scene in *The Prince of Tides* (1991) when Tom Wingo (played by Nick Nolte) finally confesses to his sister's therapist, Susan Lowenstein (played by Barbara Streisand), that he, his sister, and his mother were all raped in their home in South Carolina by escaped convicts. Lurid flashbacks to the rapes are intercut with the tranquil scene of Wingo and Lowenstein in her upscale New York office.[44] Wingo's desire to reveal the secret in order to aid Lowenstein's efforts to help his suicidal sister requires breaking a vow of secrecy his mother has insisted upon for decades, and it clashes with his desire to keep the secret so he can continue to deny that he too was raped.

These competing desires are resolved through a series of ruptures in the formalities of psychoanalytic practice (culminating in Wingo collapsing into Lowenstein's arms in her office and their ensuing love affair), just as the climactic clash in *Philadelphia* occurs through a series of ruptures in the formalities of trial procedure. As in *Metropolis*, melodramatic tension is built around a confrontation of known good and evil. And as in *Metropo-*

lis, the mediating element is passionate identification. A similar process is at work in *Philadelphia*—the jury and audience are gradually seduced by Beckett. His collapse in court (silent testimony that recalls and dramatically amplifies the earlier silent testimony his body offers on the witness stand when he exposes his lesions) completes the seduction.[45]

Ticien Marie Sassoubre's contribution to this volume trenchantly demonstrates why we should not be surprised to find elements of melodrama suffused in the formal elements of filmic representations of law that amplify the viewer's sense of realism. Here, I would add that in representations of resistance to law in the American trial film, melodrama appears to be particularly salient. Peter Brooks's work on melodrama offers a clue as to why that should be so in his suggestion that "the origins of melodrama can be accurately located within the context of the French Revolution and its aftermath."[46] Brooks is formally concerned with what he calls "the final liquidation of the traditional Sacred and its representative institutions (Church and Monarchy) . . . [and] the dissolution of an organic and hierarchically cohesive society."[47] The distinctive appeal of melodramatic "rituals" under such conditions of ethical and legal uncertainty is that they "involve the confrontation of clearly identified antagonists and the expulsion of one of them."[48] Both the anxiety and relief elicited by melodramatic confrontation rest in this clarity.

In democratic societies, and particularly pluralistic democratic societies buffeted by rapid technological and economic change such as the United States, the revolutionary and postrevolutionary emergencies with respect to the authority of any ethical system do not end in the creation of a constitutional order and the rule of law. Nor do contests between the ethical and legal end. The orders of legality attendant to and arising from foundational acts themselves repeat and express the initial emergencies in every genuinely disputed case.[49] Melodrama not only provides a reassuring aesthetic framework for exploring both petit and grand versions of this irreducible moral and legal indeterminacy, it offers a rich visual and emotional register for representations of the experience of injustice. It makes sense, from this perspective, that so many of the outbursts that punctuate representations of trial and adversarial exchange in American trial dramas stage emergencies of moral and legal authority, as well as the anxieties they evoke, in the cathartic register of melodramatic confrontation. As Brooks summarizes: "Melodrama starts from and expresses anxiety brought by a frightening new world in which the traditional patterns of moral order no longer provide the necessary social glue. It plays out the force of that anxiety with the apparent triumph of villainy, and it dissipates it with the eventual victory of virtue."[50]

As *The Wrong Man* powerfully shows, not every "eventual victory" is complete in trial dramas. Manny should never have faced the "meat grinder" of trial, and had he avoided it, his wife's protracted mental deterioration might have been avoided.[51] The point is simply that melodrama provides a relatively safe and compelling narrative device for representing (indeed, playing upon) anxieties that are generated by the persistent gap between the law and contested views of what is just, what is good, what it means to suffer injustice, what it means to see that justice is done.

Conclusion

I want to close by considering two remaining issues. The first is how to position the disorder in court depicted in trial dramas in relation to the kind of extrajudicial resistance to law depicted in films that concern vigilantism. The second is how disorder in court, as depicted in trial films, relates to the profound ambivalence Americans have historically expressed regarding the adversary system. The two issues are obviously connected since vigilantism is a long-standing and deeply culturally salient alternative to adversarial trial.

On the first point, both representations of disorder in court and vigilantism typically implicate the desire to see justice done in the face of the limitations or failures of the formality of ordinary legal process. Clint Eastwood's character in *Dirty Harry* (1971), like countless protagonists in other cop films and westerns, is determined to bring a criminal to justice even if that means resorting to wildly extralegal tactics.[52] And like many other films concerned with vigilante justice, the impotence of ordinary legal process is offered to establish not only that vigilantism is necessary but that it is justified. What seems to distinguish scenes of disorder in trial dramas is the comparative repression and displacement of physical violence. In *The Verdict*, for instance, Frank Galvin bangs his fist on the judge's desk during his tirade in chambers after the judge has interfered with his direct examination of his medical expert. But it is the judge who deserves to be struck.[53] In *Young Mr. Lincoln*, Palmer Cass is physically restrained as he attempts to leave the courtroom and as Lincoln pressures him to confess. But Cass is huge and clearly not limited in his movement by the arm bar as much as by the moral force of Lincoln's piercing cross-examination and the confrontation with his guilt it provokes. And of course, whenever speech and movement become too unruly in the trial drama, there is the fall of the gavel and the voice of the judge. The gavel—its fall often isolated by the camera in close-up—operates as a synecdoche for the order of court, the judge's power of contempt, and ultimately, for the sovereignty of law as reasoned argument.

In the depiction of vigilante justice, by contrast, viewers are typically exposed to orgies of violence. The violence is often excessive or disproportionate rather than repressed, and it usually finds its proper target in the end, rather than being displaced. Critics such as Anthony Chase have argued that representations of vigilantism are explicitly concerned with vindicating alternatives to ordinary legal process—either as fantasies of "crime control" or of civil disobedience and "a popular 'jurisprudence' of opposition to formal state power and its legal apparatus."[54] In either case, it is the claimed superiority of these alternatives to ordinary legal process, and to a lesser extent the conservative-liberal political valence of the specific alternative depicted, that drives his analysis.[55]

But this approach ignores the fact that the same underlying anxieties about the authority and determinacy of ethical and legal standards animate both trial dramas and films concerned with vigilante justice. And it matters too that in both genres the viewer is invited to take pleasure in resistance to law and to participate in a form of popular justice, indeed, to rule as a "juror" unconstrained by the formal X-not-X structure of adversarial exchange. (Nor should we forget that actual jurors are permitted to do this as well by the secrecy of jury deliberation and the opacity of the general verdict). To be sure, what might be called the "impersonation of sovereignty" offered in *Dirty Harry* is more thoroughgoing, more Leviathan-like, than feeble old Frank Galvin or the silent jurors (and viewers) before whom he is making his case.[56] But focusing on scenes of disorder in trial dramas shows that it is a mistake to see the trial drama and representations of vigilantism as opposites—the vigilante, after all, always borrows attributes and rules of ordinary legal process so that his actions can be understood as legitimate, even as he exceeds them, and trial dramas, as we have seen, depend upon disorderly conduct in a range of ways to help the jurors/viewers reach a judgment.

With respect to the second problem, it is noteworthy that Clover, along with many law and humanities scholars, relies upon Tocqueville's famous quote about how the adversary system, and particularly the jury trial, serve to make law a "vulgar tongue" in American culture. "There is virtually no political question in the United States that does not sooner or later resolve itself into a judicial question. . . . Jury duty makes people of all classes familiar with legal ways. In a sense, the language of the judiciary becomes the vulgar tongue. Thus, the legal spirit, born in law schools and courtrooms, gradually spreads beyond their walls. It infiltrates all of society, as it were, filtering down to the lowest ranks, with the result that in the end all the people acquire some of the habits and tastes of the magistrate."[57] The core of Tocqueville's argument, both here and in the chapter in which it appears in *Democracy in America*, is not merely that jury trials popularize the law, making it accessible and an object of popular fascination, but that in a democratic society the vulgarization of law has a taming effect. By learning to translate all manner of social, political, and economic concerns into the language of law, the law becomes a primary mediating device in society.

But that essentially conservative theory fits awkwardly with the structural function of outbursts in the trial drama. And indeed, it ran against popular sentiments about the adversary system at the time Tocqueville visited America. Tellingly, Tocqueville spoke primarily with Whig-Federalist lawyers during his visit—lawyers who were engaged in a decades long struggle to defend the adversary system against populist critiques that it was too costly, too time consuming, obtuse, and antidemocratic.[58] On the latter point, populists criticized the system's reliance on elite lawyers trained in obscure pleading rules and Latin; common law doctrine derived from the country's former colonial oppressor rather than local, democratically accountable legislatures; and judges who had no direct accountability to the communities in which they held office. Moreover, the primary alternative with which the adversary system had to compete was never really the more restrained methods of the continental inquisitorial system but rather vigilantism and other forms of self-help.[59] Hence, perhaps, the persistence of the vigilante hero in American film.

Against this historical backdrop, it seems clear that when trial dramas stage resistance to law in the form of disorder in court (resistance to the formalities of X-not-X presentation of proof, to the epistemological boundaries of relevance and materiality, to the process of trial itself, and to the narrow theory of justice as rectification) they are drawing upon a deeply embedded ambivalence in Americans' attitudes about the adversary system. The representation of trials in film may also have the effect of taming viewers in the same way Tocqueville suggested that watching actual trials does—perhaps all the more so in an era in which actual trials have become vanishingly rare and public experiences of trial are therefore more frequently imaginary (literally screened) than real. The trial drama may itself be in the process of becoming an epistemological remainder of a relationship to the actual practice of justice we have lost. But it matters that scenes of disorder in court depict the law being tamed too—without that element, American viewers might well wonder why they should "sit here and listen to this."

Notes

1. Herbert Brean, "A Case of Identity," *Life Magazine*, June 29, 1953, 97.

2. Alfred Hitchcock, dir., *The Wrong Man* (1956; New York: Warner Bros., 2004), DVD.

3. Jean-Luc Godard, "The Wrong Man," in *Godard on Godard*, ed. and trans. Tom Milne (New York: Da Capo Press, 1972), 48.

4. Ibid., 50.

5. Ibid.

6. Published decisions involving juror outbursts during trial are fairly rare, see People v. Wiggins, 132 A.D. 3d 514 (N.Y. App. 2015), but there are numerous published authorities regarding how courts handle expressions of bias by potential jurors during voir dire. See United States v. Vergara-Riveira, 207 F. App'x 995 (11th Cir. 2006) (a prospective juror was excused for making comment during voir dire that it is "common practice" for Spanish-speaking immigrants to sell drugs, where the defendant, a Spanish-speaking immigrant, was charged with selling drugs); State v. Kilby, 947 P.2d 420 (Idaho Ct. App. 1997) (the defendant was not denied right to fair trial by a potential juror's outburst during voir dire that the defendant was a pedophile; trial court properly dismissed the potential juror and asked the other jurors to disregard the comment).

7. As the Supreme Court put it, "the pretrial deposition-discovery mechanism established by Rules 26 to 37 is one of the most significant innovations of the Federal Rules of Civil Procedure. . . . The various instruments of discovery now serve . . . to narrow and clarify the basic issues between the parties, and . . . as a device for ascertaining the facts . . . relative to those issues. Thus civil trials in the federal courts no longer need be carried on in the dark. . . . Mutual knowledge of all the relevant facts gathered by both parties is essential to proper litigation. To that end, either party may compel the other to disgorge whatever facts he has in his possession. The deposition-discovery procedure simply advances the stage at which the disclosure can be compelled from the time of trial to the period preceding it, thus reducing the possibility of surprise." Hickman v. Taylor, 329 U.S. 495, 500–507 (1947). On the risks of surprise at trial arising from the period in between the adoption of civil discovery in common law cases and the abolition of the writ system, see William E. Nelson, *Americanization of the Common Law: The Impact of Legal Change on Massachusetts Society, 1760–1830* (Cambridge, MA: Harvard University Press, 1975), 86–87. Discovery practice in criminal cases was much slower to emerge, but as Lawrence Friedman contends, "it was a blood brother of plea bargaining and the decline of trial by jury." Lawrence M. Friedman, *Crime and Punishment in American History* (New York: Basic Books, 1993), 387.

8. A bare 1.8 percent of federal civil cases were disposed of by trial in 2002,

compared with 11.5 percent in 1962, and 18.9 percent in 1938. Mark Galanter, "The Vanishing Trial: An Examination of Trials and Related Matters in Federal and State Courts," *Journal of Empirical Legal Studies* 1 (2004): 461, 464. In federal criminal cases, disposition by trial in 2002 were under 5 percent compared with 15 percent in 1962, ibid., 493. Figures at the state level are comparably low. One study tracking "trial activity in state courts of general jurisdiction in the 75 most populous counties in the years 1992, 1996, and 2001," found a "47 percent reduction" in civil trials, ibid., 508–10. In another study covering twenty-one states between 1976 and 2002 found a decline from 1.8 to 0.6 percent in dispositions by jury trial and a decline from 34.3 percent to 15.2 percent in bench trials, ibid., 508. Criminal trials in the states fell over the same period from 8.5 percent to 3.3 percent of dispositions, ibid., 510. On the gradual redistribution of power from jury to judge in American trials, see Norman W. Spaulding, "Due Process without Judicial Process: Antiadversarialism in American Legal Culture," *Fordham Law Review* 85 (2017): 2249, and "The Enclosure of Justice: Courthouse Architecture, Due Process, and the Dead Metaphor of Trial," *Yale Journal of Law and Humanities* 24 (2012): 311.

9. See Galanter, "Vanishing Trial."

10. Compare Gilster v. Primebank, 747 F.3d 1007 (8th Cir. 2014) (a new trial was warranted in a sexual harassment suit when the plaintiff's counsel told the jury during closing arguments a personal story indicating that she herself had been sexually harassed and, unlike the plaintiff, was not courageous enough to file a complaint); Sanders-El v. Wencewicz, 987 F.2d 483 (8th Cir. 1993) (denial of new trial motion was reversed when defense counsel "dramatically dropped a lengthy computer printout in front of the jury" with the "manifest intent . . . to arouse the prejudices of the jury by leading it to believe Sanders-El had the conviction record of a veteran vocational criminal"); Cadorna v. City and County of Denver, 245 F.R.D. 490 (D. Colo. 2007) (the defendant's motion for a new trial was granted due to the plaintiff's counsel's "disrespectful cockalorum, grandstanding, bombast, bullying, and hyperbole" throughout trial); People v. Burtron, 877 N.E.2d 87, 89 (Ill. Ct. App. 2007) (a trial judge's ruling declaring a mistrial was affirmed due to defense counsel's improper conduct during criminal trial, including repeated improper commentary and an outburst asking the court in front of the jury to administer a polygraph test of the defendant); with First Nat. Bank of La Grange v. Glen Oaks Hosp. and Med. Ctr., 829 N.E.2d 378 (Ill. Ct. App. 2005) (motion for a new trial was denied when the plaintiff's counsel engaged in improper conduct during trial, including dropping books loudly on the table or floor while questioning a witness, and seizing an exhibit from a witness and waving it in front of the jury); Boyd v. Manhattan and Bronx Surface Transit Operating Auth., 912 N.Y.S.2d 196 (App. Div. 2010) (holding that the trial court erred in setting aside a verdict due to defense counsel's improper remarks, which in-

cluded asking the court to tell the plaintiff's counsel to "shut her mouth"); Willis v. Lepine, 687 F.3d 826 (7th Cir. 2012) (holding that no new trial was warranted when defense counsel's improper objections during closing argument suggested that 42 U.S.C. § 1983 plaintiffs were either gangbangers or drug dealers). On the disruption of trial by other participants, see Ashley v. Delaware, 798 A.2d 1019 (Del. Sct. 2002) (outburst by spectator and former victim of defendant "Don't think he's not guilty, he stabbed me in the back 14 times" grounds for mistrial); Taylor v. Delaware, 690 A.2d 933 (Del. Sct. 1997) (emotional outburst by witness, mother and grandmother of victims, who burst into tears and screamed at defendant, not sufficiently prejudicial to require mistrial); Robinson v. Texas, 2013 WL 2424133 (Tex. App. June 5, 2013) (unpublished) (attempt by spectator, son-in-law of victim, to attack defendant in presence of jury while screaming profanities, did not require mistrial; noting that timing, content, inflammatory effect, and response of trial court are relevant to determination).

11. Spaulding, "Enclosure of Justice," 340–41.

12. On the relationship between participation and the democratic legitimacy of law, see Tom R. Tyler, *Why People Obey the Law* (Princeton, NJ: Princeton University Press, 2006).

13. *Fury*, directed by Fritz Lang (1936; Beverly Hills, CA: Metro Goldwyn Mayer, 2005), DVD; *Young Mr. Lincoln*, directed by John Ford (1939; Century City, CA: 20th Century Fox, 2006), DVD; *12 Angry Men*, directed by Sidney Lumet (1957; Century City, CA: 20th Century Fox Home Entertainment, 2008), DVD; *The Verdict*, directed by Sidney Lumet (1982; Century City, CA: 20th Century Fox Home Entertainment, 2002), DVD; *A Few Good Men*, directed by Rob Reiner (1992; Culver City, CA: Columbia Pictures, 2007), DVD; *Philadelphia*, directed by Jonathan Demme (1993; Hollywood, CA: TriStar Pictures, 2002), DVD.

14. Carol Clover, "Law and the Order of Popular Culture," in *Law in the Domains of Culture*, ed. Austin Sarat and Thomas R. Kearns (Ann Arbor: University of Michigan Press, 1998), 99.

15. Ibid., 102, 118.

16. Ibid., 107. In a footnote, Clover says that her theory is particularly apt as applied to "whodunit" films. I think this is right and that the parallels between the X-not-X of adversarial exchange in court most closely parallels the X-not-X structure of scenes out of court in that specific genre of trial films.

17. Ibid.

18. Ibid.

19. Ibid.

20. Ibid., 102n10.

21. Even this oscillation is drained of uncertainty after the first scene in the police station when we see that Manny's handwriting matches that of the perpetrator and that he has made a similar spelling error. The audience knows both

that he is innocent and, from that moment on, that it will be exceedingly difficult to prove.

22. Godard, "Wrong Man," 49.

23. Clover, "Law and the Order," 104.

24. Ibid. On Clover's thesis of the central role of the juror-viewer substitution, see Carol Clover, "'God Bless Juries!'" in *Refiguring American Film Genres: Theory and History*, ed. Nick Browne (Berkeley: University of California, 1998), 255.

25. Ibid.

26. See ibid., 102–3n12, 104, 116.

27. On the epistemological relationship between law, curiosity, and literary realism, with a few gestures to film, see Hilary Schor, *Curious Subjects: Women and the Trials of Realism* (Oxford: Oxford University Press, 2013).

28. See Norman W. Spaulding, "The Luxury of the Law: The Codification Movement and the Right to Counsel," *Fordham Law Review* 73 (2004): 983; Robert C. Post, "On the Popular Image of the Lawyer: Reflections in a Dark Glass," *California Law Review* 75 (1987): 379; Charles M. Cook, *The American Codification Movement: A Study of Antebellum Legal Reform* (Westport, CT: Greenwood Press, 1981); Lawrence M. Friedman, *History of American Law*, 2nd ed. (New York: Simon and Schuster, 1985).

29. Clover, "Law and Order," 104.

30. Michel de Certeau, *The Writing of History* (New York: Columbia University Press, 1988), 4.

31. See United States v. Lawson, 677 F.3d 629, 641 (4th Cir. 2012) (a new trial was warranted when jurors used Wikipedia to research the definition of an element of an animal fighting offense); Anderson v. Ford Motor Co., 186 F.3d 918 (8th Cir. 1999) (grant of a new trial was upheld based on the admission of a juror that he conducted an out-of-court test of a faulty seat belt system in violation of court directive); People v. Vigil, 191 Cal. App. 4th 1474 (2011) (a new trial was warranted when a juror conducted a "homemade experiment" regarding a crucial issue at trial); People v. Wadle, 97 P.3d 932 (Colo. 2004) (grant of new trial was affirmed in a child abuse case where a juror conducted Internet research regarding a drug allegedly taken by the defendant). On facts similar to those in *12 Angry Men*, see Hill v. United States, 622 A.2d 680 (D.C. 1993) (a new trial was warranted due to a juror's visit to the crime scene to observe lighting conditions; the juror discussed the visit with other jurors and lighting was a crucial factual issue before the jury); People v. Redd, 561 N.Y.S.2d 439 (App. Div. 1990) (an alternate juror's unauthorized visit to the crime scene warranted a new trial when the alternate reported impressions from the visit to the jury).

32. Clover, "Law and Order," 102n10.

33. The later monologue strongly implies that the law Kaffee seeks to enforce

through the courtroom trial stands only to frustrate the colonel's higher charge of protecting the nation from external threats.

34. Disruptions of the proceedings mount from this point to a complete subversion of the trial: one woman passes out during the screening of the jail burning; another exits the room screaming that she is guilty too and begging forgiveness; finally, Joe Wilson, the lynching victim whose death the trial was held to punish, walks in as the verdict is read. See Ticien M. Sassoubre, "The Impulsive Subject and the Realist Lens: Law and Consumer Culture in Fritz Lang's *Fury*," *Southern California Interdisciplinary Law Journal* 20 (2011): 325.

35. In an early scene, Lincoln looks up from *Blackstone's Commentaries* and remarks "By gee, that's all there is to it, right and wrong."

36. As in the outburst from *The Verdict*, Miller's outburst establishes for the audience and Beckett Miller's full investment in the case.

37. The prosecutor's homily on lynching in America in *Fury* is strikingly similar, drawing on the outbursts of spectators and an objection of the defense counsel to place the community's (and the audience's) amnesia and apathy regarding its complicity in lynching.

38. Clover, "Law and Order," 114.

39. On the distinction between justice as rectification and as recognition of misfortune, see Judith N. Shklar, *The Faces of Injustice* (New Haven, CT: Yale University Press, 1990).

40. Witnesses and parties to a case have lost consciousness in actual trials. For a provocative example reproduced in a film, consider the sensation caused when the author and Holocaust survivor Yehiel De-Nur passed out while giving testimony at the trial of Adolf Eichmann in 1961, and the decontextualized reproduction of documentary footage of that event in the film *Hannah Arendt*, directed by Margarethe von Trotta (2012; Zeitgeist Films), DVD. See Iris Milner, "The 'Gray Zone' Revisited: The Concentrationary Universe in Ka. Tzetnik's Literary Testimony," *Jewish Social Studies* 14 (2008): 115.

41. Beckett's collapse is among the most powerful examples, but there are many others. In *The Verdict*, the attending nurse, who exposes the doctor's false defense, cries out at the end of her cross-examination "Who *were* these men? I wanted to be a nurse!" And the mother's pleas from the witness stand in *Young Mr. Lincoln*, along with Lincoln's homily, are powerful melodramatic appeals, as is the "I want the truth! . . . You can't handle the truth!" exchange between witness and attorney in *A Few Good Men*.

42. On the relationship between situation and rupture in melodrama, see Lea Jacobs, "The Woman's Picture and the Poetics of Melodrama," *Camera Obscura* 31 (1993): 121–47.

43. Fritz Lang, dir., *Metropolis* (1927; Babelsberg, Germany: UFA, 2004), DVD.

44. Barbara Streisand, dir., *The Prince of Tides* (1991; Culver City, CA: Columbia Pictures, 2002), DVD.

45. It matters of course that Beckett goes to court to stage the passionate identification that brings the reversal of shame and stigma, whereas Wingo goes to therapy and Feder goes underneath the city in search of a mysterious woman. Though of course the failure to involve the police and the courts by Wingo's mother and the utter absence of law to mediate the labor/capital dispute suggest that law operates in the shadows of these films as well. Wingo needs the therapist and Feder needs Maria because the law has already failed, is already corrupt.

46. Peter Brooks, "The Melodramatic Imagination," in *Imitations of Life: A Reader on Film and Television Melodrama*, ed. Marcia Landy (Detroit, MI: Wayne State University Press, 1991), 60.

47. Ibid.

48. Ibid., 71.

49. See Bonnie Honig, *Emergency Politics* (Princeton, NJ: Princeton University Press, 2009); Patricia Ewick and Susan S. Silbey, *The Common Place of Law: Stories of Everyday Life* (Chicago: University of Chicago Press, 1998); Norman W. Spaulding, "The Historical Consciousness of the Resistant Subject," *U.C. Irvine Law Review* 1 (2011): 677

50. Brooks, "Melodramatic Imagination," 64.

51. Other examples include *Philadelphia*, where Beckett's partner repeatedly suggests that the trial itself is costing Beckett his life, or in *Fury*, where (Sassoubre has shown) the victory is pyrrhic. See Sassoubre, "Impulsive Subject and the Realist Lens."

52. *Dirty Harry*, directed by Don Siegel (1971; Warner Brothers), DVD.

53. This is not the only incident of physical violence in the film. Galvin strikes the defense mole Laura Fisher out of court, but it is of course he who deserves to be struck for being so oblivious to the stratagem employed by the defense. And early on he strikes his head in a drunken stupor in his own office—a metaphor for the general stupor into which he has fallen. Thus, in each instance, the violence is enclosed, singular, displaced, and surrounded by repressive signs.

54. Anthony Chase, "Popular Culture/Popular Justice," in *Legal Reelism: Movies as Legal Texts*, ed. John Denvir (Champaign: University of Illinois, 1996), 134, and *Movies on Trial: The Legal System on the Silver Screen* (New York: New Press, 2002), 68.

55. Chase, "Popular Culture Popular Justice," 134.

56. For evidence that this interdependence was a distinctive feature of nineteenth-century legality in American culture, see Norman W. Spaulding, "Impersonating Justice: Lynching, Dueling, and Wildcat Strikes in Nineteenth Century America," in *The Routledge Research Companion to Law and Humanities in the*

Nineteenth Century, ed. Nan Goodman and Simon Stern (Oxford: Routledge Press 2017).

57. Alexis de Tocqueville, *Democracy in America* (New York: Literary Classics, 2004), 310–11, quoted by Clover, "Law and Order," 101, and in Clover, "God Bless Juries!," 255.

58. See Nelson, *Americanization of the Common Law*; Norman W. Spaulding, "Luxury of the Law," 983; Cook, *American Codification Movement*; Friedman, *History of American Law*.

59. See Spaulding, "Impersonating Justice"; Amalia Kessler, "The Nineteenth-Century Rejection of a European Transplant and the Rise of a Distinctively American Ideal of Adversarial Adjudication," *Theoretical Inquiries in Law* 10 (2009): 423.

5
"I Am Here. I Was There."

Haunted Testimony in *The Memory of Justice* and *The Specialist*

Katie Model

In Nuremberg, Nazi war criminals repeatedly and consistently denied their culpability in front of the court and the cameras. This Nazi testimony, first launched into circulation through newsreels at the time of the proceedings, constitutes the ground zero for what I call "filmic denial testimony." Denial testimony continues to arise in numerous documentaries about a wide variety of atrocities. Any post-Nuremberg documentary interview, in which a Nazi claims innocence or ignorance before a camera, has become on one level a reenactment of the ur-declaration of Nazi denial at Nuremberg. Moreover, Nuremberg denial testimony also haunts interviews with perpetrators worldwide. Haunting—in this context, a ghostlike echo of the Nuremberg trials, where the guilty repeatedly disowned any responsibility for one of the greatest atrocities in human history—can arise seemingly unintentionally in works featuring denial testimony and can be used deliberately as a tool to probe, discredit, or unsettle testimony. This type of filmic haunting contaminates the individual testimony, inviting in voices from other times and places, interconnecting various historical and political events to give a sense of the copresence of the past, present, and even future, creating an uncanny feeling that history is almost being repeated. Deliberate haunting can be produced through multiple means such as montage, cutting between distinct historical-political footage to encourage juxtaposition and comparison, staging mise-en-scène that overlays an interview with filmic intertexts or inclusion of verbal or sonic echoes within an interview. What haunted spaces share is a copresence of temporalities, a loosening of an image's tether to a particular time and place and a disquieting layering of the interview filmic space with other spaces/times.[1]

For Paul Ricouer, the witness's fundamental phrase is the triple deictic, "I was there." This three-word statement captures the particular space-time of testimony. As Ricouer notes, the "imperfect tense indicates the time, and the adverb marks the space."[2] To "I was there" we can add "I am here." Someone cannot testify in your place, as Paul Celan hauntingly declares:

"No one bears witness for the witness."[3] Or, as Derrida remarks, "one cannot send a cassette to testify in one's place."[4] Additionally, the specific date, location, and identification required of legal testimony, and customary of any testimony, establish a particular time, space, and identity. The witness's oath to speak the truth, in theory, binds testimony to veracity.

While these testimonial codes attempt to fix time, space, identity, and truth, testimony's very being relies on a paradoxical relationship to temporality and unicity: it must be, as Derrida has articulated, both unique and exemplary, singular and repeatable, nonsubstitutable and replaceable. Furthermore, testimony's veracity is contingent upon the instant—testimony must be enunciated in the here and now—but it becomes believable through its capacity for reiteration.[5]

When testimony is filmed, further complexity is introduced. For isn't "I am here; I was there" as much the fundamental phrase for film—its indexical contract—as it is for testimony: the promise that a person (or thing) once stood where there is now a flickering shadow? If this is true for film in general, it is all the more so for documentary, whose tie to the "once was" remains one of its primary components. When testimony and film are brought together, a double entreaty ensues. "Believe me" the witness implores; "suspend disbelief" the moving still images exhort. When testimony moves into film, the temporality and ontology particular to testimony encounters the temporality and ontology particular to film. Traditional documentaries tend to seal over the breaches that filmic witnessing opens up in a space/time continuity; some works, however, opt to lay them bare. These films blur, complicate, or expand the seemingly discrete spatial and temporal particularities of testimony and challenge the unicity—the *singularity* and *uniqueness*— of the testifying "I." Through strategic haunting, these films contest two unicities: the testifying subject becomes fragmented and the unique event becomes a part of an iterative pattern.

This chapter argues that the original statements made by Nazi defendants in Nuremberg continue to haunt perpetrator testimony in documentaries about state crimes committed in many parts of the world. Furthermore, it argues that testimony of perpetrators of subsequent crimes can retroactively haunt Nazi testimony in documentaries. I examine how filmmakers, in their cinematic study of perpetrators and atrocities, can powerfully employ this strategic multidirectional haunting.

I juxtapose two films that are exemplars of this type of deliberate haunting: Marcel Ophüls's *The Memory of Justice*, on the Nuremberg trials (the first trials filmed), and Eyal Sivan's *The Specialist: A Portrait of a Modern Criminal*, on the Adolf Eichmann trial (the first trial to be filmed in its entirety and broadcast). These works are part of a group of films, a documentary subgenre in its own right, that investigate state crimes and focus on perpetrator testimony. Directors within this subgenre, including Errol Morris, Marcel Ophüls, Eyal Sivan, Avi Mograbi, Barbet Schroeder, Joshua Oppenheimer, Hans-Jurgen Syberberg, Emile de Antonio, and Michael Moore, eschew the transparent, seemingly objective style of many conventional documentaries, instead drawing our attention to the director's hand. Films in this subgenre may or may not include trial footage, but they reverberate with Nazi denial testimony. They share a particular epistemology, one distinct from that of the trial film genre identified by Carol Clover in her well-known essay "Law and the Order of Popular Culture."[6]

Clover finds that the Anglo-American adversarial system pervades a "broad stripe of American popular culture."[7] Indeed, she argues that the particular narrative and epistemological structure of the trial "are so deeply embedded in our narrative tradition that they shape even plots that never step into the courtroom."[8] This narrative, which both the trial and many mainstream American movies follow, consists of a long examination "bookended" by a "paratactic" opening and closing, with the verdict, or film ending, as a coda. The prosecution's story (X) generally dominates the first half of the film, while the defense's narrative, what Clover calls "not-X," dominates the latter part of the film. As viewers, Clover maintains, we are positioned as jury members, "rhythmically pulled back and forth, in the almost machinelike alternation of direct examination with cross-examination."[9] The trial films' underlying epistemological structure is summed up in Clover's memorable sentence as "fragmented, evidence-examining, forensically visualized, back-story driven, X-not-X-structured, polygraphically photographed, intricately plotted, doubt-cultivating, and jury directed."[10]

As Jennifer Petersen points out in this volume, Clover describes a mode of reception "organized around a set of puzzles or cognitive activities aimed at providing narrative and epistemological coherence." Yet, citing Janet Staiger, Petersen stresses that "such cognitively driven, problem-solving activity is only one of many modes of film reception." She maintains however that "this mode of reception *is* a dominant one in documentary." In numerous trial documentaries, she notes, the viewer is positioned as juror and asked to piece together conflicting evidence and testimonies and to form hypotheses. While the cognitive model, drawing on the detective film, is a productive one for many works fitting into the "trial documentary" category, state-crime, perpetrator-focused documentaries do not adhere to this underlying epistemological structure. For starters, the guilt of perpetrators of state-sanctioned atrocities is a foregone conclusion. As Martha Umphrey has noted, the very term "perpetrator testimony" announces the difference—and change in temporality—between the documentary testimony and the actual trial.[11] Whereas in court, the perpetrator is always referred to as "the accused," directors and scholars, when discussing documentaries, use the term "perpetrator." The audience of these films is not hailed as juror but instead pulled into an unnerving and uncanny encounter. We move out of the juridical mode and into a phenomenological and ontological mode. Furthermore, Ophüls's and Sivan's films underscore what I argue are fundamental epistemological differences between interviews with perpetrators and interviews with victims. The films also serve to highlight a crucial difference between filmed trial testimony and documentary interviews with perpetrators and victims.

Clover asserts that "trials are already movie-like to begin with and movies are already trial-like to begin with."[12] Both *The Specialist* and *The Memory of Justice* speak to the interpenetration of trials and documentary, yet a basic difference between the trial and victim testimony-based documentaries—which makeup the vast majority of interview documentaries and have received the most attention in the critical literature—is that in the trial, victims, if put on the stand, are cross-examined, whereas in interview documentaries they rarely are since that technique, in the context of an interview, would seem to be cruel and out of place.[13] This encouragement of viewer belief in documentary interview testimony (largely because of the lack of cross-examination and adherence to conventional documentary realist codes) has prompted critics like Bill Nichols to be highly critical of the interview mode. One of Nichols's main objections to interview films is that they induce too much credibility in the interviewees (who have been carefully selected for their performance).[14] However, interviews with perpetrators, regardless of the directorial interventions, immediately put pressure on these documentary conventions and frustrate our desire for what Nichols has called "epistephilia." Since credibility is immediately at stake with perpetrators, these perpetrator-centered documentaries destabilize speech and testimony. This destabilization can also encourage us to question conventional documentaries that present testimony as transparent and unmediated.

Importantly, in the courtroom both victims and perpetrators are subject to this destabilization if they are put on the stand because of the structure of cross-examination, but the documentary genre, more than the law, often fixes victim testimony as truth. Interviews with perpetrators, on the other hand, lead us to rethink identification in documentary. Elizabeth Cowie and Brian Winston,[15] among others, assert that interview films encourage our empathy and belief in the witness and ground us in a knowable world. Encounters with perpetrators, on the other hand, offer radically different viewing experiences, as we are not offered a comfortable subject with whom to identify. Interviews with perpetrators often flicker between conveying a sense of the world as knowable and as unknowable. They also shift between inviting viewers to imagine themselves in the interviewee's world and dramatically blocking empathy. Documentary perpetrator testimony challenges the interview mode as one of communication, information, and revelation and as a vehicle for testimonial truth. Without a witness who seems reliable and worthy of empathy, we are no longer grounded in a knowable world. The testimony can flicker between being comfortably familiar and disturbingly strange. Our oscillating feelings of familiarity and estrangement can give rise to a radical skepticism, a feeling that we cannot know others' minds. This skepticism can contaminate the filmic medium as a whole, since film relies on a fundamental disavowal, an "I know what's before me are flickering shadows, moving still images, but still." When skepticism invades the medium, it can give rise to an unsettling sense of uncanniness, which jolts us out of the pleasurable indulgence of disavowal.[16] This sense of discomfort and skepticism forcefully disrupts the pleasing disavowal when there are *two* simultaneous "believe me" requests in filmic testimony—the witnesses and the film's.

Interestingly, Clover sees the fetishistic state of believing and disbelieving simultaneously as "the heart of the jury experience" yet does not remark on the doubling, which occurs with the film viewer as juror. When we as viewers are confronted with haunted perpetrator testimony, as with the group of films I discuss here, we move out of the cognitively satisfying fact-finding and evidence-weighing mode of juridical spectatorship and into the viscerally discomfiting arena of the uncanny. As Austin Sarat suggests, this filmic haunting can double back onto actual trials themselves. Martha Umphrey has described actual trials themselves as "productions of the uncanny," sites of performance[17] where the "real" is often eminently elusive.[18] As the number of perpetrator documentaries mount and Nazi denial testimony is strategically mobilized in both fiction and nonfiction films for various ends, the echoes and images of Nazis in Nuremberg can invade the courtroom, particularly in recent events such as International Criminal Tribunals on Rwanda and the Extraordinary Chambers on the Khmer Rouge.

Upon their release, both *The Memory of Justice* and *The Specialist* generated considerable controversy. Ophüls and Sivan, a generation apart, both wield the cinematic medium to challenge received truths and official history.[19] Both filmmakers investigate testimony as a mode and emphasize their own presence within their films; at the same time, they use the testimonial form to intervene politically and historically. Ophüls's *The Memory of Justice* strategically mobilizes previously unavailable newly synched Nuremberg footage to haunt interviews with Nazis and perpetrators of subsequent atrocities in Algeria and Vietnam. Sivan's *The Specialist* uses different cinematic techniques to achieve a sense of haunting. A filmic adaptation of Hannah Arendt's *Eichmann in Jerusalem: A Report on the Banality of Evil*, *The Specialist* reconfigures the Eichmann trial footage to place the perpetrator, not the survivor-witnesses, at the center of the trial. Haunted by the cinematic past and future, Eichmann's testimony becomes a palimpsest, acquiring multiple layers of uncanniness. Both *The Memory of Justice* and *The Specialist* marshal expressly cinematic devices to interrogate testimony's fundamental statement: "I am here. I was there."

The Holocaust/Testimony/Unicity

To hear the echo of Nazi denial at Nuremberg in the testimony of a witness discussing atrocities committed in Algeria and Vietnam (as in *The Memory of Justice*) and to conjure filmic depictions of Nazis and images of corporate criminals as we watch Eichmann speak (as in *The Specialist*) are both tantamount to diluting the specificity of the testifying "I" and to challenging the absolute uniqueness of the event. When dealing with the Holocaust this can be especially complicated because the singularity and uniqueness of the Holocaust has long been "critical doxa."[20] The Holocaust's singularity has been wrapped into its narrative since the Eichmann trial and the Holocaust narrative's mode sine qua non since the Eichmann trial is testimony. In other words it is *through* survivor testimony that the narrative of the Holocaust, with its uniqueness, is developed and transmitted at the 1961 Adolf Eichmann trial in Jerusalem.[21] The "era of the testimony," in Annette Wieviorka's phrase, was ushered in by the Eichmann trial.[22] Hence, the birth of the Holocaust as we know it and the emergence of the era of testimony were simultaneous and indivisible. While a Holocaust testimonial genre—written memoirs and first-person testimonies—had already been established in literature before the Eichmann trial (Primo Levi's *If This Is a Man* appeared in 1947; the English translation of Elie Wiesel's *Night* met with enormous success in 1960), it is hard to overstate the impact the Eichmann trial had on our current understanding of testimony and the Holocaust. With the explicit goal of establishing a *Holocaust narrative*—a narrative that the 1945 document-centric Nuremberg trials failed to "transmit"[23]—the Eichmann prosecution team chose to call to the stand 111 live witnesses, survivors of the Nazi Judeocide. Crucially, since the Eichmann trial was the first to be filmed in its entirety and televised, countless people in the United States and Europe, where the trial was broadcast, would hear and *view* the survivors' testimonies rather than reading them or only listening to them. The visual medium is thus a pivotal third player in this point of origin for the Holocaust and testimony. And if we find filmed testimony's emergence wrapped into the formation of the Holocaust narrative—what Jeffrey Shandler calls *"cinema verité of due process,"*—we also find the Holocaust wrapped into a film genre's emergence: cinema verité.[24] As Michael Rothberg stresses, Edgar Morin and Jean Rouch's groundbreaking *Chronicle of a Summer* (1960), a work that coined the term cinema verité, was released the same year as the Eichmann trial and contains what is considered the first documentary Holocaust testimony.[25] Claude Lanzmann's groundbreaking 1985 magnum opus, *Shoah*, of course further strengthens the already strong tie between testimony and the Holocaust.

Testimony at the Eichmann trial was elected as the mode of choice for transmitting the narrative of the Holocaust in its uniqueness and singularity. To invite analogies between the Holocaust and other atrocities, to haunt other testimonies with echoes of Nazi denial, is frequently regarded as a means of diminishing the Holocaust's singularity and engaging in facile comparison. However, often overlooked is the paradox embedded in the choice to have testimony as the Holocaust's primary narrative mode. For as we have seen, testimony itself subsists on a tension between singularity and exemplarity, uniqueness and repeatability. Furthermore, the Nuremberg trials and to a lesser extent the Eichmann trial—points of origin for documentary testimony as filmic mode—directly addressed these contradictions in the pretrial planning. *The Memory of Justice* and *The Specialist*, in haunting testimony with other times and places, bring to the fore testimony's complexity, which the law and conventional film often disavow. They draw our attention to the layered temporality and paradoxical nature of testimony—in court, on film—that Derrida has laid bare.

Here and Elsewhere

A twenty-six-second montage culled from footage of the Nuremberg trials opens Marcel Ophüls's *The Memory of Justice*. In rapid succession, we watch five high-ranking Nazi defendants (unidentified by the film) stand and make their statements before the court. "Not guilty," declares the chief of staff of the German High Command, Wilhelm Keitel; "Absolutely not guilty," states chief Nazi philosopher and Reichminister for the Eastern Occupied Territories, Alfred Rosenberg; "Not guilty as charged," proclaims president of the Reichstag, Hermann Göring. "That will be entered as a plea of 'not guilty,'" states a voice from the court. Echoes resound in this less than half-minute sequence, which begins Ophüls's study of Nuremberg and its aftermath. In each Nazi's statement following the first, we hear an echo of the former one. Together, they combine to create a chorus of denials, denials that will echo through the four-and-a-half-hour film about to enfold and reverberate through subsequent perpetrator testimonies in documentaries to come. This Nuremberg Nazi denial sequence points backward in film history as well as forward.

More than two decades earlier, another chilling montage of Nazi denial was marked by rapid editing. Alain Resnais's *Night and Fog* (1956) shows silent footage of statements given by two men in a trial of lower-ranking Nazis. As the men's mouths move, the narrator in voice-over speaks their words: "'I am not responsible' says the kapo; 'I am not responsible,' says the officer. 'I am not responsible.'" Haunted by this unforgettable sequence in *Night and Fog*, the opening moments of *The Memory of Justice* haunt the subsequent interviews in Ophüls's film. *Memory's* Nuremberg "not guilty" sequence is also overlaid with the fictional re-creation of Nazi pleas in Stanley Kramer's *Judgment at Nuremberg*, made the same year as the Eichmann trial, 1961. Moreover, *Memory's* opening minimontage is part of a larger montage, which constitutes the preface, which rapidly moves among three historical moments: the Holocaust, the French occupation of Algeria, and American bombing in Vietnam.

Immediately following the series of Nuremberg Nazi denials, the film cuts to an interview with violinist Yehudi Menuhin, who states, "You see I proceed from the assumption that every human being is guilty, by degree, by association, by being human. If they did it here, it is not that it could not happen in America. It is not that it could not happen elsewhere." As Menuhin speaks the final word of his statement—"elsewhere"—the camera cuts to an image of a young Vietnamese man, who at first appears dead but then slowly moves his head as the voice of NBC reporter Arthur Lord states, "What happened here is an accident of war," then cuts to notorious footage of a Vietnamese woman carrying in her arms her dead child, killed by an American attack. We listen to her agonizing lamentations and untranslated words as Lord continues, "Somebody made a mistake." The devastating footage is immediately followed by a clip from an interview with a former paratrooper in Algeria, Noel Favreliere, who states: "I think, maybe I'm finding excuses for them, but I must say what I think, and I think it was an accident, an accident because it was a little girl. The fact that someone was killed was no accident; that was deliberate. One of our units was approaching a village and a shape, a white shape or rather a bush moved. Then without even knowing what was in the bush, man or animal, the captain gave the order to fire, and out of the bush sprang a small white shape and started to run." While Favreliere speaks about this incident in Algeria, the film cuts back to footage of an atrocity in Vietnam—in this case a naked little girl, her clothes and skin incinerated from napalm, fleeing with a male child from an American attack. Then the film cuts to Anthony Herbert, identified by his title as "the Most Decorated U.S. Soldier in Korea," who, we later learn, was forced to leave the army for his refusal to cover up crimes in Vietnam. The shot goes back to the former paratrooper in Algeria, who closes his narration by saying that the captain jokingly offered to pay one of his "crackshot" soldiers to shoot the small, white running shape. The soldier complied, the little girl died in his arms, and the shooter later went mad.

The closing of *Memory*'s introductory montage includes clips from several interviews that will be continued later in the film. A US Army deserter explains his motives; chief Nuremberg prosecution council, Telford Taylor, states that "most of these things are not done by monsters; they are done by very ordinary people, people very much like you and me. . . . I guess I did think before that Americans had been somewhat immune to these pressures. . . . I guess I still think we try to obtain the higher values . . . and succeed less often than I thought before." A survivor and key Nuremberg witness, Marie-Claude Vaillant-Couturier, discusses the mixture of joy and sorrow that another survivor felt at the birth of her daughter after so many had died. At this point, the title, *The Memory of Justice*, the film credits, and "Part One: Nuremberg and the Germans" appear for the first time, over footage of a bombed-out German city, presumably Nuremberg. The preface has ended and the rest of the film begins.

In this opening salvo, cinema's particular power to generate links between events separated by time and space comes to the fore, its ability to connect here and elsewhere, to superimpose one image over another and in doing so create a "new dimension."[26] The string of Nazi "not guilty" pleas that begins Ophüls's film was plucked from fifteen hours of newly available Nuremberg footage. By choosing to edit them with quick cuts, which recall the sequence from *Night and Fog*, Ophüls immediately overlays the footage with a cinematic heritage distinct from its original context in the Nuremberg courtroom. Temporality is destabilized from *Memory*'s start. This Nazi Nuremberg testimony, which I call the "ground zero" of filmic denial testimony, was filmed in 1945. However, when it appears in Ophüls's *Memory*, it is haunted by Alain Resnais's masterpiece. Furthermore, the denial montage in *Night and Fog* is itself overlaid with other histories, other temporalities circulating in the film. Jean Cayrol's words, spoken by the narrator at *Night and Fog*'s closing, ripple through the Nuremberg denial sequence that opens *The Memory of Justice*. "Who among us," asks *Night and Fog*'s narrator, "is on the lookout from this strange tower to warn us of new executioners? Are their faces really different from our own? Somewhere among us, there are lucky kapos, reinstated officers and unknown informers. . . . We pretend to believe that all this happened only once, at a certain time and in a certain place, and we refuse to look around us. We who do not hear the endless cry." Resnais's narrator urges the viewer not to "pretend to believe that all this happened *only once*, at *a certain time* and in *a certain place*" (emphasis added); remarkably, in the final plea of *Night and Fog*—considered, after the liberation newsreels of the camps, the first Holocaust documentary—viewers are urged to defy the *very* codes of specificity ("on this day, at this time, in this location"), which govern testimony. The Nuremberg sequence in *Memory*, mobilized to haunt war crimes committed in Vietnam and Algeria, carries with it the endless cry of future atrocities resounding from *Night and Fog*. What's more, in a vertiginous mise en abyme, *Memory*, a film that refuses to lend a deaf ear to the endless cry and consistently challenges testimony's unicity, embeds within it references to *Night and Fog*. Resnais's statement about *Night and Fog*—"the whole point was Algeria"[27]—has been subject to numerous interpretations. It is perhaps in this final appeal to the viewer—to recognize ourselves in the faces of the new executioners and to hear the endless cry—that the implied reference to Algeria looms largest. An implied reference in *Night and Fog* to French atrocities in Algeria turns to direct engagement in *The Memory of Justice*. Significantly, *The Memory of Justice*'s final image cites *Night and Fog* as well. Ophüls concludes with a close-up on the now infamous photograph of a Warsaw ghetto boy with his hands up, an image first brought into circulation by its appearance in *Night and Fog*. The director of *The Memory of Justice* thus bookends his four-and-a-half-hour study of Nuremberg and its aftereffects with references to *Night and Fog*.

As I have argued elsewhere, Ophüls, in his most famous film, *The Sorrow and the Pity* (1969), not only echoes but *revises* Resnais's *Night and Fog* by firmly inserting the Judeocide into France's collective memory of the occupation, where *Night and Fog* had all but elided its direct reference.[28] Only after emphasizing the specific targets of the Nazi genocide in *Sorrow* does Ophüls, in his later film, *The Memory of Justice*, seem to respond to *Night and Fog*'s final plea, as if the specificity of the Nazi genocide must first be firmly imprinted in the collective consciousness before Ophüls can feel ready to juxtapose Nazi crimes to other atrocities. Former Nuremberg prosecutor Telford Taylor's statement "most of these things are not done by monsters; they are done by very ordinary people, people very much like you and me" seems to answer the narrator of *Night and Fog*'s question: "Are [the executioners'] faces really different from our own?" Yehudi Menuhin's comment "if they did it here, it is not that it could not happen in America.

It is not that it could not happen elsewhere" pushes back against the denial Resnais's narrator warns us we fall prey to if "we pretend to believe that all this happened only once, at a certain time and in a certain place."

Looking more closely at *Memory*'s preface, we can see how Ophüls uses techniques specific to film in order to prevent spatial and temporal confinement. The visual references for the shifters "here" and "elsewhere" rapidly change in the moments after the Nuremburg footage. As we hear Menuhin say "elsewhere," a cut to a severely injured Vietnamese man transports the viewer from Germany to Vietnam. Quickly, this "elsewhere" becomes "here" when Alfred Lord's American voice says, "What happened here is an accident of war," and then the film cuts to the image of the woman carrying her dead child. Now, the word "accident" is picked up and carried over from American acts of violence in Vietnam to French atrocities in Algeria. The former paratrooper, Noel Favreliere, begins his interview testimony stating that a murder of an Algerian girl by a French squadron was an "accident" only in the sense that the shooter could not see exactly what type of "game" he fired on. Favreliere's words are now attached to a new image. While he describes the Algerian girl as "small white running shape," a cut goes back to Vietnam, where there is horrifying footage of a small naked pale Vietnamese girl, clothes and skin seared from a napalm attack, running down a road with her back to the camera. In a further disturbing displacement, the "crackshot" shooter is now the cameraman, shooter of the film footage, whose point of view we share.

Through montage and sound bridges, the space/time of three distinct atrocities—the Holocaust, Algeria, and Vietnam—have been juxtaposed not, as Ophüls has repeatedly stressed and as his own fight with his producers attests, to create facile equations but to interrogate the efficacy of international law established at Nuremberg.[29] Ophüls also foreshadows through sound the upcoming insertion of the personal—himself and his own family —into the political. Over archival photographs of Jewish concentration camp detainees and Vaillant-Couturier's narration about children born to survivors, we hear lovely but at times hesitant piano music. The music at first seems to be extradiegetic, but its source is revealed a moment later— a young blond girl at a piano. Only after the opening credits, when the viewer is "included" in Ophüls's birthday party, do we learn that the girl is the filmmaker's daughter. The birthday party includes talk about the experiences of the family during the war, of Ophüls as a German Jew forced into exile and of his wife as a German Christian child with "unexceptional" parents. After the preface, the next two hours, which constitute "Part One: Nuremberg and the Germans," leave Algeria and Vietnam largely behind; however, the violence perpetrated in these countries by former Allies hovers over the interviews and trial footage on Nuremberg—specters from the future invited in by the preface.

But there is more to say about this twenty-six-second opening "not guilty" Nuremberg montage. In the first place, how did it get "here"? As Christian Delage traces in *Caught on Camera: Film in the Courtroom from the Nuremberg Trials to the Trials of the Khmer Rouge*, Justice Robert Jackson made a landmark decision before the Nuremberg trials began—he would use film as evidence and he would film parts of the proceedings for newsreels and as an archive. This "double jurisprudence," as Delage calls it, would of course have profound impact on future trials and the documentary genre. While researching for a never-made film, an imagined *Sorrow and the Pity: Part Two*, about postwar Western Europe, Ophüls, as he stated in an interview, "discovered from a French journalist that there were fifteen hours of footage done by the United States Army Signal Corps during the Nuremburg Trials, which had been used in various documentary films since the war but never with synchronized sound and picture."[30] With the release of *The Memory of Justice* in 1976, viewers for the first time heard the voices of the Nazi criminals while viewing their images. What I have called the ground zero of filmic denial testimony makes its first appearance as synched sound film footage in Ophüls's film. Our first exposure to the synched footage however is in the highly edited opening "not guilty" sequence where we are confronted not with the illusion of raw footage but rather with the imprint of three filmmakers—John Ford, who was hired by Jackson to shoot the original Nuremburg footage; Ophüls, who created the quick cuts in the preface; and Resnais, whose sequence in *Night and Fog* was evoked by Ophüls. It is befitting, since the Nuremberg footage was the first to be filmed in a courtroom, that the cinematic medium itself is foregrounded. Furthermore, since the Nuremberg footage will haunt the subsequent interviews about Vietnam and Algeria in *Memory*, the multiple temporalities in this opening footage presage the layered space to come.

A comparison with Christian Delage's 2007 documentary *Nuremberg: The Nazis Facing Their Crimes* highlights the very different ways the Nuremberg footage can be used in film. After the US Holocaust Memorial Museum transferred the twenty-five feet of Nuremberg trial film,[31] Delage drew on the archive to make his film. Billed as the "first documentary to tell the story of the Nuremberg trials from within the courtroom," *Nuremberg*, narrated by Christopher Plummer, spends much of its screen time showing the newly restored trial footage, with a special emphasis on the moments when, for the first time, film was shown as evidence in the courtroom. *Nuremberg* intersperses the trial footage with brief interviews with several people who were directly involved with the trial. The DVD booklet explains: "Director

Christian Delage wanted to reproduce the full impact of the proceedings filmed in Nuremberg, so the commentary complements and accentuates the highlights of the trials, rather than overshadowing them. . . . In terms of technical details, all of the original optical soundtracks of the film were replaced by the better-quality audio recording. . . . Damaged images were restored. Editing helped to give the feeling of continuity throughout the proceedings. For the interviews, only key figures present at the trial were selected in order to avoid reducing the archive to a mere parade of general declarations."[32] In contradistinction to *The Memory of Justice*, made over a quarter century earlier, *Nazis Facing Their Crimes* grounds, or locks, us in the space-time of the trial. Documentary filmic tools—narration, interviews, music, sound/image links, and editing—are marshaled to secure a linear temporality and allow the archival footage to come forward as historical document. While the precedents for international law set at Nuremberg are emphasized, there is no gesture outward, no invitation to make comparisons with subsequent atrocities. Although in his scholarly work on the Nuremberg trials Delage stresses the multiple temporalities introduced by the filming of the trials, his own documentary on Nuremberg submerges these complicated temporalities and instead projects a coherent space-time.

Fungibility

Toward the end of part 1, *The Memory of Justice* shows an excerpt from Chief Robert Jackson's opening speech to the military tribunal on the criminality of the indicted Nazi organizations: "These crimes with which we deal are unprecedented first because of the shocking number of victims; they are even more shocking and unprecedented because of the large number of people who united their efforts to perpetrate them: a thousand little *führers* dictated, a thousand imitation Görings strutted, a thousand Streichers stirred up hate, a thousand Kaltenbrunners tortured and killed, a thousand Speers administered." In this remarkable moment, camera and speech seem to unite in perfect harmony. As he speaks the words "a thousand imitation Görings," the camera pauses on the Nazi minister; with "a thousand Streichers," it holds the former Nazi publisher in a medium shot; with "a thousand Kaltenbrunners," there is a cut to the security chief; and at the sound of the words "a thousand Speers," the camera looks up and the architect appears. The film's focus on each Nazi criminal affixes individual image to word, fastens name to face, but even more powerfully and unusually, it underscores not the image's specificity but its fungibility. As each high-ranking Nazi's face in all its unnerving particularity is shown, we are told that there are a thousand others just like him. Here, in a series of single moments, we observe the delicate negotiation, in which both the law and documentary partake, between the particular and the general, the individual and the representative. It is striking that this gesture toward exchangeability exists in the original Nuremberg trial footage, long before excerpts will be mobilized within *The Memory of Justice* to haunt subsequent atrocities. Even as Göring, Streicher, Kaltenbrunner, and Speer appear and even as the camera encourages us to look closely at the Nazi defendants' particular expressions and movements, we are simultaneously asked to look past the image, to transpose other faces, other bodies into the film footage.

Agonistic Space

> The longer I was confronted by the task I had chosen for myself, the more aware I became that I had no right to substitute myself for trial by law.
>
> —Marcel Ophüls on *The Memory of Justice*, cited in Manchel, "War over Justice," 30

> I told them that I was not a prosecutor and that my movie was not a tribunal.
>
> —Rithy Panh, on *S21* press release, *S21: The Khmer Rouge Killing Machine,* cited in Delage, *Caught on Camera,* 231

The spatial and temporal particularities of testimony—whether on film or in court—are especially pertinent when considering the Nuremberg trials because of Jackson's critical decision to film the trials and show filmic testimony. While the "double jurisprudence" seems to be born from a belief in the power of moving images, the two rulings in fact draw on different attributes of the medium. In a discussion of archival footage and *Night and Fog*, Andrew Hebard observes, "the status of the visual archive as a form of evidence in the war crimes trials was one that stressed the indexical quality of the medium. As evidence, the visual archive allows one to definitively state 'that all this happened only once, at a certain time and in a certain place.'"[33] On the other hand, as Delage stresses, the decision to film the trial—to create a visual archive—means turning an eye (or multiple cameras) to future viewers, opening the possibility of links and connections between this trial and others, shifting somewhat away from unicity and singularity. This tension between fixing testimony and allowing for its association with other times and spaces is, as I have stated, intrinsic to testimony whether mediated through film or not. In *Demeure: Fiction and Testimony*, Jacques Derrida captures testimony's contradictory impulses:

"The singular must be universalizable; this is the testimonial condition."[34] Using language that conjures film though discussing verbal or written testimony, Derrida comments, "The moment one is a witness and the moment one attests, *bears witness*, the instant one gives testimony, there must also be a temporal sequence—sentences, for example—and, above all, these sentences must promise their own repetition and thus their own quasi-technical reproducibility. . . . As soon as the sentence is repeatable, that is, from its origin, the instant it is pronounced . . . it is already instrumentalizable and affected by technology."[35] The landmark decision to allow film into the Nuremberg trials—as evidence and as recorder of the proceedings—relies on a number of contradictory impulses in the law's relation to film, ones that continue to this day. As Jessica Silbey has emphasized, the law at times treats film as transparent (infallible evidence) and at other times as an ideal witness who is not subject to cross-examination.[36]

Bringing film into the courtroom also underscores an attribute that the law, documentary, and testimony all share: a delicate negotiation between the particular and the general, the specific and the representative. As mentioned earlier, this topic is perhaps most fraught when dealing with the Holocaust. As Lawrence Douglas has pointed out, the Nuremberg prosecution, struggling with a new legal category, "crimes against humanity," and a postwar fear of igniting anti-Semitism by focusing on the Judeocide, squeezed the Nazi's targeted extermination of Jews into legal categories of aggressive war and conspiracy.[37] As I will discuss further in this chapter, the Eichmann trial, the first trial in history to be filmed in its entirety, sought to narrate and transmit the specificity of the genocide—the Holocaust—which had been elided in the Nuremberg trial. However, while the Eichmann trial makes the specificity of the Nazi Final Solution its primary goal, it nevertheless explicitly and implicitly shuttles between the particular and general, the individual witness as *stand-in* for a larger group or concept. As David Ben-Gurion, the prime minister of Israel during the Eichmann trial, said, "It is not an individual that is on dock at this historic trial, and not the Nazi regime alone, but anti-Semitism throughout history."[38] Or as Gideon Hausner, chief prosecutor at the Eichmann trial proclaimed, "Rivka Yoselewska symbolizes the entire Jewish people."[39]

The cross-fertilization—and its attendant complications and misunderstandings—between documentary film and the law has been extensively and productively explored by legal and film scholars including Jennifer Mnookin, Jessica Silbey, Bill Nichols, and Kristen Fuhs. Documentaries have famously freed unjustly imprisoned men (Errol Morris's *The Thin Blue Line* and the West Memphis 3 documentaries by Joe Berlinger and Bruce Sinofsky), and "raw" footage has equally famously indicted men (the

George Halliday footage of the Rodney King beating). In different ways, both *The Memory of Justice* and *The Specialist* urge us to consider the movement in documentary from the courtroom to the interview and back again. Interviewers, like prosecutors, often confront their subjects with court testimonies or incriminating documents from their past, and interviewees will also draw on the law and their sentencing or acquittal to expiate themselves. Interview-filmmakers like Ophüls and Rithy Panh, whose extraordinary film *S21* orchestrated harrowing encounters between victims and torturers in the former Khmer Rouge prison, are often compared to prosecutors. At the same time, as their epigraphs attest, both Ophüls and Panh take pains to distinguish themselves and their work from the law; Panh, as Delage points out, refused to offer his footage from *S21* to the Khmer Rouge tribunal, arguing it was a "personal work" not "documentary material."[40] What I would like to look at in *The Memory of Justice* is the opposing ways the law is staged by Nazis and Ophüls. In a number of moments in *The Memory of Justice*, Ophüls confronts former Nazis with documents from Nuremberg. The director also visually interrupts interviews with former Nazis by cutting to Nuremberg trial footage showing the interviewee as defendant. In doing so, *Memory* replicates a strategy used in the trials. At Nuremberg, the Nazis were repeatedly confronted with their cinematic images (often Nazi-made propaganda films); their reactions were carefully studied by trial attendees and written about evocatively by trial reporters. Even the courtroom architecture, as Delage notes, was strategically altered to allow a view of both the Nazis, illuminated by spotlight, and the films.[41] At times in *Memory*, former Nazis refer back to the trials to iterate that "they served their time" or "they were found innocent" as if the legal filmic space and the documentary interview spaces were interchangeable. However, the filmic interview space is a plastic entity not ruled by juridical codes. And in *The Memory of Justice*, the interview space often becomes an agon, with Ophüls and the interviewee pulling in opposing directions, struggling to impose different frames. The Nazi, clinging to an imagined legal frame of closure and a linear temporality, points back to the trials in order to close the door on the past. Ophüls, on the other hand, *reaches* back, *unlocks* the footage from the chain of the past, so that it contaminates and haunts the interview filmic space, thus blurring past, present, and future. By additionally intercutting atrocity footage from Vietnam as the Nazi speaks, Ophüls also charges the United States with violating the very codes they established at Nuremberg.

Although some cultural scholars, notably Shoshana Felman, have drawn sharp distinctions between art and law, arguing that the law is a mode of closure and distance and art is a medium of open temporality and intimacy, *The Memory of Justice* brings this diametrically opposed paradigm into question. For it is not "the law" but the Nazi who attempts to impose a linear temporality onto the interview, one where adjudicated crimes remain in the past and do not haunt the present. Ophüls seizes on the trial footage—created in Nuremberg precisely with an eye to the future—to bring the past into the film's present.

While *Memory* does not explicitly discuss Nuremberg's groundbreaking use of film (as evidence and witness), Ophüls's work addresses the difficult relationship between the Holocaust and film. Paradoxically, although the camp liberation footage, along with Nazi propaganda, was used as filmic evidence against the Nazi war criminals at Nuremberg, these same images left a stain on the moving image, one that has not fully lifted even today. *The Sorrow and the Pity*, as I have argued elsewhere, implicates itself in the history it tells of French collaboration. Ophüls reminds us of film's complicity throughout his work, most obviously through his recontextualizing of archival propaganda newsreels and films, notably scenes from the French production of Viet Harlan's anti-Semitic spectacle *Le Juif Suss*. More subtly Ophüls, in his treatment of the interview, encourages us not to be credulous even as he pursues historical truth through the very same device. In *The Memory of Justice*, Ophüls engages in a more overt self-reflexivity to thwart passive credulity. Film-within-film moments recur in *Memory*, and, though devoid of didacticism, act as miniessays on reading images. Indeed, taken together, we could regard these moments as illustrative examples of the wide range of interpretations filmic testimony and evidence can yield, whether in documentary or in court. At the same time, they also (in some instances in a manner amusingly reminiscent of silent films with narrators) draw our attention to the way that explanatory frames shape the way we view images. With famed Nazi hunter Serge Klarsfeld, Ophüls (and the viewer) watch surreptitious footage of a Nazi industrialist, Ophüls's camera lingers on the projector, before closing in on the image on screen as Klarsfeld narrates "look how he runs!" Disturbingly, after interviewing Albert Speer, infamous Nazi architect, Ophüls is invited to the former Nazi's home to watch home movies of Hitler, Speer and his children, and other Nazis carousing and laughing at an informal gathering. Again, we view a close-up of the projector, and again, the shooter of the film, this time Speer, not Klarsfeld, offers a narration for Ophüls. At another moment while interviewing Speer, Ophüls reflexively interrogates the interview and testimony as devices. Almost midsentence the director stops and asks, "Herr Speer, why do you give these interviews? It must not be very pleasant standing here, with the spotlight on you, forced to again and again answer these questions." Speer responds that his motivation is "to let the world know the truth." But it seems too easy a response. Ricoeur and Derrida both assert that testimony, despite its commitment to the precise instant, gains its veracity through repetition.[42] Perhaps somehow through the repetition, Speer will feel not only exonerated but credible. Ophüls's questions remind us of the mediated and performative quality of testimony whether in court or in a documentary. Even as we look for a possible original revelation in the interviews Speers grants to Ophüls, we are reminded that he has repeated the statements on camera numerous times before and he will probably repeat them again afterward. In a clever subterfuge at one point in *Memory*, the film cuts again to Nuremberg footage of the Nazi war criminals. We watch the footage, now familiar through its reappearance in *Memory*, for a moment. Suddenly, the camera pulls back to reveal a small television screen where we see the same Nuremberg footage we were seeing seconds before now playing on the monitor. Standing in front of it are Ophüls's wife, Regine, and several Yale students. Together they talk about the Nuremberg trials. Regine confesses to a hazy memory of the proceedings when she was living in Germany; the students discuss their perception of the successes and failures of the trial. The Nuremberg footage here has shifted from filmic specter haunting subsequent testimonies to object of scholarly analysis. Mutating from instrument to catch Nazi perpetrators, to recorder of Nazis at "play," to object of analysis, film testimony, in Ophüls's dexterous hands, shows itself to be a quicksilver being that demands, in addition to our embrace, our active attention and at times vigilance.

Sharing Space with *The Specialist*

In *The Memory of Justice*, Ophüls mobilizes the Nazi Nuremberg testimony to haunt the testimonies of subsequent atrocities in Algeria and Vietnam. In *The Specialist*, Eyal Sivan haunts Eichmann's Nazi testimony with subsequent perpetrator testimony. In *The Memory of Justice*, as I have discussed, the trial and interview oppose each other agonistically; in *The Specialist*, the original trial footage is reconfigured to phenomenologically become more like an interview. Part of what makes this Sivan work so uncomfortable to view is that in addition to repositioning Eichmann at the center of the trial, the film also breaks down the boundary between us and the perpetrator. What arises is a spatially and temporally un-delimited filmic space. The film's title, *The Specialist: Portrait of a Modern Criminal*, echoes the title of Hannah Arendt's work *Eichmann in Jerusalem: A Report on the Banality of Evil* of which it is an adaptation, or visualization. *The Specialist* consists exclusively of selections from the original Eichmann trial footage.

In 1960, Eichmann, the notorious Nazi "specialist" on Jewish affairs and later on Jewish transport, was captured by Israeli Mossad agents in Buenos

Aries and brought to Jerusalem. The Israeli government hired renowned American documentarian Leo Hurwitz to shoot the ensuing eighth-month trial that led to Eichmann's death sentence. Some thirty years later, Sivan sifted through the countless hours of trial video and selected and restored footage for his 127-minute compilation documentary.

Whereas the Eichmann trial centered on survivor testimony, with 111 witness-survivors called to the stand, *The Specialist*, like Arendt's essay, re-orients the trial's focus from victim to perpetrator testimony. In doing so, Sivan's film allows us to see for the first time extended portions of Eich-mann's testimony. Indeed, much of *The Specialist's* unnerving quality arises from this intimacy with the perpetrator. At the same time, *The Specialist*, as I will discuss, powerfully and deliberately challenges testimony's "I am here. I was there." Whereas *The Memory of Justice* mobilized the Nurem-berg court footage to haunt subsequent interviews with Nazis and atroci-ties in Vietnam and Algeria, cutting among the 1945 footage, interviews conducted by Ophüls and news and archival footage, *The Specialist* never leaves the courtroom. However, through a variety of filmic techniques—special effects, editing, lighting, sound, and voice manipulation—Sivan's film haunts the Eichmann footage with cinematic and historical associa-tions from the future. The film produces the unsettling effect of forcing us to share space with the perpetrator and at the same time contaminates the Nazi's testimony with other voices, other places, other films.

The Specialist lays bare issues central to testimony, whether in court or in a documentary interview. The film helps us to work toward a different way of seeing documentary interviews and filmed trial testimony. I believe a re-training of the eye and a denaturalizing of the testimonial mode are needed in order for us to see conventional documentary testimony anew. The ques-tions "what do we see?" and "whom do we hear?" are foregrounded from the start in *The Specialist*. The difficulty we have in answering them alerts us to how deceptively simple these questions can be in relation to testimony.

Sivan went to great lengths to restore Hurwitz's grainy videotapes, which were languishing in archives. The exquisite, hyperreal clarity of Sivan's im-ages, which confront us in *The Specialist* depart from the conventions of re-alism that traditionally code "original footage." Sivan's restoration coats the original Eichmann trial footage with a sheeny patina that simultaneously allows us to see more clearly and disturbs our sense of security about what we see: is this, in fact, actual footage or is it partially digitally fabricated? This destabilization is furthered by the doubleness of authorship: are the cuts, zooms, and directorial flourishes Sivan's or Hurwitz's? When Sivan, in the prologue to the film, intercuts a clip of what appears to be the origi-nal, unrestored, grainy videotape, he plays with the notion that there is an authentic "real" image behind the restored one. The imperfect black and white image, a documentary signifier for "reality" and "truth," creates a hierarchy of reality between the restored and original image. In commentary on the film, we learn Sivan has played a trick on us—this "original" scratched and grainy footage was in fact digitally fabricated to look like an archival fragment. However, in a further irony, this seeming dichotomy of constructed and real, as Sivan's film will emphasize, is yet another illusion since the "real" of the Eichmann trial itself consists of construction and performance—an aspect that Sivan, through his manipulation of the footage, is at pains to display. The very hyperclarity of the image undermines the reliability of vision and plays with notions of surface and depth since what lies behind the restored image contains more artifice. *The Specialist* invites us to winnow out the cinematic manipulation in order to grasp some elusive reality even as we know this is an exasperating and fruitless task since the original trial is steeped in performance. We know, but still . . .

The Specialist, in its very first moment—the opening credits—draws attention to issues of performance. Historical figures are introduced as characters in a play or fictional film: "Adolf Eichmann—The Accused; Gideon Hausner—The Attorney General." The blurring of documentary and fiction styles is furthered by the announcement that *The Specialist* is "based on the book *Eichmann in Jerusalem: [A Report on] The Banality of Evil* by Hannah Arendt," as if the film were an adaptation of a novel. As the credits continue, we hear snippets of Eichmann's indictment in male and female voices overlaying each other speaking Hebrew, English, French, and German. We read that the film "was produced entirely from footage recorded in Jerusalem by Leo Hurwitz." A prologue then begins, which compresses many of the central historical and theoretical issues that the main body of the film will confront. The first image we see, in the striking sharpness of the restored videotape, is rows of empty seats. Guards wander around in the empty space. The camera cuts to an empty glass booth, then to a close-up of a stack of books. Then, reflected in the glass of the booth, we see crowds filling the theater/courtroom. Moments later, the three judges enter and take their seats on the enormous stage, which towers over the lawyers and audience. The attorney general, Gideon Hausner, begins his opening speech, which we read in subtitles. But midway through, the subtitles abruptly halt; ominous extradiegetic music suddenly begins to amplify; and Hausner starts to move in slow motion. As the music crescendos and abruptly stops, the image suddenly shifts from hyperreal sharpness to the grainy, scratched "original" video. In place of the intrusive extradiegetic music, we hear the familiar sound of static that often accompanies archival footage. The subtitles return in time for English speakers to read the final moments of the opening speech: "I therefore ask you to sentence this man to death." As the camera pulls back to reveal the courtroom in all its theatrical monumentality, the music recommences. The words "The Specialist" then appear on the screen before an abrupt cut to black. Just as abruptly, an image of Adolf Eichmann appears, staring at and through us in a medium close-up, which begins the main body of the film.[43]

Sivan's gestures toward the theatrical in the opening credits are not facile blurrings of reality and fiction but a foregrounding of the multiple layers of performance embedded in the Eichmann trial itself. Unveiling these layers necessitates consideration of the event of which the Eichmann trial is both a continuation and a reaction against: the 1945 Nuremberg trials. Despite sentencing and putting to death some of the most notorious Nazis and establishing the precedent of "crimes against humanity," the Nuremberg trials failed to communicate to an international public the unimaginably horrific story of the Holocaust. The Eichmann prosecution team and most scholars attributed this failure of transmission to the tribunal's choice to favor stacks of incriminating Nazi documents over survivor testimony. Fearing that survivors could be made to appear "biased" or unreliable under harsh cross-examination, and thus become fodder for Holocaust denial, the prosecution instead presented what they viewed as irrefutable, hard evidence. But, since the trials were stripped of the human component, a number of reporters found them boring, and countless individual stories of unspeakable suffering were lost under the mounds of documents. David Ben-Gurion, the prime minister of Israel at the time of Eichmann's capture, hoped that the trial could be a corrective to the failings of Nuremberg. Shoshana Felman, in *The Juridical Unconscious*, articulates a "crucial difference of perspective" between the two trials. "Whereas the Nuremberg trials view murderous political regimes and their aggressive warfare as the center of the trial, . . . the Eichmann trial views the victims as the center."[44] Ben-Gurion forcefully stated the objectives of the trial: "It is . . . the duty of the State of Israel . . . to see that the whole of this story, in all of its horror, is *fully exposed*. . . . It is not the penalty to be inflicted on the criminal that is the main thing— no penalty can match the magnitude of the offence—but the *full exposure* of the Nazi regime's infamous crimes against our people.[45] He continued, "It is not an individual that is at the dock at this historic trial, and not the Nazi regime alone, but anti-Semitism throughout history. The judges whose business is the law and who may be trusted to adhere to it will judge Eichmann the man for his horrible crimes, but responsible *public opinion* in the world will be judging anti-Semitism" (emphasis added).[46] Ben-Gurion sought to fully "expose" the world to the Nazi atrocities whether they were present at the trial or watching the broadcast. Differing forms of mediation—from carefully selected courtroom architecture to television—would assist in this full exposure. The bifurcated goals of trying Eichmann and *transmitting*, in Shoshana Felman's word, the horror of the Holocaust to the world led to a fundamental shift in the way in which information was communicated. In direct opposition to the document-centric Nuremberg trials, victim testimony became the "evidence" in the courtroom. And television, which had developed in the intervening years between the Nuremberg and the Eichmann trials, became an ideal medium for transmitting the survivor testimonies to the public, a medium that Israel seized upon. Treating the audiovisual medium as one that transparently records reality, the court states that cameras would record the proceedings "far more accurately than the written word."[47] As Jeffrey Shandler cites in *While America Watches: Televising the Holocaust*, the decision to televise the trial provoked considerable controversy and objection from the defense counsel, Robert Servatius, who argued that the witnesses might "play act" for the cameras. Israeli judges ruled in favor of the prosecution and cited jurist Jeremy Bentham on British law regarding publicity and equitable trials: "Where there is no publicity there is no justice. It keeps the judge himself, while trying, under trial. The security of securities is publicity."[48] This legal statement, striking in its own right and all the more so as a means to support the televising of the Eichmann trial, avers that under the gaze of the camera the judge becomes the apotheosis of judges and that the watchful eyes of countless viewers guarantee justice. Rather than "performing" for the cameras, the Eichmann court implied—in a theory that Edgar Morin and Jean Rouch would similarly espouse the same year in their cinema verité work *Chronique d'été* (1960), where the staged encounter between interviewee and interviewer would provoke an authentic truth—the Holocaust survivor witnesses would instead become more authentically themselves under the camera's gaze. As we now know, an alarming extension of Bentham's notions of publicity and justice, of the salutary force of "being watched," gave rise to the Panopticon prison, made infamous by Michel Foucault. Publicity quickly turns to surveillance.

Ben-Gurion's pronouncements of his pedagogic goals for the trial and Israel's decision to broadcast it earned the Eichmann trial the moniker "show trial." Adding another stratum to the layers of performance, authenticity, and spectatorship is the court's ruling that the television cameras be hidden rather than exposing the apparatus as Morin and Rouch insisted in *Chronicle*. Capital Cities Broadcasting Corporation, the American production company hired by the Israeli government to record the trial, set up cameras flanking the tribunal stage. A cordoned off control room housed director Leo Hurwitz and the camera crew, who selected what to record from the continuous feed streaming in on the monitors.[49] The court stated, "We have satisfied ourselves that these machines stand concealed behind netted apertures, and that the persons operating them are likewise concealed; the machines record pictures by the ordinary lighting in the room and make no noise whatsoever. In this respect, i.e., as regards the possibility of a disturbance during the proceedings, we are absolutely satisfied that there will be none."[50]

Thus, a certain disavowal hovered over the proceedings: everyone knew the cameras were there, but their presence was masked. The television crew functioned as an invisible textual voice in the Eichmann trial. Jeffrey Shandler comments: "The decision to conceal the cameras placed the television crew in the posture of a hidden surveillance team. Their absence from the spectacle . . . indicates the court's inability to acknowledge the connection television provided [to external spectators] let alone to recognize the implications of the camera's presence."[51]

Jennifer Mnookin has argued that both documentary and the trial "overtly aspire to the truth" and both "processes by which they are constructed are somehow hidden in plain sight."[52] The Eichmann court literalizes and instantiates this "hiding in plain sight" by concealing the cameras, those very apperatuses they deem most accurate recorders of the proceedings. While Sivan and many other filmmakers working within but challenging the conventions of the documentary medium do not "overtly aspire to the truth" in the same way, their films show up this generic tendency to hide the underlying construction. *The Specialist* exposes at once the construction in *both* documentary and trial processes.

One of the most virulent critics of the trial's performative nature and overall approach was the eminent German Jewish philosopher Hannah Arendt, sent by the *New Yorker* to write weekly dispatches of the momentous event's unfolding. Two years later, she would convert her series of articles into a book, published in the United States in 1963 under the title *Eichmann in Jerusalem: A Report on the Banality of Evil*. The book provoked considerable controversy (and continues to do so to this day) and lost Arendt a number of friends and collegial relationships. It was not translated into Hebrew and made available in Israel for many years. "Whoever planned this auditorium," she wrote, "had a theater in mind, complete with orchestra and gallery, with proscenium and stage, and with side doors for the actors' entrance. Clearly, this courtroom is not a bad place for the show trial David Ben-Gurion, Prime Minister of Israel, had in mind when he decided to have Eichmann kidnapped."[53] Arendt saw the government-hired prosecutor, Gideon Hausner, as the mouthpiece for Israeli prime minister David Ben-Gurion, who is, for Arendt, the "invisible stage manager" of the trial. Felman identifies Arendt's role in the trial as "the critical historian," in the Nietzschean sense—one who judges and condemns the past rather than aggrandizing it in the tradition of the monumental historian.[54] Much of Arendt's withering and incisive critique of the trial involves peeling back the layers to reveal the orchestrations beneath. She aims to fragment the projected image of a unified Israel by emphasizing the fissures in the community. Her emphasis on Jewish collaboration under Nazism remains one of the book's more controversial assertions.[55] Arendt excoriates the victim-centered focus of the trial, which she feels departs from the goal: to try Eichmann. She is particularly unforgiving of Hausner's choice of witnesses, many of whom are prominent Jews who she feels have a prepackaged, well-rehearsed testimony. Ben-Gurion and Hausner, on the other hand, seem to share the belief of many documentarians that a partially staged and scripted reality with twin goals of didacticism and full exposure does not jeopardize truth. Hurwitz's footage of the trial captures the many tiers of performance within it. Shandler emphasizes the impact that filming the trial had on witness selectivity: "One significant effect the televising had on the trial was in Hausner's choice of witnesses." Hausner sought "effective performers, choosing those who seemed 'less tongue-tied' after a 'preliminary sifting' of candidates."[56] Shandler notes that the trial's emphasis on publicity also affected the mode of address in the trial: "The multiple audiences that the trial addressed also challenged the effectiveness of its storytelling. From a legal perspective, the proceedings were directed solely at three men—the Israeli judges who sat on the bench and eventually handed down the verdict. As a public event, however, the trial was generally acknowledged to have a wide array of audiences, both within Israel and around the world. Catering to these various audiences posed a challenge to the prosecution in determining what stories to tell, who should tell them, and how they should be told."[57] Shandler observes that the prosecution addressed themselves more "to its invisible legion of auditors and viewers than to the adjudicating tribunal."[58] Eichmann and the judges on the other hand addressed each other and seemed to tune out the external viewers. Crucially, as *The Specialist* makes abundantly clear, each person in the tribunal speaks from a marked position of power.

Ylana Miller asserts that "although the testimony, as it unfolded, thus contributed to the construction of a collective memory, it remained limited as a historical contribution, among other reasons because of the criteria that determined inclusion as well as exclusion."[59] The selectivity of witnesses has continued to have great bearing on the history narrated in subsequent interview documentaries on the Holocaust. Arendt's criticism of the choice of witnesses and the move away from prosecuting Eichmann brings to the fore the complications in testimony. Sivan, through selective use of footage and editing, in effect, remakes the trial the way that Arendt felt was judicially correct. Like *Eichmann in Jerusalem*, *The Specialist* recenters the trial on Eichmann and away from witness testimony (at points survivors are brutally cut off by Sivan's editing). Sivan also seems to respond to the sleight of hand Arendt perceived in having Hausner be the mouthpiece for Ben-Gurion, "the invisible stage manager," by continually drawing attention to Hausner's directorial presence. Throughout the documentary, Sivan exploits the intrinsic theatricality of the trial through generous use of lighting, camera angles, music, and special effects.

If Arendt's *Eichmann in Jerusalem* is critical history, Sivan's adaptation of the trial report is haunted history. Inflected by Nuremberg Nazi denial footage that preceded the Eichmann trial and by filmic images of Nazis in both fiction and documentary works subsequent to the trial, *The Specialist* is a palimpsest, with Leo Hurwitz and the original trial itself peeking through. In this sense, we can consider it vertical haunting as opposed to *The Memory of Justice*'s horizontal haunting. *Memory* moves back and forth on a horizontal axis between three historical atrocities; *The Specialist* instead layers each moment with multiple temporalities and associations while never showing us anything other than the (manipulated) Eichmann trial footage. Gal Raz also points to a "historical vertigo," which Sivan creates by leaving out crucial dates and information surrounding the trial.[60] Another "historical vertigo" occurs when viewing the Hurwitz footage in *The Specialist*. Sivan's film is haunted by Nazi and Holocaust films, many of which were made well after the Eichmann trial. His subtitle, *Portrait of a Modern Criminal*, also overtly and provocatively contests the singularity of Eichmann's testimony, framing it instead as that of an *example* of a "modern criminal." Furthermore, because Sivan chooses to abstain from voiceover or verbal commentary, one has the vertiginous sensation of accessing historical footage inflected with the history that succeeded it. When Eichmann sits behind his mounds of papers and methodically adjusts his glasses, the image takes on iconic value, marked by the many nonfictional and fictional images of the bureaucratic Nazi that appeared after the Eichmann trial. Similarly, Eichmann's utterances of denial and his willful deferring of responsibility to a higher up circulate amid the countless proclamations of ignorance by Nazis. Furthermore, *The Specialist* itself leaves an imprint on subsequent documentaries; it adds to the echo of Nazi denials, which began at Nuremberg. The Eichmann trial was the first recorded trial with a single Nazi perpetrator, as opposed to the lineup of war criminals at the Nuremberg trials; however, as I have mentioned, the trial's focus on survivor testimony—and the circulation of now iconic moments of filmed survivor testimony at the Eichmann trial—meant that the greatest impact was on victim-survivor testimony not perpetrator testimony. *The Specialist*, in restoring never-before-seen footage and recentering the trial on Eichmann, as Arendt did in her trial report, exposes viewers for the first time to extended Nazi perpetrator testimony. In doing so, it plays its own part as haunter in works that follow it.

The Specialist, in recentering the trial on Eichmann and in its frequent use of close-ups and focus on the perpetrator, turns the trial space into interview-like space. The agonistic tension between the Nazi and Ophüls in *The Memory of Justice* opposes trial and interview space. *The Specialist*, on the other hand, turns the trial footage into an intimate encounter with the perpetrator: we have the same unnerving response watching Eichmann in *The Specialist* as one does watching interviews with perpetrators. Forcing the viewer to share space with the perpetrator, ostentatiously using filmic devices, playing with archival and doctored film footage, encouraging us to conjure other voices of denial (whether Nazis, corporate criminals, or perpetrators of other atrocities), and vertiginously playing with temporality—all of these things alarmingly shake up any comfortable notions we hold about the past, testimony, and truth.

Face-to-Mediated-Face Encounter

Sivan jars us at the start of the film when he cuts to a close-up of Eichmann. But, significantly, we view Eichmann through an encasing, a bulletproof glass structure. This extraordinary structure, which led many reporters at the time to assign the Nazi the sobriquet "The Man in the Glass Box," suggests that Eichmann existed on a different ontological level than the judges, lawyers, and audience present in the courtroom. Sivan exploits the presence of this transparent cage, superimposing reflections on the glass, which gesture toward another screen embedded in the one that appears before the viewer. While Hurwitz's/Sivan's camera allows us imaginary entrance into Eichmann's space, the box simultaneously maintains a separation between "us" and the Nazi criminal. The glass case invites the desire to shatter this wall and break through the web of lies and denial on display but it also disallows too much familiarity. The director's camera—a Metzian all-seeing eye—all the more omnipotent since it is never clear whether the movements are authored by Hurwitz or Sivan, moves through the glass to close-ups of Eichmann's face, a face we scour for some glimpse into the nature of this man. Yet, the camera's ability to pierce the glass, bringing Eichmann's face into close-up, undermines the revelatory potential of film. For Eichmann remains stubbornly impassive and the close-up only exacerbates his unreadability. Sergei Eisenstein avers that physiognomy returned with new force with the invention of cinema. The close-up revealed a "soliloquy of the silent language of the face."[61] Jean Epstein famously panegyrized on Greta Garbo's face, revealed in all its glory through the close-up. And for Walter Benjamin, the last vestige of the withering aura was the photograph of the human face. But Eichmann's face is the antiauratic face—blank, expressionless. He is the faceless bureaucrat.

Jeffrey Shandler cites the preoccupation, during the original Eichmann trial, with Eichmann's face. Because Eichmann had never been seen in photographs or footage, there was a fixation with laying eyes on him. Shandler notes that "the act of seeing Eichmann was so important that looking, watching, and witnessing became central motifs of the trial's press coverage. . . . In their quest for insight into Eichmann—and all that came to embody—through their attention to his body, observers scrutinized his presence for revealing minutiae, his behavior for involuntary betrayals of inner monstrosity."[62] But the curiosity soon turned to frustration as Eichmann's face and body stubbornly refused to reveal any signs that might in some infinitesimal way offer insight into his or the Nazi character. Shandler cites a number of journalists' and writers' reactions at the time. Elie Wiesel articulates the general disbelief of the perpetrator's seemingly "normal" appearance: "He *must* have a different appearance: he *must* display some sort of nervousness, some sort of hatred, some sort of madness, that would mark him as different from other human beings."[63] A reporter for the *Forward* commented that "our eyes never leave him, and he remains for us an impenetrable psychological riddle. . . . Let us at least see one pulsation of an artery behind this heavy mask!" Television close-ups of Eichmann did not "provide the viewer with an advantage over the courtroom spectator, but only emphasized Eichmann's inscrutable ordinariness and made his presence seem that much more remote."[64] A *New York Times* article commented that "Eichmann himself is watched by Mr. Hurwitz with hungry attention, but there is not a whole lot to see on the rather ordinary face. . . . He has been a disappointment."[65]

Part of the disappointment of Eichmann's inscrutability is in the failure of the mimetic medium, the medium that, in Eisenstein's estimation, reincarnated physiognomy, the science of reading the face. What Peter Brooks calls the "the tyranny of transparency" in contemporary society has been particularly linked to confession and revelation in tell-all talk shows and documentaries. Brooks asserts that the "truth *of* the self and *to* the self have become the markers of authenticity, and confession—written or spoken —has come to seem the necessary, though risky, act through which one lays bare one's most intimate self, to know oneself and to make oneself known."[66] Vestiges of the Enlightenment's fervent belief in "power through transparency" and "fear of darkened spaces, of the pall of gloom, which prevents the full visibility of things, men and truths" still cling to the late twentieth and early twenty-first century.[67] While all knew that the enormity of Eichmann's crimes could never be even remotely understood by a revelatory flicker on the face, the desire to see something in the close-up still persisted. Eichmann's unsettling mechanistic recitation of the horrific events he helped orchestrate leads one to search for ruptures that might betray a flicker of conscience. The camera assists us in our search by zooming in on the defendant's hands, his impassive face, his frantic scribbling, but to no avail.[68]

Eichmann's performance of impassivity is however revelatory of the Nazi "character." Performance, denial, and self-deception were parts of the very fibers of the Nazi regime and essential to its power. These layers of performance extended to the sadistic deceit in the extermination camps. The narrator in Resnais's *Night and Fog* describes a death-camp "hospital" where deathly ill "patients" were given paper band aids, as "setup and scenes."[69] Denial found its way into performance. Arendt cites an example of a former Nazi who claimed he was an "inner emigrant"—in other words, while perpetrating the most unimaginable atrocities, he simultaneously experienced an internal removal from his acts. Refusing to actually emigrate he resorted to inner emigration. The former Nazi declared that fear of revealing his hidden resistance led him to strive at all times to be "more Nazi" than the other Nazis. The infusion of performance into the everyday life of the Third Reich adds another layer of performance to the Eichmann trial and complicates Nazi testimony in general. Closely tied to performance was the essential maintenance of self-deception in the Third Reich. Arendt identifies Himmler's insidious spin on the stubborn "animal pity" many SS members inevitably experienced. "Instead of saying: What horrible things I did to the people!, the murderers would be able to say: What horrible things I had to watch in the pursuance of my duties, how heavily the task weighed upon my shoulders!"[70] Himmler, in other words, attempted to change his men from performers to audience members who passively observed the brutal acts even as they enacted them. This stepping outside the self and transformation from performer to observer in the act of perpetrating atrocities turns any after-the-fact testimony into an act of repetition or reenactment.

Although Sivan encourages us to read the verbal and visual registers separately by zooming in on Eichmann's expressions and gestures, the original layer of distance from the event frustrates a hope for revelation in these close-ups. But what appears before us in these moments is another layer of performance and deception present at the inception of the event. Rather than encountering a disjuncture between what is spoken and what we see, there is a disquieting consistency. Amid the registers and layers of theatricality on display in the film, Eichmann reveals a truth in performance by replaying his original role as audience to his own actions.

"The face is the evidence that makes evidence possible," Emmanuel Levinas gnomically pronounced. The "face," for Levinas, is an ineffable, unrepresentable figure that comes from outside and instills us with ethics. It commands us not to kill, but its precariousness incites a violence in us, and it is this struggle that humanizes us. The face depends on an other, who remains radically Other. Nazism attempted to annihilate this other and embraced an extreme narcissism. In *The Mass Ornament*, Siegfried Kracauer presciently asserts that, under fascism, "the masses are forced . . . to gaze at themselves everywhere . . . made aware of themselves in the form of an aesthetically seductive ornament."[71] Arendt asserts that Eichmann lacked, above all, empathy. His "inability to speak was closely connected with an inability to *think*, namely, to think from the standpoint of somebody else."[72] Eichmann's face then is the antithesis of the Levinas face, which relies on the other.

Particularly frustrating to the viewer's (and presumably the judges') ability to read and glean some kind of knowledge from Eichmann's testimony is that he neither confesses nor fully denies his culpability. Arendt emphasizes that Eichmann does not proclaim his innocence but instead makes the mysterious assertion that "he was not guilty in the sense of indictment."[73] Throughout the trial, he neither consistently lies nor consistently tells the truth. Therefore, although *The Specialist* cuts out or interrupts almost all survivor testimony to center the film on Eichmann, we cannot come away with knowledge about the defendant in the traditional sense.

Throughout the film, viewers of *The Specialist*, while unnerved by the encounter with the perpetrator, also feel themselves safely distanced from the glass enclosure that surrounds Eichmann. At one point in the trial, Eichmann unnervingly breaks the proscenium of the glass box and steps out into the main area of the courtroom. Sivan punctuates this moment with ominous music, which further exacerbates our discomfort. Watching Eichmann step out of the glass box and mingle with the tribunal provokes an unnerving closeness between this man and us. The opening of the glass cage partakes of radical film aesthetics by breaking the boundary between viewer and projected spectacle. The moment is particularly disorienting because we watch, in slow motion and to the sound of otherworldly music, Eichmann trace out the annexed Nazi territories on an imposing map. Maps in classic documentaries are traditional signifiers of facts and history, grounding

us in a knowable world. Elizabeth Cowie identifies the coexistence and interrelation of two desires for reality that the documentary film provokes,
"on the one hand . . . a reality as reviewable for analysis . . . a world of evidence confirmed through observation and logical interpretation" and on the
other "the desire for the real not as knowledge but as image, as spectacle."[74]
In this moment reality as spectacle collides with reality as reviewable for an
analysis. Eichmann, suddenly one ontological level closer to us, calmly and
methodically delineating with a pointer which areas of Europe were annexed by the Nazis conveys "facts" and yet the actions are thought defying.

Sivan's film also lays bare issues of address and power, which are often
submerged in filmic testimony. The courtroom design clearly and hierarchically demarcates the position of the participants. The three judges tower
over the auditorium, the prosecutor and defense attorney flank the "stage";
Eichmann resides in his box in the peripheral foreground; and the audience
sits behind. The prosecutor addresses the defendant as a single-minded
monster and viewers may watch Eichmann in these moments through a
similar lens. However, when the judges cross a seemingly impassable divide
to ask Eichmann their own questions, they attempt to get some inkling of
an understanding.

Sivan's manipulation of the Eichmann trial footage unveils links between power, speaking, and modes of address that are collapsed in the traditional documentary interview. It is as if the many subterranean mechanisms
of power, language, and enunciation in the ostensibly two-person documentary have become instantiated in the many people in the courtroom.[75]

At the end of a discussion on testimony with Bernard Stiegler, Derrida
makes a provocative statement: "The unconscious, the taking into account
of a topic of ipseity, the differentiation or the scission of agencies, the fact
that the ego is only one agency or can be a dissociated agency, all of this . . .
remains massively ignored by juridical discourse. . . . .Better-or worse-this
discourse is built on disavowal. . . . And in the long, very long, term this
situation will have to change. When it does, we will inhabit, our inheri-
tors will inhabit a complete different world. But it's beginning, slowly."[76]
Whether the law cannot account for these schisms in the "I," these challenges to testimonial's unicity, its "I am here. I was there." is hard to determine. But in one astounding moment in the Eichmann trial, presiding
judge Landau states, "I will permit myself to depart from the habitual procedure to abandon Hebrew to address the accused in his own language."
Looking directly at Eichmann, he continues in German "Did you ever experience a conflict, what one would call a conflict between your duty and
your conscience?" Eichmann's response articulates the textbook state of denial: "One could call it a state of being split, a case in splitting where one

could flee from one side to the other. . . . It was necessary to abandon one's conscience." Landau listens intently.

Coda: Haunting 2.0, Simultaneous Atrocities

In 2012, filmmaker Eyal Sivan launched *Montage Interdit* (*Forbidden Montage*), which he describes as a "web-based documentary practice [in progress]."[77] The web project places disparate but often interlocking histories together on one screen, reifying what has existed, as I have been arguing, in inchoate form—as haunting—throughout the history of the documentary interview film. The technology of new media enables Sivan to create an interactive website with cross-referenced footage and interviews such that violent histories spanning from the distant past to the present, separated by time and space, become literally linked with the click of a user's hand. We ourselves can create montages, often "forbidden" ones, by clicking within an interview, interrupting its unfolding to cut to another clip or interview. Sivan's web project allows us to see multiple histories together on one plane.

The title of Sivan's project refers to the 1956 debate between André Bazin and Jean-Luc Godard, which appeared in the pages of *Cahiers du Cinema*. Bazin, in his essay "Montage Interdit," argues for the long take over editing, whereas in "Montage, mon beau souci" ("Montage, my beautiful care"), Godard maintains that montage is the essence of cinema. Sivan's project extracts numerous clips from Godard's oeuvre and embeds multiple interviews with filmmakers and scholars, who discuss the work. Sivan's project is visually vertiginous on first encounter; we are confronted with a screen that looks like multiple horizontally arranged film strips. Scattered here and there over some of the strips are white-boxed uppercase words: ALGERIA, ANTISEMITISM, ARAB, AFRICA, CHRISTIANITY, GENOCIDE, FASCISM, ISLAM-MUSULMAN, ISRAEL, JLG CONTROVERSY, MONTAGE/IMAGE, NATIVE AMERICAN, NAZISM, OCCIDENT/WEST, PALESTINE, TERROR, *SHOA/NAKBA*. All refer to issues taken on in Godard's films. Clicking on a frame near one of the words will activate an interview, usually conducted by Sivan over Skype, on the topic. With a click, the selected frame enlarges and slowly slides across the screen as the interview proceeds. Clicking other nearby frames will bring up related interviews or clips from relevant films. Multiple clicks by the user will give rise to two or more interviews playing simultaneously in adjacent moving squares accompanied by more white-boxed titles. It becomes clear that there are numerous combinations of clips and interviews and numerous mini "documentaries" the user can generate from the material. While one interview on a particular topic may focus our gaze, the words in capital letters on various historical and theoretical issues and the still images ready to come alive with a click never leave our purview. It is in this way that Sivan (through Godard) powerfully realizes the "montage interdit"—visually placing discrete but related historical traumas adjacent to one another, often encouraging forbidden comparisons such as *Shoa/ Nakba*, Algeria and anti-Semitism, Islam-*Musulman*. Although the interviews and clips themselves move from left to right across the screen, the visual space creates connections and linkages vertically, horizontally, diagonally, and all across the site. Rather than ghostly echoes haunting a filmic interview space, here we create interrelations between historical events and view testimony of disparate but interconnected atrocities simultaneously.

Notes

1. Haunting has been discussed by a number of scholars, each with a particular understanding of the term. Jacques Derrida, in *Specters of Marx: The State of Debt, the Work of Mourning and the New International,* trans. Peggy Kamuf (New York: Routledge, 1994), draws on Marx's statement that "a specter is haunting Europe, a specter of communism," and introduces the neologism "hauntology." While Marx sees Communism's eventual realization as means for putting the ghosts to rest, for Derrida, haunting is an essential part of justice. In *Echographies of Television,* Derrida states "as soon as one calls for the disappearance of ghosts, one deprives oneself of the very thing that constitutes the revolutionary movement itself, that is to say, the appeal to justice, what I call 'messianicity' . . . which is a ghostly business, which must carry beyond the synchrony of living presents." (Jacques Derrida and Bernard Stiegler, *Echographies of Television,* Trans. Jennifer Bajorek. Cambridge, UK: Polity Press, 2007, 128). In *Ghostly Matters,* Avery Gordon argues that the past always haunts the present and we ignore our societies' ghosts at our own risk. (Avery Gordon, *Ghostly Matters: Haunting and the Sociological Imagination.* Minneapolis: University of Minnesota Press, 2008). Of course, any consideration of haunting can find its way back, however circuitously, to Sigmund Freud's work on the uncanny and the return of the repressed. My use of *haunting* is both indebted to the many previous scholars' work on the topic and distinct in the way I am understanding it in documentary.

2. Paul Ricoeur, *Memory, History, Forgetting,* trans. Kathleen Blamey and David Pellauer (Chicago: University of Chicago, 2004), 163–64.

3. Paul Celan, cited in Shoshana Felman and Dori Laub, eds. *Testimony: Crisis of Witnessing in Literature, Psychoanalysis and History* (New York: Routledge, 1991), 3.

4. Maurice Blanchot and Jacques Derrida, *The Instant of My Death/Demeure: Fiction and Testimony*, trans. Elizabeth Rottenberg (Stanford, CA: Stanford University Press, 2000), 30.

5. See ibid., 41.

6. Carol Clover, "Law and the Order of Popular Culture," in *Law in the Domains of Popular Culture*, ed. Austin Sarat and Thomas R. Kearns (Ann Arbor: University of Michigan Press, 1998).

7. Ibid., 109.

8. Ibid.

9. Ibid., 116–17.

10. Ibid., 127.

11. Martha Umphrey, comment made at "Trial Films on Trial" conference held at Amherst College, November 14–15, 2014.

12. Clover, "Law and Order," 108.

13. As Ticien Sassoubre pointed out at the Amherst College "Trial Films on Trial" conference, victim impact statements can be presented in court at the time of ruling to avoid placing the victim on the stand and subjecting them to potentially brutal cross-examination.

14. See Bill Nichols, "The Voice of Documentary," *Film Quarterly*, vol. 36 no. 3 (Spring 1983): 17–30.

15. See Elizabeth Cowie, "The Spectacle of Actuality," in *Collecting Visible Evidence*, ed. Jane M. Gaines and Michael Renov (Minneapolis: University of Minnesota Press, 1999), and Brian Winston, "The Tradition of the Victim in Griersonian Documentary," in *New Challenges for Documentary*, ed. Alan Rosenthal (Berkeley: University of California Press, 1988).

16. Christian Metz discusses films' fetishistic disavowal in *The Imaginary Signifier: Psychoanalysis and the Cinema*, trans. Celia Britton, Annwyl Williams, Ben Brewster, and Alfred Guzzetti (Bloomington: Indiana University Press, 1977).

17. Jennifer Mnookin notes in "Reproducing a Trial: Evidence and Its Assessment in Paradise Lost" that the fact that "trials, too, are 'productions'—elaborate staged dramas whose relation to the real is very far from indexical—almost goes without saying." In *Law on the Screen*, ed. Austin Sarat, Lawrence Douglas, and Martha Merrill Umphrey (Stanford, CA: Stanford University Press, 2005), 157.

18. Austin Sarat and Martha Umphrey, comments made at the "Trial Films on Trial" conference.

19. Not surprisingly, Sivan cites Ophüls as an inspiration for his work. The directors share an interest in perpetrator testimony and a willingness to ask hard questions of history and contemporary political situations. In 2013, Sivan and Ophüls appeared at a number of film festivals and events together to discuss their work and screen *The Memory of Justice*. Their conversation at the Courtisane du Gand festival was filmed and is available on Vimeo, https://vimeo.com/65969200.

20. Michael Rothberg, Debarati Sanyal, and Max Silverman, "Editor's Note," in *Noueds de mémoire, Yale French Studies*, January 2011, 118–119.

21. Photographs taken by the Allies and film footage of the camps at their liberation circulated in 1945, exposing much of the Western world for the first time to the Nazi atrocities. However, at the Nuremberg trial the specificity of the Judeocide was not emphasized for fear it could ignite more anti-Semitism. Instead the prosecution focused on war crimes, conspiracy, and the new legal category "crimes against humanity." It was an overt goal of the Eichmann trial to establish and transmit the story of the Holocaust—the Judeocide—as a narrative separate from war crimes because the Nuremberg trials had failed to do so.

22. See Annette Wieviorka, *The Era of the Witness*, trans. Jared Stark (Ithaca, NY: Cornell University Press, 2006).

23. Shoshana Felman identifies the inability to *transmit* the story of the Holocaust as one of the Nuremberg trials' failings in *The Juridical Unconscious: Trials and Traumas in the Twentieth Century* (Cambridge, MA: Harvard University Press, 2002), 112.

24. Cited in Michael Rothberg, *Multidirectional Memory: Remembering the Holocaust in the Age of Decolonization* (Stanford, CA: Stanford University Press, 2009), chapter 6, Kindle DX, retrieved from www.amazon.com.

25. Ibid.

26. See Sergei Eisenstein, *Film Form: Essays in Film Theory*, trans. Jay Leyda (New York: Harcourt Press, 1969), 4, on filmic mechanics and "new, higher dimensions."

27. Sandy Flitterman-Lewis, "Documenting the Ineffable: Terror and Memory in Alain Resnais's *Night and Fog*," in *Documenting the Documentary*, ed. Barry Keith Grant and Jeannette Sloniowski (Detroit, MI: Wayne State University Press, 1998). 215fn11.

28. Numerous scholars have discussed *Night and Fog*'s lack of specifying the Jews as the Nazi's genocidal target, many contextualizing this surprising omission in the postwar France context and pointing out that the Holocaust as a narrative was only formed in the 1961 Adolf Eichmann trial. See Debarti Sanyal's essay on *Night and Fog*'s lack of specificity and use of allegory in "Auschwitz as Allegory in *Night and Fog*" in *Concentrationary Cinema: Aesthetics as Political Resistance in Alain Resnais's "Night and Fog,"* ed. Griselda Pollock and Max Silverman (New York: Berghahn Books, 2011).

29. See for example the contentious exchange between Ophüls and Harold Rosenberg in "*The Memory of Justice*: An Exchange," in *New York Review of Books*, March 17, 1977, editorial page.

30. Quoted in Frank Manchel, "A War over Justice: An Interview with Marcel Ophüls," *Literature/Film Quarterly* 6, no. 1 (Winter 1978): 27.

31. As Christian Delage points out in the booklet accompanying his docu-

mentary *Nuremberg: The Nazis Facing Their Crimes*, there are in fact twenty-five feet of Nuremberg trial film, which were transferred to video by the US Holocaust Memorial Museum. It seems likely that when Ophüls was making *The Memory of Justice* the footage had not all been compiled in one place.

32. Christian Delage, dir., *Nuremberg: The Nazis Facing Their Crimes* (Santa Monica: Lions Gate, 2007), DVD.

33. Andrew Hebard, "Disruptive Histories: Towards a Radical Politics of Remembrance in Alain Resnais's *Night and Fog*," in Pollock and Silverman, *Concentrationary Cinema*.

34. Jacque Derrida, *Demeure: Fiction and Testimony*, trans. Elizabeth Rottenberg (Stanford, CA: Stanford University Press, 2000), 41.

35. Ibid., 70.

36. See Jessica Silbey, "Judges as Film Critics: New Approaches to Filmic Evidence," *University of Michigan Journal of Law Reform* 37 (2004); "Videotaped Confessions and the Genre of Documentary," *Fordham Intellectual Property, Media and Entertainment Law Journal* 16 (2006); "Cross-Examining Film," *University of Maryland Law Journal Race, Relations, Gender and Class* 8 (2008) (symposium issue); "Evidence Verité and the Law of Film," *Cardozo Law Review* 31 no.4 (2010).

37. Lawrence Douglas, *The Memory of Judgment: Making Law and History in the Trials of the Holocaust* (New Haven, CT: Yale University Press, 2001), 55.

38. Cited in Felman, *Juridical Unconscious*, 120.

39. Douglas, *Memory of Judgment*, 121.

40. Christian Delage, *Caught on Camera: Film in the Courtroom from the Nuremberg Trials to the Trials of the Khmer Rouge*, trans. Ralph Schoolcraft and Mary Byrd Kelly (Philadelphia: University of Pennsylvania Press, 2013), 233.

41. Ibid., 112.

42. See Derrida, *Demeure*, and Ricoeur, *Memory, History, Forgetting*.

43. Eyal Sivan, dir., *The Specialist: Portrait of a Modern Criminal* (1999; New York: Kino International, 2002), DVD.

44. Felman, *Juridical Unconscious*, 112.

45. David Ben-Gurion, *Israel: A Personal History*, trans. Nechemia Meyers and Uzy Nystar (New York: Funk and Wangalls, 1971), 575; cited in Felman, *Juridical Unconscious*, 218n24.

46. Ben-Gurion, 559; cited in Felman, *Juridical Unconscious*, 221n41.

47. Cited in Delage, *Caught on Camera*, 170.

48. Cited in Horace Sutton, "Eichmann Goes on Trial: The Charged Air," *Saturday Review* 44, no. 14 (8 April 1961): 60; article cited in Jeffrey Shandler, *While America Watches: Televising the Holocaust* (Oxford: Oxford University Press, 1999), 277n21.

49. Shandler, *While America Watches*, 106.

50. Cited in Delage, *Caught on Camera*, 169.

51. Shandler, *While America Watches*, 131.

52. Mnookin, "Reproducing a Trial," 157.

53. Hannah Arendt, *Eichmann in Jerusalem: A Report on the Banality of Evil* (New York: Penguin Books, 1977), 4.

54. Felman, *Juridical Unconscious*, 111.

55. The controversy caused by Arendt's writing led to attempts to mute her voice. Ylana N. Miller, in "Creating Unity through History: The Eichmann Trial as Transition," *Journal of Modern Jewish Studies* 1, no. 2 (2002), cites an organized attempt by the Israeli government to discredit and suppress her work. The need for a united history, Miller argues, superseded the allowance of polyphony.

56. Shandler, *While America Watches*, 127.

57. Ibid., 130.

58. Ibid., 132.

59. Miller, "Creating Unity through History," 143.

60. Gal Raz, "Actuality on Banality: Eyal Sivan's *The Specialist* in Context," *Shofar: An Interdisciplinary Journal of Jewish Studies* 24, no. 1 (Fall 2005): 8.

61. Sergei Eisenstein, *Film Form,* 127; cited in Michael Taussig, *Defacement: Public Secrecy and the Labor of the Negative* (Stanford, CA: Stanford University Press, 1999), 23.

62. Shandler, *While America Watches,* 107.

63. Elie Wiesel, *The Jewish Daily Forward*, April 12, 1961, 1, cited in ibid., 109.

64. Shandler, *While America Watches*, 111.

65. Lawrence Fellows, "TV Makes Its Israeli Debut with a Tragedy," *New York Times,* July 2, 1961, sec.2, p.9,; cited in ibid., 106.

66. Ibid, 9.

67. Thomas R. Flynn, "Foucault and the Eclipse of Vision," in *Modernity and the Hegemony of Vision*, ed. David Michael Levin (Berkeley: University of California, 1992), 275.

68. The frustration of contemporary viewers of the Eichmann trial shows up the failure of the camera to give us clues, offer some inkling of an answer. The viewers hope the camera will act as it does within the trial genre's exemplar *Basic Instinct*, where, as Clover describes, the cinematography, in becoming "increasingly polygraphic in its close-up probe of faces—searching the for signs of lies and truth," often does gratify our desire for some answer or clue, and in doing so reaffirms our faith in the camera's revelatory powers. Clover, "Law and Order," 125.

69. Jay Cantor, "Death and the Image," in *Beyond Document: Essays on Nonfiction*, ed. Charles Warren (Hanover, NH: Wesleyan University Press, 1996), 27.

70. Arendt, *Eichmann in Jerusalem*, 106.

71. Siegfried Kracauer, "The Mass Ornament," in *Critical Theory and Society: A Reader*, ed. Stephen Bronner (New York: Routledge, 1989), 316.

72. Arendt, *Eichmann in Jerusalem*, 42.

73. Ibid., 21.

74. Cowie, "Spectacle of Actuality," 19.

75. Shoshana Felman argues in *The Juridical Unconscious* that a trial needs closure and "art" is what refuses to be closed. "A trial is presumed to be a search for truth, but technically, it is a search for a decision and thus, in essence, it seeks not simply truth but a finality: a force of resolution" (54–55). Literature "wrenches apart what was precisely covered over . . . by the legal trial" (95). Citing Freud's notion that "historical events are inherently dual in nature and truly register in history only through the gap of the traumatic repetition"(62), Felman emphasizes that in order for a trial to be a great historical event it must be "cross-legal," or refer to another trial. She asserts the ocularcentric aspect of the trial: "The rules of evidence . . . are . . . based on seeing. The strongest proof admitted by the court is proof corroborated by the eye; the most authoritative testimony in the courtroom the eyewitness. Every trial, therefore, by its very nature as a trial, is contingent on the act of seeing" (81). Pointing to the Eichmann trial and Claude Lanzmann's 1980 film *Shoah*, Felman stresses the interlink between the trial and the work of art. Since law, in Felman's estimation, distances us and art brings us closer, the Holocaust becomes accessible, "*precisely in this slippage. But it is also in this space of slippage that its full grasp continues to elude us*" (107). Citing Paul Valery, she argues that repetition is necessary when an act has not been comprehended.

While Felman points to a crucial dialectic and contact between the trial and the artwork, she does not attend to the particularly vexed role that documentary plays in this drift from trial to artwork and back again. She also elides all but entirely a consideration of repetition of denial on the part of the perpetrator, centering instead on the victim and the abyss that trauma reveals.

76. Derrida and Stiegler, *Echographies*, 98–99.

77. See http://montageinterdit.net/.

6
The Appearance of Truth
Juridical Reception and Photographic Evidence in *Standard Operating Procedure*

Jennifer Petersen

There's this crazy thinking that style guarantees truth. You go out with a hand-held camera, use available light, and somehow the truth emerges.

The only thing I do that's different from other people is I call attention to the fact that I have a point of view. I call attention to the fact that how we see, what we see, is constructed, and that looking at how it's constructed is often a useful exercise.

I think people want the appearance of truth. They don't necessarily want the truth.

—Errol Morris quoted in Anderson, "Of Crime and Perception"

Within military court proceedings, the photo is considered evidence from within a frame of potential or actual legal proceedings is already framed within the discourse of law and of truth. The photo presupposes a photographer, and that person is never shown in the frame. The question of guilt has been juridically restricted to those who committed such actions or who were responsible for those who did commit those actions. And these prosecutions have been limited to the most well-publicized cases.

—Judith Butler, "Torture and the Ethics of Photography"

Errol Morris's documentary on the Abu Ghraib scandal, *Standard Operating Procedure*, is not a typical trial film. It does not depict a trial, though many of the people involved were tried and are repeating testimony that they may have given in court. It does, however, draw on the trial form identified by Clover, and it has something to show us about that form. The film and its critical reception highlight the disciplinarity of the trial form—in particular, the way it directs and circumscribes the use of images as evidence. Analyzing the film within the context of its ambivalent critical reception suggests that what many viewers wanted from this documentary, if not all documentaries, was remarkably similar to what we want from trials: to know what happened, who was culpable, how to allocate guilt and innocence. Despite Morris's attempts to use photographic images otherwise, audiences wanted them to stand as evidence. That *Standard Operating Procedure* attempts to evade these expectations is its central distinction and its perversity.

The film focuses on the photographs at the heart of the Abu Ghraib scandal, in which pictures of soldiers abusing and humiliating Iraqi detainees surfaced in the news (specifically in reports on *60 Minutes* on April 28, 2004, and in the *New Yorker* on April 30, 2004). While allegations of prisoner abuse had been made by Amnesty International and the Associated Press several times in the previous year, the abuse did not become a major story, and scandal, until the circulation of the photographs. Images of two soldiers, Specialist Lynndie England, holding a leash attached to an Iraqi prisoner lying on the ground, halfway out of his cell, and Specialist Charles Graner, mounted atop a pyramid of naked Iraqi men, circulated as evidence of sexualized humiliation and torture at the Abu Ghraib detention center and seemed to expose the corruption and abuses taking place within the military and the invasion.

Rather than investigating how the abuses came to take place or whether higher-ups might take the blame, Morris made a somewhat open-ended movie about the role of photography in the scandal.[1] In doing so, the film perversely refuses the epistephilia that social problem documentaries usually feed: the desire to know, to leave the film with a sense of having gained, or mastered, some set of knowledge.[2] In refusing this desire, the film denies audiences the closure, moral, or perspective that we so often desire from documentaries.[3] It does not offer insight into where culpability for the abuse lies. It does not give a clear overview of the abusive events at Abu Ghraib, tie the abuse to the timeline of the war in Iraq, or provide much information on the worse abuses (both not caught on camera and those in photographs that were not released to the public). It does not even leave a strong statement about the role or power of photographs but rather attempts to open questions about photographs as evidence. Querying the status of photographs as proof in documentary is a difficult tactic, given that the form is constructed around visual evidence. Morris, in effect, highlights the incompleteness of the very building blocks of documentary through the use of these same blocks.[4]

The film parallels discussions of the partiality and fallibility of photographs as evidence that have taken place in documentary studies, visual culture, and some critical legal scholarship. Yet, it does so in a medium where this message is much harder to convey. In attempting to make arguments that others have more and less successfully made in written tracts in the form of a documentary film, Morris ends up with a conflict between content and form. He attempts to critique the idea of photographic evidence within a form that is built on the assertion of photographic evidence as privileged proof. The film in a sense failed its critical mission. This failure was due to the fundamental conflict and to the ways that audience expectations—modes of reception—limit what can be said, or more properly, understood.

Documentaries and the Trial Form

In the essay around which this book is convened, Carol Clover argues that films and trials are united by their orientation toward a particular mode of reception—a judging audience testing out different hypotheses. Each asks its audience members to spin out possible scenarios in their minds, arranging pieces of potential evidence (e.g., close-ups of facial expressions, implied causal relations).[5] The mode of reception for both trials and films is organized around a set of puzzles or cognitive activities aimed at providing narrative and epistemological coherence. Yet, as Janet Staiger points out, such cognitively driven, problem-solving activity is only one of many modes of film reception. It is, however, the one that is most often assumed as universal within film theory (i.e., that much of film theory generalizes from a type of reception most closely attuned to the detective film).[6]

While this mode of reception may not be the only or most important one in attempting to understand the interpretation or effects of film as a whole, it *is* a dominant one in documentary. One of the key things that determine the boundaries of documentary and other films is audience expectations.[7] When films are classified as documentary, audiences approach them with a specific set of expectations and reading strategies. They understand that the film is supposed to point to the shared historical world[8] and are invited to test out what they see against experiences in that (shared) historical world.[9] This understanding is part of the inclusion of documentary among what Bill Nichols terms "discourses of sobriety," such as economics, politics, law, and science (such discourses are lexicons that are culturally understood to have instrumental power or the ability to intervene in the world).[10] As texts that bear the claim and responsibility to represent and, per the tradition of social documentaries to intervene in the world (specifically, to intervene in policy decisions, social conditions, and cultural attitudes), documentaries consistently call upon audiences to attend to their content and claims, doing the particular work of testing and judging that

Clover identifies with the trial form. In particular, documentaries' use of film footage as evidence hails the audience as members of a jury, providing viewers with various different scenarios whose truth must be tested: the match between what is heard and what is said probed, the authenticity or believability of the images tested.

Given this consonance between documentary and the trial as a narrative form (or more pointedly, as a mode of reception), it is not surprising that many documentaries have made this similarity explicit. A number of recent documentaries have taken the courtroom as a model for how they present and narrate the events. In this, I mean to include not only documentaries organized around trials (e.g., *Paradise Lost*) but also those organized as an array of conflicting testimony presented to the audience, which is positioned as jury. In films like *The Thin Blue Line, Capturing the Friedmans,* and (arguably) *The Act of Killing*,[11] the trial operates as the organizing mode of discourse, in the way that the poem, the journalistic report, and the diary do for other genres and subgenres of documentary (poetic, expository, performative).[12] For documentarians interested in using the instrumental potential of nonfiction film, borrowing from the law makes sense. And the most dramaturgical aspect of the law is the trial. These films not only involve the audience in making sense of the evidence presented before them through the spinning out of different hypothetical narratives but in fact are expressly organized around them: testing each narrative against common sense and the other testimony and evidence supplied in the film, testing out theories of guilt and innocence.

Morris employs a juridical, even forensic voice. In particular, *Standard Operating Procedure* is composed of testimonial-style interviews, which the audience is invited to evaluate. Whereas in earlier films like *Thin Blue Line* and *The Fog of War*, this invitation enabled a judgment (of guilt or innocence), *Standard Operating Procedure* in many ways frustrates desires to reach a verdict. What audiences were invited to judge was less the guilt or innocence of the low-level military personnel on display in the film and more the role of the camera in the scandal. The testimony of the personnel called less for judgment and more for identification, a point that disturbed many commentators.

As the critical reception of *Standard Operating Procedure* attests, modes of reception can be disciplinary. They focus our expectations and attention on some aspects of what we view over others, priming us as to what should be salient and defining the boundaries of permissible, or intelligible, discourse. When statements do not fit within the parameters of expectation, they fail, either not achieving illocutionary force or simply not making sense. Given this, what can the critical reception of *Standard Operating*

Procedure tell us about the circumscriptions of Clover's juridical mode of reception? Are there limits on what one can say to an audience that experiences itself as a judging one?

Standard Operating Procedure on Trial

Morris's concern is for the ability of photographs—specifically the photographs of US soldiers abusing detainees at the Abu Ghraib prison—to speak for themselves in the court of public opinion and the court of law, to ask us to reconsider what we believe to be true. These photographs were at the heart of the scandal that erupted over the abuse and of the legal charges levied (and not levied) against those involved. The photographs, depicting American soldiers humiliating and abusing Iraqi detainees in a variety of ways, provided undeniable evidence of some level of misconduct in Abu Ghraib. They also illustrated a common way that we relate to photographs. Despite the fact that many people (in the academy and outside of it) have sophisticated takes on the limited ability of photographs to reveal truth, the photographs were widely discussed as incontrovertible proof[13] of the existence of inhumane (and possibly illegal) terms of engagement, of the existence of some very "bad apples," or in the hands of Susan Sontag, of a flaw in national culture and character.[14]

Morris takes on this reaction in the film, as various paratexts (from interviews to posters) attest and as the film itself attests in content and form. He sets out to show how these photographs functioned simultaneously as "expose and cover up."[15] As exposé, the photographs made pressing and real the conditions at Abu Ghraib (these conditions were known and reported before the photos were leaked, but the photos focused public attention on the abuses). As cover-up, the photographs focused attention on the actions of the soldiers pictured in them, away from the agencies authorizing the abuses pictured and much worse ones that were not pictured. As cover-up, the photos made real only a small portion of what was going on, but given the reality effect of these photos, the public felt that it had sufficient knowledge. This operation of the photos enabled impunity and operated against justice in many instances; for example, an army reservist pictured next to the dead body of a detainee was tried for mistreatment of the body, while those responsible for the death of the detainee did not face any legal charges.

By taking such a controversial topic, and one that audiences so strongly desired to know about, and refusing to satisfy this desire, Morris made a highly perverse film.[16] This perversity, Morris's refusal to satiate the audience's epistephilia on such a controversial topic, registered in the critical reactions to the film. As something of an auteur, Morris's films are generally well received. While *Standard Operating Procedure* received fairly positive reviews (an 84% percent score on the "Top Critics" section of Rotten Tomatoes),[17] many of these reviews were ultimately quite ambivalent on the film, recommending it but at the same time critiquing it for what it failed to do: reveal guilt and apportion blame.[18] Reviewers decried the film's inability to deliver any further information about the scandal; the *Washington Post* called it scattered "footnotes, the intellectual underpinnings of an argument about the war" that someone else would make at a later date.[19] Reviewers compared the film unfavorably to *Taxi to the Dark Side* and the *Ghosts of Abu Ghraib* (two films that had tried to investigate torture in the Iraq war),[20] in all bemoaning the failure of the film to shed more light on what had happened and who was responsible. In addition, many reviewers (most prominently, J. Hoberman's scathing review in the *Village Voice* and Manohla Dargis's tepid one in the *New York Times*) objected to the reenactments, as "aestheticizing" or fetishizing the images and events they depicted. The use of a top Hollywood composer, Danny Elfman, for the obtrusive film score drew similar criticism. This was in part an effect of the long American tradition of distrusting showiness or aesthetic style as a detraction from the truth function of documentary images[21] and in part a sense that such images were, in the case of images of torture, in poor taste. As one reviewer put it, "what's the point of a beautiful image of ugliness?"[22]

In addition to film critics, several prominent film scholars, including Bill Nichols and Jonathan Kahana, panned the film's politics, arguing that it worked to "fetishize" the photographs and detract from the structural and political issues at stake or to in some way excuse the soldiers. Nichols veered from reserved academic language to describe his visceral "revulsion" at the movie's lack of political responsibility (for not questioning the guards and their rationalizations, for not letting the Iraqis speak, among other things).[23] The responses from film scholars are particularly telling, given that they are among those in theory most sympathetic to the argument and reading that Morris encourages through various paratexts, from interviews and promotional materials to extras on the DVD. In that Morris attempts to intervene in a discussion about the photographs as evidence, and so many of the reviewers' critiques are made on other (often very compelling) grounds, the film seems to have missed its mark, failing in a rather different way than its critics contended.[24] In the next section, I analyze the text of the film for the different statements it attempts to make. Reading these against the background of the critical reviews summarized above, I offer an explanation for why these statements failed their mark.

Argument and Evidence in *Standard Operating Procedure*

The film begins with a disorienting introduction to Abu Ghraib, Saddam Hussein's former prison center taken over by the US military for prisoner detention and interrogation. The film is structured on the timeline of the photographs of abuse, detailing the background of each event captured in the widely publicized photos, based on the timeline put together by the forensic technician Brent Pack. It is also structured, as most of Morris's films, as a mystery—or twin mysteries: Why did these soldiers take these photos, and what do they tell us? Borrowing from the style Morris established in *Thin Blue Line* and *The Fog of War*, much of *Standard Operating Procedure* consists of interviews and stylized reenactments illustrating the testimony of the interviewees; these are interspersed with images of the Abu Ghraib photographs. These elements are arranged both chronologically (upon the logic provided by a specialist within the film) and around the unspoken questions of why and what they tell us.

As with most of Morris's films, *Standard Operating Procedure* relies heavily on talking head interviews.[25] The film begins midinterview, with a man we later learn was a professional interrogator. The first words we hear are "Charlie foxtrot for sure," military slang for clusterfuck, a situation in which multiple things have gone awry. After a brief discussion of how the military came to take over the notorious prison and how the reservists who took the photos came to the prison (where military intelligence already had detainees shackled naked with women's underwear over their heads), we are introduced to some of the key figures in front of and behind the cameras and the photos themselves. Lynndie England tells of her victimization at the hands of a charismatic and untrustworthy man, Megan Ambuhl and Javal Davis of justifiable actions within the context of war, Sabrina Harmon of being trapped in an unbelievable situation and of being both an accomplice and a witness to it.

These stories are profoundly unsatisfying. In the face of images of torture and violence, we tend to want clear answers, to know what happened and who is responsible.[26] Others in this volume contend that what we want from trials, on film or not, is a clear rendering of guilt and innocence (as in the privileged moral voice of the outburst in trial films discussed by Norman Spaulding or the rhyming of melodrama and popular notions of justice in Ticien Sassoubre). If this is so, then an audience primed to view *Standard Operating Procedure* juridically, to evaluate the truth value or plausibility of the testimony in the film, will be frustrated. This testimony of the film reveals less about guilt or innocence and more about the context of the abuse and the personas and self-understandings of the characters at the center of the scandal.

The film, like many of Morris's other films, dwells on characters—the humans at the center of the action and the stories they tell themselves/ they tell about themselves. At one point, Morris even said he thought of England as a "character" out of a Theodore Dreiser novel.[27] In this, *Standard Operating Procedure* is more like a character-driven film than a traditional American documentary. The interviews are intimate and in them each participant spins out his or her own version of what happened and why. We get bitter recitations of being railroaded, explanations of the conditions that brought on anger and extreme actions. From almost all, we get the repetition that the actions they staged or captured on camera were not all that bad, that they humiliated the detainees but did not seriously hurt them. These stories, the intimacy of the interviews, and the effect of the recreations are most likely what led some reviewers to say that the movie humanized the abusers, or worse, acted as a vehicle for their rationalizations.[28] The intense intimacy of the interviews invites empathy, if not identification. As in his other films, the interviewees in *Standard Operating Procedure* are not immediately identified. This tactic deemphasizes the professional authority of the speaking subjects and emphasizes their performance of personality. We are invited to attend to not an avatar of expertise but to attend to a person with a particular body, history, and perhaps facial and vocal tics.[29] Our trust in what is said is based less on the location from which the interviewee speaks than on how the interviewee speaks. All of the other images in the film elaborate on or illustrate what these subjects say, either through reenactment and symbolic rendering of what is said (e.g., semitransparent men walking the halls of Abu Ghraib to illustrate the existence of shadowy representatives of the FBI and CIA) or through display of the Abu Ghraib photos themselves.[30]

Given that the only speakers in the film are the perpetrators, they are the only available subjects for identification or empathy. This is an uncomfortable position. As Susan Sontag points out in discussing lynching photographs, we would much rather identify with the victim, even or precisely when this identification actively obscures our implication in unjust histories and relations of power.[31] Rather than provide an opportunity to fantasize that we feel the pain of the victims, we are invited into intimate proximity with low-level perpetrators. These perpetrators do not explicitly refuse dialogue or flatly deny their actions, as in the Nazi perpetrator interviews analyzed by Katie Model in this volume, but rather contextualize and rationalize. Given the intimate aesthetics of these interviews (and the simulation of dialogue in interviews for which Morris is known), this discursive tactic has a very different effect. It allows for a sense of getting to know these perpetrators, even of asking oneself what would I have done in their shoes. They do not refuse or elude understanding so much as invite it. This of course is precisely what disturbed so many reviewers, who critiqued the way the film allowed the perpetrators to speak without contradiction, in particular from the Iraqi detainees.[32]

It is true that there are no speaking Iraqi subjects. This both does not allow the audience to hear about the physical and affective experiences of the abuse and thus risks deemphasizing its severity and does not allow viewers the option of identification with the victims. The use of images, both the actual Abu Ghraib photographs, and the reenactments, can be read as anchoring and realizing the soldiers' stories, making them more vivid and affectively compelling. They can also be read as relativizing them, reminding that the photographs show us moments of events taking place in time and that the stories we hear are subjective and partial memories.[33]

A clear illustration of how the actual photographs of the abuse at Abu Ghraib will be used in the film comes during the interview with Sabrina Harmon, about ten minutes into the film. When she first appears on screen, Harmon is midstory, a tactic to cue viewers in that we are not hearing the full story but an edited one (this point is further conveyed through the use of jump cuts and even black screens during the interviews). She is explaining why she started to take the pictures. She recounts a story in which she comes into a cell to find a detainee handcuffed to a bed, arms outstretched behind him, crucifixion-style, naked with women's underwear on his head. At first, she said, recounting the story she wrote home to her wife, she thought it was funny and went to get the camera to take a snapshot. Then, when another specialist began to poke at the detainee's penis with her baton, Harmon recounts thinking "that's a form of molestation." She says she began taking the photos to document what was going on. Harmon goes on to say she took the pictures as proof, saying no one would believe her if she told them the "shit" that went on at the facility. She wanted, she says, to be able to say, "Look, I have proof; you can't deny it."

The display of photographs within Harmon's testimony is in many ways similar to the standard use of visual evidence in the dominant modes of Anglo-American documentary, yet the visual bracketing calls attention to the photograph as artifact (denaturalizing it while still reminding of its indexicality). In the expository and observational documentaries—the dominant modes of documentary in the United States and the United Kingdom —photographic images are naturalized as privileged evidence or proof, anchoring the spoken word.[34] Yet, *Standard Operating Procedure* in many ways reverses the typical relation of word and image, using the words to query the photos. While the photos appear in the documentary alongside the spoken testimony, they are stylistically denaturalized, marked as objects of inquiry rather than verification of what is said. When Harmon describes the man handcuffed to the bed, we see a photo of the scene described, seemingly endorsing the status of the photos as proof. The photo, however, is visually bracketed. It does not fill the full screen but appears with white borders, as in an old-fashioned photographic print. The use of these borders on the soldier photos clearly brackets them; digital photos like those taken at Abu Ghraib do not have such borders and so the borders are clearly a special effect, calling attention to the artifactuality of the photograph. This effect, and the grainy texture and poor focus of the photographs, differentiates them from the other visual imagery in the documentary.

The interviews and reenactments are highly produced, glossy images with often-obtrusive style, all of which differentiate what we are seeing from the verité aesthetics of observational documentary. Its aesthetics remind, like the white borders on the photographs, that the interviews and reenactments are mediations and not reality captured on the fly. From the heavy use of jump cuts during the talking head interviews, which serves as a constant reminder of the presence of a filmmaker editing the testimony recorded, to the intrusive score by veteran Hollywood composer Danny Elfman, the film is constantly pointing to its own construction. The interviews and re-creations fill in the gaps around the frames of the photographs, attempting to convey what happened before, after, and on the sidelines. In contrast to the grainy amateur photographs, the reconstructions are immersive, filling the screen with highly produced beautiful images. Most offer tightly composed perspective shots that highlight detail. They eschew realism and the omniscient point of view in favor of tight focus on detail and odd camera angles, a film convention for portraying a subjective perspective. It is one of the hallmarks of Morris's style to use these subjective visualizations to point to the partiality of memory and testimony, to simultaneously illustrate spoken testimony and remind us that it is not a perfect record.

While they are stylistically similar, the reconstructions in *Standard Operating Procedure* often work in the opposite manner to those he is most known for, in *The Thin Blue Line,* where the reenactments point to the subjective nature of the testimony of different witnesses and visually focus attention on discrepancies and lies.[35] In *Standard Operating Procedure,* the reenactments often seem to amplify and underscore what is said rather than to draw attention to lies. Perhaps because there are no strongly divergent memories pictured, perhaps because of the desire to know what happened, it is easy to read these scenes as exposing what happened rather than remediating the words and memories of highly partial and incomplete testimony.

Still highly subjective, the reenactments seem to fill in what the photos do not say, what they cannot say. Both stills and moving images, the recreations are lush, highly produced scenes, offering a strong sense of verisimilitude. Morris in fact spent almost $5 million on *Standard Operating Procedure*,[36] much of that on an elaborate reconstruction of the buildings at Abu Ghraib in order to film the reconstructions. Attesting to the complexity of the shoot and the production values of these reconstructions, the credits list includes set and costume designers, an art department, a visual effects department, casting, and a stunt man. In part because of these high production values, the reconstructions in *Standard Operating Procedure* are more detailed than the actual photographs. For example, the photographic image of a bloody cell where a prisoner was shot shows the doorway into a room, with blood smeared on the concrete, seeming to indicate that someone had been dragged across the floor through the blood. Because of the framing and lighting of the photo, however, we can see little else (the interior of the room is shrouded in darkness). The photograph, bracketed against the black background, fades into a full-screen re-creation of the scene. We see the inside of a jail cell, containing a metal bunk bed, from an angle near the floor of the back of the cell (looking toward the door). The scene is rich in tone and texture. Light and shadow illuminate the beige and yellow walls. Red blood is pooled and smeared across the concrete floor, and arcs of blood spatter the beige cinderblock. This still fades to a set of a man in an orange suit in tightly composed shots: falling to the floor in prayer, lifting and aiming a pistol at a guard outside the cell. The visuals provide extra information that the photos deny, but also the very resolution and texture of the images seem more complete and thus more real than the photograph. We can see the arcs of blood but also details like particles of dust caught in the light. The reenactment seems to provide what happened beyond the moment caught on film—or to extend the temporal boundaries of the photograph beyond the frame. Between the audience's desire to know what happened, the use of high-resolution cameras that provide rich visual detail, and the promise of documentary film to capture reality, the re-creations work against the larger aim of the film, seeming to give us the real (through photographic media). In *Thin Blue Line*, the reenactments were used to highlight inconsistencies in testimony (and thus the fact that someone must be lying), making a clearer point about the miscarriage of justice. Given the desire to know what happened and the lack of any contradictory testimony, in *Standard Operating Procedure* it is easy to see the re-enactments as providing evidence for the perpetrator's testimony. This slippage helps to explain why so many critics who lauded Morris's earlier use of reenactments were uncomfortable with those in *Standard Operating Procedure*. For Nichols and Kahana, the focus on the perpetrators and the visualization of their testimony served only to support and endorse the soldiers' rationalizations. The *Hollywood Reporter* reviewer wrote that in the face of so much existing photographic evidence, the re-creations were unnecessary.[37] Other reviewers wrote that the reenactments were in bad taste or fetishized the scenes of violence.[38]

Part of the film's difficulty in engaging its audience in questions about what they think they know lies in the very form of documentary and its modes of reception. New media theory can help elaborate this. Kris Fallon, applying the work of Lev Manovich, argues that the movie's central concern is the translation of the Abu Ghraib photographs from the symbolic form of the database to that of narrative.[39] The collection of photographs, like the database, is a grouping without necessary connection, hierarchy, chronology, or cause and effect. Such a collection, with no causal or temporal order imposed on it, cannot meaningfully tell us anything—it is not representational.[40] Within the symbolic form of narrative, on the other hand, there is a definite beginning, middle, and end. Further, within the narrative form, we read cause and effect and engage in evaluations.[41]

This process of translation is not only depicted in the film, it is the narrative or structural logic of the film. That is, it provides the structure around which the shots are edited into a text that conveys meaning. In the title credits of the film, often a place where the themes are telegraphed visually, we see a sea of photographs, floating with no particular order or connection: a visual representation of the database. Slowly, these photos literally fall into line, placed into a timeline: a visual representation of the narrative form.[42] The use of the photos to create a timeline and to suggest cause and effect is precisely the kind of thing that Morris warns us of, yet the film centers on this assembly as a central visual organizing trope (and Morris goes further on his website, using the software to bring photographs together to re-create events and rooms, tagging these images to testimony).[43] Morris wants viewer to read the photographs as something like data points, small moments that do not reveal the whole story we seek.[44] But documentaries must work within the symbolic form of narrative in order to engage viewers, suggest connections (notably, the causes and effects of which both narrative and argument are made), and cohere. So, *Standard Operating Procedure*, rather than making the photographs into data points, simply places the photographs into another narrative, providing a different set of potential motivations and relationships within which to read them.

It is not only the film that must assemble the photographs into a narrative (an alternative hypothesis). Army forensic investigator Brent Pack is shown in the film searching through and making sense of the photos through relations of space and time. Using metadata about the time the photographs were taken, he creates a timeline and a re-creation of the physical space in which the photographs were taken. Just as Morris must translate the images from database to narrative in order for his documentary to work, in order for the photographs to become evidence in a court of law, they must be translated from one form to the other, taking on the symbolic trappings of narrative.[45] Just as in other arenas (such as documentary, anthropology, and police work), photographs must conform to cultural-aesthetic forms external to the law in order to function as legal evidence.[46] In discussing the photographs as evidence, Pack slides between the two symbolic forms, arguing that a photograph can only provide basic facts (data) all the while inferring relationships and causality derived from his narration of them, making statements about the apparent amusement of the soldiers and, ultimately, labeling their actions as either criminal conduct or just standard operating procedure.

To say that photographs must be translated from the symbolic form of the database to that of the narrative in order to take on any evidentiary power adds a twist to John Tagg's take on the documentary power of photographs. Tagg argues that photographs did not self-evidently or naturally become evidence[47] but rather that the evidentiary status of photographs is the result of the fact that they were taken up and used by institutions such as the police: "Photography as such has no identity. Its status as a technology varies with the power relations which invest it. Its nature as a practice depends on the institutions and agents which define it and set it to work. Its function as a mode of cultural production is tied to definite condition of existence, and its products are meaningful and legible only within the particular currencies they have. . . . [Its power is] not the power of the camera but the power of the apparatuses of the local state which deploy it and guarantee the authority of the images it constructs to stand as evidence or register a truth."[48] In other words, the cultural status of photographic and filmic media as evidence is a product of their use as a means of surveillance and record by institutions such as the police;[49] he reminds of the institutional aspect of those discourses external to the film or photo itself that supply its meaning.[50] The technical, mimetic capacities of film are a key part of why we view photographs as evidence, yet we regularly overestimate the ability of photographs to represent and identify.

Documentary films as a genre ask viewers to read their filmic contents as a type of inscription, or simple record, of what happened with little to no human (or authorial) intervention. Both making and viewing documentaries equally depend on a willingness to use/see film footage in this way.[51] For Tagg, this means that the progressive potential of documentary will always be hamstrung because the power of photographs to document is an artifact of their use by repressive state apparatus (their rhetoric of realism thus always ends up subjecting those they want to uplift; a tendency of subjection Brian Winston terms "the tradition of the victim").[52] In asking audiences to view the subjects and events in the film as evidence of real events, the filmmaker is inadvertently asking the viewer to mobilize ideas about the camera as a tool of surveillance, to view the subjects of the film through the lens of mug shots and the scientific racism of salvage ethnography.[53]

The twist on Tagg's institutional historiography is this: photographic (or filmic) images in documentary film borrow not only from the apparatus of the state but the apparatus of cinema. Invoking the apparatus of cinema draws attention to films not as individual texts, or works of art, but as institutionalized discourse with a particular built-in ideology (built in through conventions of editing, the technology and use of the camera, and conventions of semiotics).[54] One of the features of the apparatus of cinema conferred upon documentary is narrative, in particular the use of moving images and edits to convey the passage of time, salience, relationships, and causality or motive. In documentary, as a form of film, photographic images are pressed into service precisely through their insertion into this narrative form rather than, per the terminology of Tagg and Nichols, discourse. It is not only that documentaries depend upon existing epistemes for what they can say (their statements must fit within contemporaneous discourses, or notions of truth which are always external to the documentary) but that the dominant form of documentary can only make these statements through the narrative conventions and audience expectations supplied by cinema.[55]

The power (and work) of the visual in documentary film is thus conferred by two very different sets of institutions: the state and the (technological, aesthetic, and commercial) institution of cinema. The marriage of these two sets of institutions promises both knowledge and pleasure: the pleasure in knowing that documentary films promise, and the pleasure of the spectacle through which they deliver that knowledge.[56] Visual evidence, argument, and spectatorship combine to provide a sense of not only knowledge but also completion or sufficient knowledge—in a word, mastery. For *Standard Operating Procedure*, this means that the documentary fights against itself or more precisely against the institutional determination of the form of documentary. It asks us to view photographs as incomplete evidence within a form (documentary film) predicated upon a particular way of viewing images as evidence, in which images verify words and provide ultimate proof (sufficiency of the narrative). The institutionally inculcated expectations of such relationships led reviewers to fault the film for not offering a moral voice or a political argument, despite the film's central conceit of querying the photos and its visual and structural emphasis on testimony.

If one of the lessons of *Standard Operating Procedure* is that evidence is always narrativized, either by the lawyer presenting the pictures to the court or by the person creating and editing the film, then the other lesson is that attempts to ask juries, judges, and lawyers to be more conscious and literate about the mediation and persuasion may fail to gain traction. The first lesson comes within the film, through Pack's meditations on and arrangement of the photographs into a chronology that also connotes causality and motive (it is, he says, the expressions on their faces that really damned them). The second comes in the reception of the film, in its failure to effectively frame the film as an interrogation of the photographs and a meditation upon the cultural and psychological conditions that led to them. The expectations that photographs are solid evidence are as entrenched as expectations that visual images within documentary film will reveal the truth. Such is the power of the juridical mode of reception.

The Disciplinary Nature of Juridical Reception

The argument—or utterance—*Standard Operating Procedure* attempts to articulate is then made within a context that hampers its illocutionary force. The same point can be made about arguments within the courtroom. Specifically, the institutional setting of the courtroom and expectations of truth, proof, and decidability that attend it make it difficult to denaturalize, or cross-examine, photographic and filmic evidence. Given that the reception of visual imagery within documentaries and of visuals (and other evidence) within the trial are both institutionally conditioned (by the documentary form and the law, respectively), photographs arrive on each scene within the frame of truth, evidence, and the limited scope of responsibility described by Judith Butler at the beginning of this chapter.

Photographs did not, of course, arrive on the scene of the courtroom as evidence, but rather as Tagg and others have shown, needed to be articulated and guaranteed as evidence through alignment with science and law enforcement. Late nineteenth-century legal practitioners were in fact unsure of how to use photographs as evidence; there was a debate about whether photographs should be treated as hearsay or as testimony.[57] Photographs were both potentially untrustworthy (their provenance and accuracy needed verification) and too powerful, threatening to take over the work of the court by showing guilt and innocence in perfect verisimilitude. It took a few years for the new technology to be "domesticated" into a category of evidence that merely illustrated or supported other evidence (e.g., testimony).[58] In practice, however, photographic evidence is often used not to merely illustrate but also to make statements or to stand on its own. However, because they are labeled as merely representative, photographs are generally not subjected to the same critical evaluation and cross-examination as other types of substantive evidence; the cultural status of photographs as "real" often leads legal practitioners to conflate the narrative or discourse in which the photographs are inserted with the event they depict.[59]

Despite their formal legal status, and despite the fact that we know that photographs are not complete representations, they still are used as privileged evidence, if not perfect reference, in the courtroom. The appearance of photographs in the courtroom frames them within the discourse of evidence and marshals what can be overblown expectations of their ability to represent an event.[60] Motion pictures, or film, entered the legal landscape as evidence only in the 1920s, inheriting many of the problems of photographs and incurring others.[61] As Jessica Silbey points out, film is treated much the same way as photographic evidence even though the two forms convey meaning very differently; namely, conventions of viewing lead us to read the sequence of images in film as chronological and causal.[62] Legal practice and categories have yet to acknowledge the particular persuasive capacities brought into the courtroom via reading images (e.g., of a surveillance video or a crime scene video) through the lens of narrative conventions that emphasize causality and psychological realism. One of the key problems of film as evidence is that this narration is accomplished by someone other than the lawyers present and may not be recognized as persuasion at all.[63] In response to this problem, legal scholars such as Silbey and Richard Sherwin suggest methods of critical visual analysis and cross-examination of the different sorts of film employed as evidence in trials.[64]

The expectations of photographs to act as proof, even a privileged form of proof, was key to the legal repercussions of the Abu Ghraib photographs—namely, their use to selectively prosecute military personnel for the abuses. While the prosecution of only lower-level military was no doubt politically and pragmatically motivated, it proceeded through the logic of photographic evidence. That is, the use of the photographs to assign blame followed the juridical mode of reception, the expectation that these photographs would provide evidence of guilt or innocence. Even though there were many voices clamoring for more extensive prosecutions, the expectation that the photographs would and could stand as evidence became the grounds of legitimation for the prosecution. In this way, the photographs operated, in Morris's terms, as a cover-up.[65]

Despite testimony and other evidence that worse abuses had taken place out of the photographic frame, legal charges were brought primarily against those implicated in the photographs, and it was only those in the pictures, or the events pictured, who were punished. Twelve military personnel had legal charges filed against them; of these, four pled guilty and eight went to trial, most sentenced for relatively short periods of time (less than one year). Specialist Charles Graner was sentenced to ten years and Staff Sgt. Ivan Frederick to eight years. The only senior ranking officer among these twelve to face legal charges (court-martial) was Lt. Col. Steven Jordan, who was not in any pictures and did not take any pictures. Jordan was accused of torture and of ultimate responsibility for the acts of those under him and for willfully disobeying an order not to talk about the abuse at Abu Ghraib. The military jury found Jordan not responsible for training of supervising the soldiers pictured in the photographs and not present on the evening photographs were taken of naked or nearly naked prisoners being intimidated by (and in one case, bitten by) dogs.[66] He was acquitted on all charges but those related to speaking out about the abuse. This acquittal meant that no officers were found legally responsible for the abuse. Two more senior officers, Col. Thomas Pappas and Brig. Gen. Janis Karpinski, were given administrative penalties but faced no legal charges.[67] No one above the rank of sergeant faced any legal penalties; likewise, no one from nonmilitary arms of the government (FBI, CIA) or civilian interrogators faced legal charges.[68] Journalists have traced official sanctioning of many of the abuses detailed in the Abu Ghraib photos—and at issue in these trials. Karpinski claims that Donald Rumsfeld ordered the use of torture techniques, and the ACLU released army documents (acquired via FOIA) implicating Lt. Gen. Ricardo Sanchez in encouraging abusive behavior. The ACLU documents also demonstrated that the government knew about the abuses before the photographs came out and was actively investigating sixty-two instances of prisoner abuse (twenty-six of which had resulted in the death of the prisoner).[69] The *Washington Post* reported on documents showing that Sanchez had approved techniques such as temperature extremes, sleep deprivation, the use of dogs, food deprivation (bread and water diets), and sensory deprivation in Iraqi prisons.[70]

Many of these reports were made before the completion of the trials of military personnel. Yet, they did not make their way from press reports into the legal proceedings. Those tried and found guilty were those in the pictures. Many abuses at Abu Ghraib detailed in government documents (including the deaths of twenty-six prisoners, sexual assault, threatening to kill a child in order to "send a message," and interrogating prisoners at gunpoint)[71] were never photographed. Likewise, the fact that many of the people who were subject to this treatment (including Gus, the man on the end of the dog leash in the famous photograph with Lynndie England) were not combatants but rather civilians who had been drinking or out after dark or were picked up in sweeps (including children) and that these people were being held in a dangerous combat zone were not so easy to picture.[72] And in the end, what was not pictured—what was out of the frame—was not prosecuted.

The limited photographic record became, per the record of prosecutions, the evidence of abuse. Within the visual economy of the scandal, what was not caught or not available for photographic capture by the camera was not prosecutable (there being no public evidence). The photographs did not give us the chain of command, the context, or whether the military personnel were simply carrying out orders. The photos stood in for the entirety, screening out what was not pictured. If we think that we believe what we see, the (near) opposite is also true: what we cannot see is open to doubt. This was the lesson of Abu Ghraib, according to Heidi Viterbo. Viterbo suggests that the very types of film and photograph that count as good visual evidence are those that bear no traces of mediation—those which can seem to be a "transparent" representation or a perfect mimetic copy.[73] These are of course the type of images that are labeled as most suspect by many scholars of documentary film.[74] In an argument that parallels the critique of realism in documentary representation, Viterbo argues that the very types of photographic images that meet the criteria of good evidence are those most likely to obscure context and, worse, to misdirect. The existence of seemingly solid visual evidence for some types of torture can lessen the possibility of the recognition or prosecution of other types of torture (namely, psychological torture, which is harder to picture).[75] This is not a problem of pictures per se but of our expectations of visual proof and the abuses to which these expectations can be exploited. It is, in short, a problem of reception.

If a number of critics faulted *Standard Operating Procedure* for failing to show what really happened, or to take more of a stand, this shows a strong expectation that documentary will lead us to what happened, rather than open questions about what we know. This expectation originates in the institutional history of documentary photography but also in more recent documentary conventions of situating the audience as a jury, evaluating the evidence presented in filmic form. The film asked the audience-as-jury to step back and question the meaning of the evidence before their eyes. The difficulty of making this request, both formally in the text and in practice as registered by the ambivalent critical reception, highlights the way that expectations borne of institutionalized conventions act as constraints on communication. As noted above, the ease with which we read photographs and film as evidence owes as much to their institutional entanglements as to the technical capacities of cameras. Especially when primed to a juridical orientation, audiences expect answers and arguments rather than questions. The juridical mode of reception is oriented toward judgment rather than complication. The parallel between the work of the audience and that of the jury identified by Clover thus suggests that the very site and modes of reception associated with the courtroom itself may hinder attempts to cross-examine or otherwise critically engage the evidentiary status of photographic media.

Notes

1. The critics differed on the message of the film. Where some saw a strong condemnation of the military chain of command and indictment of the higher-ups, others saw Graner as the chief villain of the film. Others saw no moral or political stance.

2. Generally, in the Anglo-American tradition defined by John Grierson, documentaries have centered on publicizing a social problem, ideally a hidden or "invisible" one.

3. Bill Nichols, *Representing Reality: Issues and Concepts in Documentary* (Bloomington: Indiana University Press, 1991); Elizabeth Cowie, *Recording Reality, Desiring the Real* (Minneapolis: University of Minnesota Press, 2011).

4. Other reflexive documentaries make similar interventions. Most notably, Trinh Minh-ha's *Surname Viet, Given Name Nam* uses breaks from realism, sound-image mismatch and re-creations to critique the authority of the interview within documentary, and Chris Marker's *Sans Soleil* meditates on the paradoxes of visual history. Trinh Minh-ha, dir., *Surname Viet, Given Name Nam* (New York: Women Make Movies, 1989), VHS. Chris Marker, dir., *Sans Soleil* (New York, NY: Criterion Collection, 2007), DVD.

5. Carol Clover, "Law and the Order of Popular Culture," in *Law in the Domains of Culture,* ed. Austin Sarat (Ann Arbor: University of Michigan Press, 1989), 97–120.

6. Janet Staiger, *Perverse Spectators: The Practices of Film Reception* (New York: New York University Press, 2000).

7. Dirk Eitzen, "When Is a Documentary? Documentary as a Mode of Re-

ception," *Cinema Journal* 35, no. 1 (1995): 81–102; Bill Nichols, *Blurred Boundaries: Questions of Meaning in Contemporary Culture* (Bloomington: Indiana University Press, 1995).

8. Nichols, *Representing Reality.*

9. Hector Amaya, "Racialized Documentary Reception in Ken Burns' Jazz" *Television and New Media* 9, no. 2 (2008): 111–30.

10. Documentaries may be at the edges of such discourses rather than the center. Nichols, *Representing Reality.*

11. Errol Morris, dir., *The Thin Blue Line* (Santa Monica, CA: Metro Goldwyn Mayer , 2005), DVD.; Andrew Jarecki, dir., *Capturing the Friedmans* (2003; New York: HBO Pictures, 2004), DVD.; Joshua Oppenheimer, dir., *The Act of Killing* (Copenhagen, Denmark: Final Cut for Real, 2012), DVD.

12. Bill Nichols argues that documentaries borrow from other types of texts (like the exposé or the poem). Bill Nichols, *Introduction to Documentary,* 2nd ed. (Bloomington: Indiana University Press, 2010).

13. Given that we know that photographs are partial yet treat them as if they were if not objective at least sufficient, our relation to photographs parallels the operation of contemporary ideology, which no longer requires belief. We may know better, but we do it anyway. Slavoj Zizek, *Sublime Object of Ideology* (London: Verso, 1989).

14. Susan Sontag, "Regarding the Torture of Others," *New York Times*, May 23, 2004, http://www.nytimes.com/2004/05/23/magazine/regarding-the-torture-of-others.html.

15. Errol Morris, "Standard Operating Procedure: Synopsis," http://www.errolmorris.com/film/sop.html.

16. Thank you to Barry Langford for pointing out this perversity.

17. *Standard Operating Procedure*, Rotten Tomatoes (Top Critics), accessed August 1, 2018, https://www.rottentomatoes.com/m/standard_operating_procedure/reviews/?type=top_critics.

18. Based on a survey of twenty-nine reviews in US newspapers (the combined results of a Lexis-Nexis search for reviews of the film between April and June 2008 and those available on Metacritic).

19. Phillip Kennicott, "The War Comes Home: Two Iraq Documentaries Attempt to Engage Us in a Now-Distant Conflict," *Washington Post*, April 2, 2008, Lexis-Nexis Academic.

20. Joe Williams, "Documentary Only Muddles Abu Ghraib Scandal," *St. Louis Post-Dispatch,* May 23, 2008, Lexis Nexis Academic. Chris Hewett, "'Standard Operating Procedure': Better Never than Late," *St. Paul Pioneer Press*, May 22, 2008, Lexis Nexis Academic. Anne Thompson, "The Wages of War," *Variety,* April 21, 2008, Lexis Nexis Academic. Bob Strauss, "Standard Operating Procedure Is No Ordinary Documentary," *Daily News of Los Angeles*, May 2, 2008,

Lexis Nexis Academic. Manohla Dargis, "We, The People behind the Abuse," *New York Times,* April 25, 2008, Lexis Nexis Academic.

21. Susan Sontag, *Regarding the Pain of Others* (New York: Picador Press, 2003).

22. Hewett, "'Standard Operating Procedure.'"

23. Bill Nichols, "Feelings of Revulsion and the Limits of Academic Discourse" *Jump Cut* 52 (2010), http://ejumpcut.org/archive/jc52.2010/sopNichols/index.html; Jonathan Kahana, "Speech Images: Standard Operating Procedure and the Staging of Interrogation" *Jump Cut* 52 (2010), http://ejumpcut.org/archive/jc52.2010/sopkKahana/index.html.

24. This failure is directly proportional to the perversity of the film. In the introduction to the *Jump Cut* article on the Society for Cinema and Media Studies meeting at which Kahana and Nichols critiqued the film, David Andrews contrasted the contentious panel at which these high-profile American scholars discussed the film and another panel on the film, populated by European scholars. The discussion was less heated at this panel. These scholars, less implicated in the abuses, may have had less of a pressing desire for the ultimate responsibility to be revealed. David Andrews, "Conference Report: Reframing 'Standard Operating Procedure': Errol Morris and the Creative Treatment of Abu Ghraib" *Jump Cut* 52 (2010), http://ejumpcut.org/archive/jc52.2010/sopAndrews/index.html.

25. Interestingly, given the centrality of photographs, the film is anchored not by visuals, but by the testimony of those who took the photos, the military personnel in the pictures, and those who analyzed them, and those who were taken down by them; none of the pictured prisoners speak in the film. Yet, the film is not as hopeful (or naive) about witness testimony as are many other recent documentaries (e.g., Spike Lee's *When the Levees Broke* [2006]). For more on the role of testimony in contemporary documentary, see Bhaskar Sarkar and Janet Walker, eds., *Documentary Testimonies: Global Archives of Suffering* (New York: Routledge, 2009).

26. Sontag, *Regarding the Pain of Others*; Valerie Hartouni, *Visualizing Atrocity: Arendt, Evil, and the Optics of Thoughtlessness* (New York: New York University Press, 2012).

27. Sheila Johnson, "The Dark Side of Democracy," *Daily Telegraph,* May 30, 2008, Lexis Nexis Academic.

28. Similar reactions plagued *The Act of Killing*, another documentary perversely interested less in documenting the abuses committed by its subjects than in exploring their psyches and the culture of impunity in which they exist.

29. As in the outbursts examined elsewhere in this volume by Norman Spaulding, the bodies of the speakers and their affect become the locus of cinematic focus here.

30. Toward the end of the movie, there is a departure from this logic of illus-

tration and evidence, a sort of visual metaphor, in which one of the "most wanted playing cards" (distributed by the US Army) with Saddam's face on it falls to a wooden floor and then a weighted rope falling through trap doors as if we were witnessing a hanging from below. This scene does not reenact or illustrate but rather alludes to the hanging of Saddam Hussein.

31. Sontag, *Regarding the Pain of Others*. A similar avoidance of implication is at work in American rhetorics of witnessing; see Carrie Rentschler, "Witnessing: U.S. Citizenship and the Vicarious Experience of Suffering," *Media Culture and Society* 26 (2004): 296–304.

32. This decision not to include detainees as speaking subjects also meant that there were no victims for audiences to identify with.

33. The use of Sabrina Harmon's letters home is an exception. These letters, which we are told were written at the time, are employed as visual proof of Harmon's motivations and state of mind, legitimizing her testimony.

34. In the dominant expository and observational modes of Anglo-American documentary, photographic images are naturalized as privileged evidence, or proof. In the expository mode, or the version of documentary that most closely resembles a lecture or textbook, film footage clinches or proves the argument spoken in the voice over. The observational mode, in which there is no voice-over argument and no (or few) interviews, the editing of the film footage and natural dialogue constitutes the argument; authority in this mode is premised on the idea that such footage is more authentic and accurate than testimony (whether voice-over, expert, or witness testimony).

35. See Linda Williams, "Mirrors without Memories: Truth, History, and the New Cinema," *Film Quarterly* 46, no 3 (1993): 9–21.

36. Michael Cieply and Ben Sisario, "Film on Abu Ghraib Puts Focus on Paid Interviews," *New York Times*, April 26, 2008, http://www.nytimes.com/2008/04/26/movies/26morris.html?pagewanted=all.

37. John Anderson, "Of Crime and Perception at Abu Ghraib," *New York Times*, April 20, 2008, Lexis Nexis Academic.

38. Lisa Kennedy, "The Shame of Abu Ghraib," *Denver Post*, May 23, 2008, Lexis Nexis Academic; Hewett, "'Better Never than Late'"; Stephen Hunter, "A Pieced-Together Picture of the Scandal at Abu Ghraib" *Washington Post*, May 23, 2008, Lexis Nexis Academic; Dargis, "We, The People"; Williams, "Documentary Only Muddles."

39. Kris Fallon, "Archives Analog and Digital: Errol Morris and Documentary in the Digital Age" *Screen* 54 (2013): 20–43.

40. Ibid.

41. Lev Manovich, "Database as a Symbolic Form," *Millennium Film Journal* no. 34 (1999): http://www.mfj-online.org/journalPages/MFJ34/Manovich_Database_FrameSet.html.

42. Fallon, "Archives Analog and Digital."

43. Ibid.

44. Philip Gourevitch and Errol Morris, *Standard Operating Procedure* (New York: Penguin Press, 2008). Michael Meyer, "Recovering Reality: Errol Morris on Abu Ghraib," *Columbia Journalism Review*, March 5, 2008. http://www.cjr.org /behind_the_news/recovering_reality.php.

45. For more on narrative and the law, see Anthony G. Amsterdam and Jerome Bruner, *Minding the Law* (Cambridge, MA: Harvard University Press, 2000).

46. For more on how photographs must conform to discourses external to themselves in order to operate as evidence, see: Bill Nichols, "The Question of Evidence, the Power of Rhetoric and Documentary Film," in *Rethinking Documentary: New Perspectives, New Practices*, ed. Thomas Austin and Wilma de Jong, 33–39 (Maidenhead, UK: Open University Press/McGraw Hill, 2008); John Tagg, *The Burden of Representation: Essays on Photographies and Histories* (Minneapolis: University of Minnesota Press, 1993), 63–64.

47. Indeed, there was debate in the late nineteenth century about the use of photographs in court; namely, whether photographs could be considered hearsay or legitimate evidence. Thomas Thurston, "Hearsay of the Sun: Photography, Identity, and the Law of Evidence in the 19th Century," Hyptertext Scholarship in American Studies, *American Quarterly* (1998), http://chnm.gmu.edu/aq /photos/index.htm. For a more general discussion of photography and evidence in law in the nineteenth century, see Jennifer Mnookin, "The Image of Truth: Photographic Evidence and the Power of Analogy," *Yale Journal of Law and the Humanities* 10, issue 1 (1998): 1–74.

48. Tagg, *Burden of Representation*.

49. This is echoed by Allan Sekula, "The Body and the Archive" *October* 39 (1986): 3–64. Similarly, the evidentiary status of documentary relied on anthropological knowledge and practices. Assenka Oksiloff, *Picturing the Primitive: Visual Culture, Ethnography, and Early German Cinema* (New York: Palgrave, 2001).

50. Bill Nichols, "Question of Evidence." This does not mean that films and photographs cannot to be trusted or that they do not have evidentiary power but instead that these forms must be evaluated with an understanding of these mediating discourses and institutions. After all, other forms of testimony, evidence, and perception (including sight itself) are subject to similar shaping by discourse. Carl Plantinga, "'I'll Believe It When I Trust the Source': Documentary Images and Visual Evidence," in *The Documentary Film Book,* ed. Brian Winston (London: British Film Institute, 2013), 40–47.

51. Brian Winston, *Claiming the Real: The Griersonian Documentary and Its Legitimations* (London: British Film Institute, 1995).

52. Brian Winston, "The Tradition of the Victim in Griersonian Documentary," in *New Challenges for Documentary*, ed. Alan Rosenthal (Berkeley: Univer-

sity of California Press, 1990): 269–87. Winston is not drawing on Tagg or any other Foucaudian notions of surveillance but rather critiquing the efficacy of documentary in achieving social change and pointing to the unintentional exploitation of subjects by well-meaning progressive documentarians. Tagg's argument, however, offers an explanation for the unintended subjectifications of documentary film.

53. Salvage ethnography was the anthropological practice of "capturing" and preserving the sounds and images of what were thought to be "dying" races (i.e., Native Americans) around the twentieth century, a practice that relied heavily on new recording media of photograph and phonograph. See Oksiloff, *Picturing the Primitive;* Jonathan Sterne, *The Audible Past: Cultural Origins of Sound Reproduction* (Chapel Hill, NC: Duke University Press, 2003).

54. See, for example, Jean-Louis Baudry, "Ideological Effects of the Basic Film Apparatus," in *Narrative Apparatus Ideology: A Film Theory Reader*, ed. Philip Rosen (New York: Columbia University Press, 1986), 286–98.

55. Of course, experimental and poetic documentaries that do not attempt to make statements in the same way do not face the same limitations. Drawing on logics of art, and examples of other cinemas (notably, early Soviet montage film), they engage in nonnarrative documentation—a documentation that as I note is sometimes lost on casual viewers.

56. On epistephilia and its difference from scopophilia and other pleasures usually described by film theory, see Nichols, *Representing Reality;* Cowie, *Recording Reality, Desiring the Real* (Minneapolis: University of Minnesota Press, 2011); and Michael Renov, "Toward a Poetics of Documentary" in *Theorizing Documentary*, ed. Renov (New York: Routledge, 1993): 12–36.

57. Thurston, "Hearsay of the Sun."

58. Mnookin, "Image of Truth."

59. Ibid.; Jessica Silbey, "Evidence Verité and the Law of Film," *Cardozo Law Review* 31, no. 4 (March 2010): 1257. Neil Feigenson and Christina Spiesel, *Law on Display: The Digital Transformation of Legal Persuasion and Judgment* (New York: New York University Press, 2009).

60. Think, specifically, about the way that the Supreme Court justices assumed that the in-dash recorder in the police car in Scott v. Harris (2007).

61. Louis-George Schwartz, *Mechanical Witness: A History of Motion Picture Evidence in U.S. Courts* (New York: Oxford University Press, 2009).

62. Jessica Silbey, "Judges as Film Critics: New Approaches to Filmic Evidence," *University of Michigan Journal of Legal Reform* 37, 2 (2004): 493–571.

63. A similar point has been made about observational documentaries—that their persuasion is more manipulative than expository forms for being less obtrusive or visible.

64. Silbey, "Judges as Film Critics"; Richard Sherwin, "Imagining Law as

Film (Representation without Reference?)," in *Law and the Humanities: An Introduction*, ed. Austin Sarat, Matthew Anderson, and Cathrine O. Frank, 241–68 (New York: Cambridge University Press, 2010).

65. Dave Gilson, "Interrogating Errol Morris," *Mother Jones*, May/June 2008. https://www.motherjones.com/politics/2008/05/interrogating-errol-morris/.

66. Josh White, "Abu Ghraib Officer Cleared of Detainee Abuse," *Washington Post*, August 29, 2007.

67. In addition, four Iraqi detainees and the Center for Constitutional Rights filed a lawsuit alleging that private contractor CACI Premier Technology had tortured them. The suit was thrown out by a district court in Virginia and then appealed to the Fourth Circuit Court of Appeals, which reversed the lower court's ruling, approving the lawsuit to proceed in US courts. The outcome of this suit is still pending.

68. Gourevitch and Morris, *Standard Operating Procedure*, 270.

69. American Civil Liberties Union, "Army Documents Show Senior Official Reportedly Pushed Limits on Detainee Interrogations," May 2, 2006, https://www.aclu.org/national-security/army-documents-show-senior-official-reportedly-pushed-limits-detainee-interrogation.

70. Jeffrey Smith and Josh White, "General Granted Latitude at Prison," *Washington Post*, June 12, 2004.

71. ACLU, "Army Documents."

72. Gourevitch and Morris, *Standard Operating Procedure,* 270.

73. Heidi Viterbo, "Seeing Torture Anew: A Transnational Reconceptualization of State Torture and Visual Evidence," *Stanford Journal of International Law* 281, issue 50 (2014): 281–317.

74. For example, Nichols, *Representing Reality*; Winston, *Claiming the Real*, cf. Carl Plantinga, *Rhetoric and Representation in Nonfiction Film* (New York: Cambridge University Press, 1997).

75. Viterbo, "Seeing Torture Anew." This is not necessarily to say that no photographs are better than photographs but to caution against giving the photographs too much evidentiary weight. This is of course difficult and leaves aside the power of photographs to implicate their viewers in a relationship of vicarious witnessing.

Works Cited

Abramson, Jeffrey. *We, the Jury: The Jury System and the Ideal of Democracy.* Cambridge, MA: Harvard University Press, 2000.

Adler, Stephen J. *The Jury: Disorder in the Court.* New York: Doubleday, 1994.

Althusser, Louis. *Essays on Ideology.* Translated by Ben Brewster. London: Verso, 1984.

Altman, Rick. "Dickens, Griffith, and Film Theory Today." In *Silent Film,* edited by Richard Abel, 146–62. New Brunswick, NJ: Rutgers University Press, 1996.

Amaya, Hector. "Racialized Documentary Reception in Ken Burns' Jazz." *Television and New Media* 9, no. 2 (2008): 111–30.

American Civil Liberties Union. "Army Documents Show Senior Official Reportedly Pushed Limits on Detainee Interrogations." May 2, 2006. https://www.aclu.org/national-security/army-documents-show-senior-official-reportedly-pushed-limits-detainee-interrogation.

Amsterdam, Anthony G., and Jerome Bruner. *Minding the Law.* Cambridge, MA: Harvard University Press, 2000.

Anderson, John. "Of Crime and Perception." *New York Times,* April 20, 2008. http://www.nytimes.com/2008/04/20/movies/20ande.html?_r=0.

Andrews, David. "Conference Report: Reframing 'Standard Operating Procedure': Errol Morris and the Creative Treatment of Abu Ghraib." *Jump Cut* 52 (2010). http://ejumpcut.org/archive/jc52.2010/sopAndrews/index.html.

Arendt, Hannah. *Eichmann in Jerusalem: A Report on the Banality of Evil.* New York: Penguin Books, 1977.

Asimow, Michael. "Bad Lawyers in the Movies." *Nova Law Review* 24 (2000): 531–49.

Ball, Milner. "The Play's the Thing: An Unscientific Reflection on Courts under the Rubric of Theater." *Stanford Law Review* 28 (1975–76): 81–115.

Barthes, Roland. "Rhetoric of the Image." In *Image Music Text,* translated by Stephen Heath, 32–51. New York: Hill and Wang, 1977.

———. *S/Z.* New York: Hill and Wang, 1974.

Baudry, Jean-Louis. "Ideological Effects of the Basic Film Apparatus." In *Narrative Apparatus Ideology: A Film Theory Reader,* edited by Philip Rosen, 286–98. New York: Columbia University Press, 1986.

Bazin, Andre. "The Evolution of the Language of Cinema." In *Critical Visions in Film Theory,* edited by Timothy Corrigan, Patricia White, and Meta Mazaj, 314–24. Boston: Bedford/St. Martin's, 2011.

Benforado, Adam. "Frames of Injustice: The Bias We Overlook." *Indiana Law Journal* 85 (Fall 2010): 1333–78.

Benjamin, Walter. "The Work of Art in the Age of Mechanical Reproduction." In *Film Theory and Criticism*, edited by Leo Braudy and Marshall Cohen, 791–811. 6th ed. New York: Oxford University Press, 2004.

Benton, Robert, dir. *Kramer vs. Kramer*. 1979; Culver City, CA: Columbia TriStar Home Entertainment, 2001. DVD

Biskind, Peter. *Seeing Is Believing; or, How Hollywood Taught Us to Stop Worrying and Love the Fifties*. New York: Pantheon, 1983.

Blanchot, Maurice, and Jacques Derrida, *The Instant of My Death/Demeure: Fiction and Testimony*. Translated by Elizabeth Rottenberg. Stanford, CA: Stanford University Press, 2000.

Bordwell, David. "Classical Hollywood Cinema." In *Narrative, Apparatus, Ideology*, edited by Philip Rosen, 17–34. New York: Columbia University Press, 1986.

Bordwell, David, Janet Staiger, and Kristin Thompson. *The Classical Hollywood Cinema*. New York: Columbia University Press, 1985.

Box Office. October 15, 1955, 2–3.

Brean, Herbert. "A Case of Identity." *Life Magazine*, June 29, 1953, 97.

Brecht, Bertolt. *Life of Galileo*. Translated by John Willett. London: Methuen, 1980.

Brooks, Peter. "Melodrama, Body, Revolution." In *Melodrama: Stage Picture Screen*, edited by Jacky Bratton, Jim Cook, and Christine Gledhill, 11–24. London: British Film Institute, 1994.

———. "The Melodramatic Imagination." In *Imitations of Life: A Reader on Film and Television Melodrama*, edited by Marcia Landy, 50–67. Detroit, MI: Wayne State University Press, 1991.

———. *The Melodramatic Imagination: Balzac, Henry James, Melodrama, and the Mode of Excess*. New Haven, CT: Yale University Press, 1995.

———. *The Melodramatic Imagination: Balzac, Henry James, Melodrama, and the Mode of Excess*. New Haven, CT: Yale University Press, 1976.

———. *Reading for the Plot: Design and Intention in Narrative*. Cambridge, MA: Harvard University Press, 1992.

Burns, Ken, Sarah Burns, and David McMahon, dirs. *The Central Park Five*. 2012; Arlington, VA: PBS, 2013. DVD.

Burns, Sarah. *The Central Park Five*. New York: Vintage Books, 2011.

Butler, Judith. "Torture and the Ethics of Photography." *Environment and Planning D: Society and Space* 25, no. 6 (2007): 951–66.

Byars, Jackie. *All That Hollywood Allows: Re-Reading Gender in 1950s Melodrama*. Chapel Hill: University of North Carolina Press, 1991.

Cantor, Jay. "Death and the Image." In *Beyond Document: Essays on Nonfiction*, edited by Charles Warren. Hanover, NH: Wesleyan University Press, 1996.

Cawelti, John. "*Chinatown* and Generic Transformation in Recent American Films." In *Film Genre Reader II*, edited by Barry Keith Grant. Austin: University of Texas Press, 1995: 227–46.

Chase, Anthony. *Movies on Trial: The Legal System on the Silver Screen*. New York: New Press, 2002.

————. "Popular Culture/Popular Justice." In *Legal Reelism: Movies as Legal Texts*, edited by John Denvir, 133–53. Champaign: University of Illinois, 1996.

Chase, Richard. *The American Novel and Its Tradition*. Baltimore: Johns Hopkins University Press, 1980.

Chopra-Gant, Mike. *Hollywood Genres and Postwar America: Masculinity, Family and Nation in Popular Movies and Film Noir*. London: I. B. Tauris, 2006.

Clover, Carol. "'God Bless Juries!'" In *Refiguring American Film Genres: History and Theory*, edited by Nick Browne, 255–77. Berkeley: University of California, 1998.

————. "Judging Audiences: The Case of the Trial Movie." In *Reinventing Film Studies*, edited by Christine Gledhill and Linda Williams, 244–64. London: Hodder Arnold, 2000.

————. "Law and the Order of Popular Culture." In *Law in the Domains of Popular Culture*, edited by Austin Sarat and Thomas R. Kearns, 97–129. Ann Arbor: University of Michigan Press, 1998.

————. *The People's Plot: Trials, Movies, and the Adversarial Imagination* (provisional title). Princeton, NJ: Princeton University Press, forthcoming.

Cohen, Rob, dir. *The Fast and the Furious*. 2001, Universal City, CA: Universal Pictures Home Entertainment, 2002. DVD.

Cook, Charles M. *The American Codification Movement: A Study of Antebellum Legal Reform*. Westport, CT: Greenwood Press, 1981.

Cook, David. *A History of Narrative Film*. New York: Norton, 1981.

Cowie, Elizabeth. *Recording Reality, Desiring the Real*. Minneapolis: University of Minnesota Press, 2011.

————. "The Spectacle of Actuality." In *Collecting Visible Evidence*, edited by Jane M. Gaines and Michael Renov, 19–45. Minneapolis: University of Minnesota Press, 1999.

Cuniberti, John. "*The Birth of a Nation": A Formal Shot-by-Shot Analysis Together with Microfiche*. Ann Arbor: University of Michigan Press, 1979.

Curtiz, Michael, dir. *Casablanca*. 1942; Burbank, CA: Warner Home Video, 1999. DVD.

de Certeau, Michel. *The Writing of History*. New York: Columbia University Press, 1988.

Delage, Christian, *Caught on Camera: Film in the Courtroom from the Nuremberg Trials to the Trials of the Khmer Rouge*. Translated by Ralph Schoolcraft and Mary Byrd Kelly. Philadelphia: University of Pennsylvania Press, 2013.

————, dir. *Nuremberg: The Nazis Facing Their Crimes*. Santa Monica, CA: Lions Gate, 2007. DVD.

Demme, Jonathan, dir. *Philadelphia*. 1993; Hollywood, CA: TriStar Pictures, 2002. DVD.

Denvir, John, ed. *Legal Reelism: Movies as Legal Texts*. Champaign: University of Illinois Press, 1996.

———— ed. *Movies as Legal Texts*. Urbana: University of Illinois Press, 1996.

Derrida, Jacques. *Specters of Marx: The State of Debt, the Work of Mourning and the New International*. Translated by Peggy Kamuf. New York: Routledge, 1994.

Derrida, Jacques, and Bernard Stiegler, *Echographies of Television*. Translated by Jennifer Bajorek. Cambridge, UK: Polity Press, 2007.

Dershowitz, Alan M. "Life Is Not a Dramatic Narrative." In *Law's Stories: Narrative and Rhetoric in the Law*, edited by Peter Brooks and Paul Gewirtz, 99–105. New Haven, CT: Yale University Press, 1996.

———. *Reversal of Fortune: Inside the von Bulow Case*. New York: Simon and Schuster, 1986.

Dillon, Karen "Friends of the Court." *American Lawyer*, April 1989, 130.

Douglas, Lawrence. *The Memory of Judgment: Making Law and History in the Trials of the Holocaust*. New Haven, CT: Yale University Press, 2001.

Eisenstein, Sergei. "Dickens, Griffith, and the Film Today." In *Film Form: Essays in Film Theory*, edited and translated by Jay Leyda, 195–255. New York: Harcourt, 1977.

———. *Film Form: Essays in Film Theory*, translated by Jay Leyda. New York: Harcourt Press, 1969.

Eitzen, Dirk. "When Is a Documentary?: Documentary as a Mode of Reception." *Cinema Journal* 35, no. 1 (1995): 81–102.

Elsaesser, Thomas. "Tales of Sound and Fury." In *Movies and Methods*, vol. 2, edited by Bill Nichols, 166–89. Berkeley: University of California Press, 1985.

Ewick, Patricia, and Susan S. Silbey. *The Common Place of Law: Stories of Everyday Life*. Chicago: University of Chicago Press, 1998.

Fallon, Kris. "Archives Analog and Digital: Errol Morris and Documentary in the Digital Age." *Screen* 54 (2013): 20–43.

Feigenson, Neal R. "Accidents as Melodrama." *New York Law School Law Review* 43 (1999–2000): 741–810.

———. *Legal Blame: How Jurors Think and Talk about Accidents*. Washington, DC: American Psychological Association, 2000.

Feigenson, Neil, and Christina Spiesel. *Law on Display: The Digital Transformation of Legal Persuasion and Judgment*. New York: New York University Press, 2009.

Felman, Shoshana. *The Juridical Unconscious: Trials and Traumas in the Twentieth Century*. Cambridge, MA: Harvard University Press, 2002.

Felman, Shoshana, and Dori Laub, eds. *Testimony: Crisis of Witnessing in Literature, Psychoanalysis and History*. New York: Routledge, 1991.

Ferguson, Robert A. "Untold Stories in the Law." In *Law's Stories*, edited by Peter Brooks and Paul Gewirtz, 84–98. New Haven, CT: Yale University Press, 1996.

Fiedler, Leslie. *Love and Death in the American Novel*. New York: Meridian Books, 1960.

Field, Syd. *Screenplay: The Foundations of Screenwriting*. New York: Dell, 1984.

Fisher, George. "The Jury's Rise as Lie Detector." *Yale Law Journal* 107 (January 1997): 575–713.

Flitterman-Lewis, Sandy. "Documenting the Ineffable: Terror and Memory in Alain Resnais's *Night and Fog*." In *Documenting the Documentary*, edited by Barry Keith Grant and Jeannette Sloniowski, 204–22. Detroit, MI: Wayne State University Press, 1998.

Flynn, Thomas R. "Foucault and the Eclipse of Vision." In *Modernity and the Hegemony of Vision*, edited by David Michael Levin, 273–86. Berkeley: University of California, 1992.

Ford, John, dir. *The Man Who Shot Liberty Valance*. 1962; Hollywood, CA: Paramount Pictures, 2017. DVD.

————, dir. *Young Mr. Lincoln*. 1939; Century City, CA: 20th Century Fox, 2006. DVD.

Foucault, Michel. *Discipline and Punish: The Birth of the Prison*. Translated by Alan Sheridan. New York: Vintage, 1979.

Frankenheimer, John, dir. *The Young Savages*. 1961; New York, NY: Kino International, 2014. DVD.

Friedman, Lawrence M. *Crime and Punishment in American History*. New York: Basic Books, 1993.

————. "The Day before Trials Vanished." *Journal of Empirical Legal Studies* 1, no. 3 (2004): 689–703.

————. *History of American Law*. 2nd ed. New York: Simon and Schuster, 1985.

Gaines, Jane, and Neil Lerner. "The Orchestration of Affect." In *The Sounds of Early Cinema*, edited by Richard Abel and Rick R. Altman, 252–70. Bloomington: Indiana University Press, 2000.

Gaines, Jane, and Michael Renov, eds. *Collecting Visible Evidence*. Minneapolis: University of Minnesota Press, 1999.

Galanter, Mark. "The Vanishing Trial: An Examination of Trials and Related Matters in Federal and State Courts." *Journal of Empirical Legal Studies* 1, no. 3 (2004): 459–570.

Gallagher, Tag. *John Ford: The Man and His Films*. Berkeley: University of California Press, 1986.

Geary, Daniel. "Children of *The Lonely Crowd*: David Riesman, the Young Radicals, and the Splitting of Liberalism in the 1960s." *Modern Intellectual History* 10.3 (2013): 603–33.

Gewirtz, Paul. "Victims and Voyeurs: Two Narrative Problems at the Criminal Trial." In *Law's Stories: Narrative and Rhetoric in the Law*. New Haven, CT: Yale University Press, 1996.

Gewirtz, Paul, and Peter Brooks, eds., *Law's Stories: Narrative and Rhetoric in the Law*. New Haven, CT: Yale University Press, 1996.

Gilson, Dave. "Interrogating Errol Morris." *Mother Jones*, May/June 2008. https:// www.motherjones.com/politics/2008/05/interrogating-errol-morris.

Gledhill, Christine. "The Melodramatic Field: An Investigation." In *Home Is Where the Heart Is: Studies in Melodrama and the Woman's Film*, edited by Christine Gledhill, 5–39. London: British Film Institute, 1987.

Gledhill, Christine, and Linda Williams, eds. *Reinventing Film Studies*. London: Arnold, 2000.

Godard, Jean Luc. "The Wrong Man." In *Godard on Godard*, edited and translated by Tom Milne, 48–55. New York: Da Capo Press, 1972.

Gordon, Avery. *Ghostly Matters: Haunting and the Sociological Imagination*. Minneapolis: University of Minnesota Press, 2008.

Gourevitch, Philip, and Errol Morris. *Standard Operating Procedure*. New York: Penguin Press, 2008.

Green, Thomas. *Verdict According to Conscience: Perspectives on the English Criminal Trial Jury 1200–1800*. Chicago: University of Chicago Press, 1985.

Greenfield, Steve, Guy Osborn, and Peter Robson, eds. *Film and the Law*. London: Cavendish Publishing, 2001.

————. *Film and the Law*, 2nd ed. Oxford: Hart Publishing, 2010.

Griffin, Annaliese. "A Profile of Matias Reyes." *New York Daily News*, April 9,

2013. http://www.nydailynews.com/services/central-park-five/profile-matias
-reyes-article-1.1308560.

Griffith, D. W., dir. *The Birth of a Nation*. 1915; Chatsworth, CA: Image Entertainment, 1998. DVD.

Gunning, Tom. *D. W. Griffith and the Origins of American Narrative Film*. Champaign: University of Illinois Press, 1991.

Hale, Grace Elizabeth. *Making Whiteness*. New York: Vintage Books, 1999.

Halliwell, Martin. *American Culture in the 1950s*. Edinburgh: Edinburgh University Press, 2007.

Harris, Thomas. *Courtroom Drama's Finest Hour*. Metuchen, NJ: Scarecrow, 1987.

Hartouni, Valerie. *Visualizing Atrocity: Arendt, Evil, and the Optics of Thoughtlessness*. New York: New York University Press, 2012.

Hayes, Wendell. *Anatomy of a Murder*. screenplay, February 25, 1959. www.dailyscript
.com/scripts/anatomy_of_a_murder.pdf.

Hebard, Andrew. "Disruptive Histories: Towards a Radical Politics of Remembrance." In *Concentrationary Cinema: Aesthetics as Political Resistance in Alain Resnais's "Night and Fog,"* edited by Griselda Pollock and Max Silverman, 87–113. New York: Berghahn Books, 2012.

Hirsch, Foster. *Otto Preminger: The Man Who Would Be King*. New York: Alfred A. Knopf, 2007.

Holcomb, Mark. *"To Kill a Mockingbird." Film Quarterly* 55, no.4 (Summer 2002): 34–40.

Hitchcock, Alfred, dir. *I Confess*. 1953; Burbank, CA: Warner Bros. Pictures, 2006. DVD.

———, dir. *North by Northwest*. 1959.; Burbank, CA: Warner Bros. Pictures, 2010. DVD.

———, dir. *The Paradine Case*. 1947; Beverly Hills, CA: Anchor Bay Entertainment, 1999. DVD.

———, dir. *Rear Window*. 1954; Universal City, CA: Universal Pictures Home Entertainment, 2012. DVD.

———, dir. *The Wrong Man*. 1956; New York: Warner Bros., 2004. DVD.

Holmes, Oliver Wendell, Sr. "The Age of Photography." *Atlantic Monthly*, June 1859. http://www.theatlantic.com/ideastour/technology/holmes-full.html.

Honig, Bonie. *Emergency Politics*. Princeton, NJ: Princeton University Press, 2009.

Ivins, William, Jr. *Prints and Visual Communication*. Cambridge, MA: MIT Press, 1969.

Jacobs, Lea. "The Woman's Picture and the Poetics of Melodrama," *Camera Obscura* 31 (1993): 121–47.

Jameson, Fredric. *The Political Unconscious: Narrative as a Socially Symbolic Act*. Ithaca, NY: Cornell University Press, 1981.

Jancovich, Mark. *Rational Fears: American Horror in the 1950s*. Manchester, UK: Manchester University Press, 1996.

Jarecki, Andrew, dir. *Capturing the Friedmans*. 2003; New York: HBO Pictures, 2004. DVD.

Kahan, Dan, David A. Hoffman, and Donald Braman, "Whose Eyes Are You Going to Believe? *Scott v. Harris* and the Perils of Cognitive Illiberalism." *Harvard Law Review* 122 (2009): 837.

Kahana, Jonathan. "Speech Images: Standard Operating Procedure and the

Staging of Interrogation." *Jump Cut* 52 (2010). http://ejumpcut.org/archive/jc52.2010/sopkKahana/index.html.

Kamir, Orit. "Anatomy of Hollywood's Hero-Lawyer: A Law-and-Film Study of the Western Motifs, Honor-Based Values and Gender Politics Underlying *Anatomy of a Murder*'s Construction of the Lawyer Image." *Studies in Law, Politics and Society* 35 (2005): 35–49.

———. *Framed: Women in Law and Film*. Durham, NC: Duke University Press, 2006.

Kammen, Michael. *American Culture, American Tastes: Social Change in the 20th Century*. New York: Basic Books, 1999.

Kennicott, Phillip. "The War Comes Home: Two Iraq Documentaries Attempt to Engage Us in a Now-Distant Conflict." *Washington Post*, April 2, 2008.

Kessler, Amalia. "The Nineteenth-Century Rejection of a European Transplant and the Rise of a Distinctively American Ideal of Adversarial Adjudication." *Theoretical Inquiries in Law* 10 (2009): 423.

Kleinhans, Chuck. "Notes on Melodrama and the Family under Capitalism." In *Imitations of Life*, edited by Marcia Landy, 197–204. Detroit, MI: Wayne State University Press, 1991.

Klinger, Barbara. *Melodrama and Meaning: History, Culture and the Films of Douglas Sirk*. Bloomington: Indiana University Press, 1994.

Kramer, Stanley, dir. *Judgment at Nuremberg*. 1961; Beverly Hills, CA: Metro-Goldwyn-Mayer Studios, 2004. DVD.

Lacan, Jacques. *The Four Fundamental Concepts of Psycho-Analysis*. New York: Norton, 1998.

Lakoff, Robin Tolmach. *Talking Power*. New York: Basic Books, 1990.

Lang, Fritz, dir. *Beyond a Reasonable Doubt*. 1955; New York, NY: RKO Pictures, 2011. DVD.

———, dir. *Fury*. 1936; Beverly Hills, CA: Metro Goldwyn Mayer, 2005. DVD.

———, dir. *Metropolis*. 1927; Babelsberg, Germany: UFA, 2004. DVD.

Lang, Robert. "Birth of a Nation: History, Ideology, Narrative Form." In *"The Birth of a Nation": D. W. Griffith, Director*, edited by Robert Lang, 3–24. New Brunswick, NJ: Rutgers University Press, 1994.

Langford, Barry. "*American Graffiti*." In *America First: Naming the Nation in US Film*, edited by Mandy Merck, 157–76. London: Routledge, 2007.

———. *Film Genre: Hollywood and Beyond*. Edinburgh: Edinburgh University Press, 2005.

Laster, Kathy. *The Drama of the Courtroom*. With Krista Breckweg and John King. Sydney: Federation Press, 2000.

Ledwon, Lenora. "Melodrama and the Law: Feminizing the Juridical Gaze." *Harvard Women's Law Journal* 21 (Spring 1998): 141–78.

Leff, Leonard J. "The Breening of America." *PMLA* 106.3 (1991): 432–45.

Levi, Ross D. *The Celluloid Courtroom: A History of Legal Cinema*. Westport, CT: Praeger, 2005.

Levinas, Emmanuel. *Ethics and Infinity: Conversations with Philippe Nemo*. Translated by Richard A. Cohen. Pittsburgh: Duquesne University Press, 1985.

Library of Congress. "NAACP: A Century in the Fight for Freedom." Accessed October 25, 2014. http://www.loc.gov/exhibits/naacp/founding-and-early-years.html.

Lippmann, Walter. *Public Opinion*. New York: Harcourt, 1922.

Lumet, Sidney, dir. *12 Angry Men*. 1957; Century City, CA: 20th Century Fox Home Entertainment, 2008. DVD.

———, dir. *The Verdict*. 1982; Century City, CA: 20th Century Fox Home Entertainment, 2002. DVD.

Lykken, David. *Tremor in the Blood: Uses and Abuses of the Lie Detector*. New York: McGraw Hill, 1981.

Lynn, Jonathan, dir. *My Cousin Vinny*. 1992; Century City, CA: 20th Century Fox Home Entertainment, 2009. DVD.

Macaulay, Thomas Babington. *The History of England*. Vol. 4. Leipzig, Ger.: Bernhard Tauchnitz, 1855.

MacNeil, William. *Lex Populi: The Jurisprudence of Popular Culture*. Stanford, CA: Stanford University Press, 2009.

Manchel, Frank. "A War over Justice: An Interview with Marcel Ophuls." *Literature/Film Quarterly* 6, no. 1 (Winter 1978): 26–47.

———. "The Paradoxes of Digital Photography." In *The Photography Reader*, edited by Liz Wells, 240–49. London: Routledge, 2003.

Manovich, Lev. "Database as a Symbolic Form." *Millennium Film Journal* no. 34 (1999). http://www.mfj-online.org/journalPages/MFJ34/Manovich_Database_FrameSet.html.

———. "The Paradoxes of Digital Photography." In *The Photography Reader*, edited by Liz Wells, 240–49. London: Routledge, 2003.

Marquand, Richard dir. *Jagged Edge*. 1985; Culver City, CA: Sony Pictures, 2000. DVD.

Metz, Christian. *The Imaginary Signifier: Psychoanalysis and the Cinema*. Translated by Celia Britton, Annwyl Williams, Ben Brewster, and Alfred Guzzetti. Bloomington: Indiana University Press, 1977.

———. "Photography and Fetish." In *The Photography Reader*, edited by Liz Wells, 138–147. London: Routledge, 2003.

Mezey, Naomi. "The Image Cannot Speak for Itself: Film, Summary Judgment, and Visual Literacy." *Valparaiso University Law Review* 48, no.1 (Fall 2013): 1-39.

Miller, Ylana N. "Creating Unity through History: The Eichmann Trial as Transition." *Journal of Modern Jewish Studies* 1, no. 2 (2002): 131–49.

Mills, C. Wright. *The Power Elite*. New York: Oxford University Press, 1999.

Milner, Iris. "The 'Gray Zone' Revisited: The Concentrationary Universe in Ka. Tzetnik's Literary Testimony." *Jewish Social Studies* 14 (2008): 115.

Mitchell, William. *The Reconfigured Eye: Visual Truth in the Post-Photographic Era*. Cambridge, MA: MIT Press, 1992.

Mitchell, W. J. T. "The Fog of Abu Ghraib." *Harper's Magazine*, May 2008, 81–86.

Mnookin, Jennifer. "The Image of Truth: Photographic Evidence and the Power of Analogy." *Yale Journal of Law and the Humanities* 10, issue 1 (1998): 1–74.

———. "Reproducing a Trial: Evidence and Its Assessment in Paradise Lost." In *Law on the Screen*, edited by Austin Sarat, Lawrence Douglas, and Martha Merrill Umphrey, 153–200. Stanford, CA: Stanford University Press, 2005.

Morris, Errol. *Believing Is Seeing: Observations on the Mysteries of Photography*. New York: Penguin, 2011.

———, dir. *Standard Operating Procedure*. 2008; Culver City, CA: Sony Pictures Home Entertainment, 2008. DVD.

————, dir. *The Thin Blue Line*. 1988; Beverly Hills, CA: Metro-Goldwyn-Mayer Studios, 2005. DVD.

Mulligan, Robert, dir. *To Kill a Mockingbird*. 1962; Universal City, CA: Universal Pictures Home Entertainment, 2012. DVD.

Mulvey, Laura. "Visual Pleasure and Narrative Cinema." *Screen* 16, no. 3 (1975): 6–18.

Musser, Charles. *The Emergence of Cinema: The American Screen to 1907*. Berkeley: University of California Press, 1990.

Muybridge, Eadweard. *Animals in Motion*. London: Chapman and Hall, 1899.

Naremore, James. *More Than Night: Film Noir in Its Contexts*. 2nd ed. Berkeley: University of California Press, 2008.

Nelson, William E. *Americanization of the Common Law: The Impact of Legal Change on Massachusetts Society, 1760–1830*. Cambridge, MA: Harvard University Press, 1975.

Nevins, Francis M. "Reconnoitring Juriscinema's First Golden Age and Lawyers in Film 1928–34." *Vermont Law Review* 28 (2004): 915–55.

Nichols, Bill. *Blurred Boundaries: Questions of Meaning in Contemporary Culture*. Bloomington: Indiana University Press, 1995.

————. "Feelings of Revulsion and the Limits of Academic Discourse." *Jump Cut* 52 (2010). http://ejumpcut.org/archive/jc52.2010/sopNichols/index.html.

————. *Introduction to Documentary*. 2nd ed. Bloomington: Indiana University Press, 2010.

————. "The Question of Evidence, the Power of Rhetoric and Documentary Film." In *Rethinking Documentary: New Perspectives, New Practices*, edited by Thomas Austin and Wilma de Jong, 33–39. Maidenhead, UK: Open University Press/McGraw Hill, 2008.

————. *Representing Reality: Issues and Concepts in Documentary*. Bloomington: Indiana University Press, 1991.

————. "The Voice of Documentary." *Film Quarterly*, vol. 36 no. 3 (Spring 1983): 17–30.

————. "The Voice of Documentary." In *Movies and Methods*, vol. 2, edited by Bill Nichols, 258–73. Berkeley: University of California Press, 1985.

Oksiloff, Assenka. *Picturing the Primitive: Visual Culture, Ethnography, and Early German Cinema*. New York: Palgrave, 2001.

Ophüls, Marcel, *The Memory of Justice*. 1976; Hollywood, CA: Paramount Pictures Corporation, 1976. DVD.

Orvell, Miles. *The Real Thing: Imitation and Authenticity in American Culture, 1880–1940*. Chapel Hill: University of North Carolina Press, 1989.

Papke, David Ray. "Law, Cinema and Ideology: Hollywood Legal Films of the 1950s." *UCLA Law Review* 48 (2001): 1473–93.

Parry, Sir Edward. *The Drama of the Law*. London: Ernst Benn, 1924.

Pizer, Donald. *Realism and Naturalism in Nineteenth-Century American Literature*. Carbondale: Southern Illinois University Press, 1984.

Plantinga, Carl. "'I'll Believe It When I Trust the Source': Documentary Images and Visual Evidence." In *The Documentary Film Book*, edited by Brian Winston, 40–47. London: British Film Institute, 2013.

————. *Rhetoric and Representation in Nonfiction Film*. New York: Cambridge University Press, 1997.

Polanski, Roman, dir. *Death and the Maiden*. 1994; Los Angeles: New Line Home Entertainment, 2003. DVD.

Porter, Elizabeth G. "Taking Images Seriously." *Columbia Law Review* 114 (2014): 1687.

Post, Robert C. "On the Popular Image of the Layer: Reflections in a Dark Glass." *California Law Review* 75 (1987): 379.

Postlewait, Thomas. "The Hieroglyphic Stage: American Theatre and Society, Post-Civil War to 1945." In *The Cambridge History of the American Theatre*, vol. 2, edited by Don B. Wilmeth and Christopher Bisby, 107–95. Cambridge: Cambridge University Press, 1999.

Preminger, Otto, dir. *Anatomy of a Murder*. 1959; Culver City, CA: Sony Pictures Home Entertainment, 2000. DVD.

Public Broadcasting Service. "Q&A with the Filmmakers." Accessed December 14, 2014. http://www.pbs.org/kenburns/centralparkfive/about/filmmaker-q/.

Rafter, Nicole. "American Trial Films: An Overview of Their Development, 1930–2000." In *Law and Film*, edited by Stefan Machura and Peter Robson, 9–25. Oxford: Blackwell, 2001.

———. *Shots in the Mirror: Crime Films and Society*. 2nd ed. Oxford: Oxford University Press, 2006.

Rapping, Elayne. "Television, Melodrama, and the Rise of the Victim's Rights Movement." *New York Law School Law Review* 43, nos. 3 and 4 (1999–2000): 665–90.

Raz, Gal. "Actuality on Banality: Eyal Sivan's *The Specialist* in Context." *Shofar: An Interdisciplinary Journal of Jewish Studies* 24, no. 1 (Fall 2005): 4–21.

Reiner, Rob, dir. *A Few Good Men*. 1992; Culver City, CA: Columbia Pictures, 2007. DVD.

Renov, Michael. "Toward a Poetics of Documentary." In *Theorizing Documentary*, edited by Renov, 12–36. New York: Routledge, 1993.

Rentschler, Carrie. "Witnessing: U.S. Citizenship and the Vicarious Experience of Suffering." *Media Culture and Society* 26 (2004): 296–304.

Ricoeur, Paul. *Memory, History, Forgetting*. Translated by Kathleen Blamey and David Pellauer. Chicago: University of Chicago, 2004.

Riesman, David. *The Lonely Crowd: A Study of the Changing American Character*. 2nd ed. New Haven, CT: Yale University Press, 1961.

Robson, Mark, dir. *Trial*. 1955; Beverly Hills, CA: MGM, 2014. DVD.

Rogin, Michael. *Ronald Reagan, the Movie and Other Episodes in Political Demonology*. Berkeley: University of California Press, 1987.

Rodowick, D. N. "Madness, Authority and Ideology: The Domestic Melodrama of the 1950s." *Velvet Light Trap* 19 (1982): 40–46.

Rosen, Jeffrey. "The Bloods and the Crits." *New Republic* 215, no. 24 (December 9, 1996): 27–42.

Rosenberg, Norman. "Hollywood on Trials: Courts and Films, 1930–1960." *Law and History Review* 12 (1994): 341–67.

———. "Law Noir." In *Legal Reelism: Movies as Legal Texts*, edited by J. Denvir, 280–302. Urbana: University of Illinois Press, 1996.

Rostron, Allen. "Shooting Stories: The Creation of Narrative and Melodrama in Real and Fictional Litigation against the Gun Industry." *UMKC Law Review* 73, no. 4 (Summer 2005): 1047–72.

Rothberg, Michael. *Multidirectional Memory: Remembering the Holocaust in the Age of Decolonization*. Stanford, CA: Stanford University Press, 2009.

Rothberg, Michael, Debarati Sanyal, and Max Silverman. "Editor's Note" in *Noueds de mémoire*. *Yale French Studies*, January 2011, 118–19.

Rubin, Rachel, and Jeffrey Paul Melnick. *Immigration and American Popular Culture: An Introduction*. New York: New York University Press, 2007.

Sanyal, Debarati. "Auschwitz as Allegory in *Night and Fog*." In *Concentrationary Cinema: Aesthetics as Political Resistance in Alain Resnais's "Night and Fog,"* edited by Griselda Pollock and Max Silverman, 152–82. New York: Berghahn Books, 2011.

Sarat, Austin, ed. *Studies in Law, Politics and Society*. Bingley, UK: Emerald Group Publishing, 2009.

Sarat, Austin, and Martha Merrill Umphrey, eds. *Reimagining "To Kill a Mockingbird": Family, Community, and the Possibility of Equal Justice Under Law*. Amherst: University of Massachusetts Press, 2013.

Sarkar, Bhaskar, and Janet Walker, eds. *Documentary Testimonies: Global Archives of Suffering*. New York: Routledge, 2009.

Sassoubre, Ticien M. "The Impulsive Subject and the Realist Lens: Law and Consumer Culture in Fritz Lang's *Fury*." *Southern California Interdisciplinary Law Journal* 20 (2011): 325.

Schatz, Thomas, *Hollywood Genres: Formulas, Filmmaking, and the Studio System*. New York: Random House, 1981.

Schor, Hilary. *Curious Subjects: Women and the Trials of Realism*. Oxford: Oxford University Press, 2013.

Schwartz, Louis-George. *Mechanical Witness: A History of Motion Picture Evidence in U.S. Courts*. New York: Oxford University Press, 2009.

Sekula, Allan. "The Body and the Archive." *October* 39 (1986): 3–64.

Shandler, Jeffrey. *While America Watches: Televising the Holocaust*. Oxford: Oxford University Press, 1999.

Sherwin, Richard. "Imagining Law as Film (Representation without Reference?)" In *Law and the Humanities: An Introduction*, edited by Austin Sarat, Matthew Anderson, and Cathrine O. Frank, 241–68. New York: Cambridge University Press, 2010.

———. "Law Frames: Historical Truth and Narrative Necessity in a Criminal Case." *Stanford Law Review* 47 (1994): 39-83.

———. *When Law Goes Pop: The Vanishing Line between Law and Popular Culture*. Chicago: University of Chicago Press, 2000.

Sherwin, Richard K., Neil Feigenson, and Christina Spiesel. "Law in the Digital Age." *Boston University Journal of Science and Technology Law* 12, no. 2 (2006): 2.

Shklar, Judith N. *The Faces of Injustice*. New Haven, CT: Yale University Press, 1990.

Silbey, Jessica. "Cross-Examining Film." *University of Maryland Law Journal of Race, Relations, Gender and Class* 8 (2008) (symposium issue): 101–30.

———. "Evidence Verité and the Law of Film." *Cardozo Law Review* 31, no. 4 (March 2010): 1257–99.

———. "Filmmaking in the Precinct House and the Genre of Documentary Film." *Columbia Journal of Law & the Arts* 29, no. 2 (2006): 107–80.

———. "Judges as Film Critics: New Approaches to Filmic Evidence." *University of Michigan Journal of Legal Reform* 37, 2 (January 2004): 493–571.

———. "Patterns of Courtroom Justice." In *Law and Film*, edited by Stefan Machura and Peter Robson, 97–116. Oxford: Blackwell, 2001.

———. "Videotaped Confessions and the Genre of Documentary." *Fordham Intellectual Property, Media and Entertainment Law Journal* 16 (2006): 789–807.

Simonett, John E. "The Trial as One of the Performing Arts." *American Bar Association Journal* 62 (1966): 1145–47.

Singer, Ben. *Melodrama and Modernity*. New York: Columbia University Press, 2001.

Sivan, Eyal, dir. *The Specialist: Portrait of a Modern Criminal*. 2013; New York, NY: Kino International, 2002. DVD.

Sklar, Robert. *Movie-Made America: A Cultural History of American Movies*. New York: Vintage Books, 1994.

Smith, Matthew Wilson. "American Valkyries: Richard Wagner, D. W. Griffith and the Birth of Classical Cinema." *Modernism/Modernity* 15, no. 2 (April 2008): 221–42.

Sobchack, Vivian. *Screening Space: The American Science Fiction Film*. 2nd ed. New Brunswick, NJ: Rutgers University Press, 1987.

———. "Toward a Phenomenology of Nonfictional Film Experience." In *Collecting Visible Evidence*, edited by Jane Gaines and Michael Renov, 241–54. Minneapolis: University of Minnesota Press, 1999.

Soderbergh, Steven, dir. *Erin Brockovich*. 2000; Culver City, CA: Columbia TriStar Home Entertainment, 2000. DVD.

Solomon, Alisa. "Who Gets to Be Human on the Evening News?" *PMLA* 121, no. 5 (October 2006): 1585–92.

Sontag, Susan. *Regarding the Pain of Others*. New York: Picador Press, 2003.

Spaulding, Norman W. "Due Process without Judicial Process: Antiadversarialism in American Legal Culture." *Fordham Law Review* 85 (2017): 2249.

———. "The Enclosure of Justice: Courthouse Architecture, Due Process, and the Dead Metaphor of Trial." *Yale Journal of Law and Humanities* 24 (2012): 311–44.

———. "The Historical Consciousness of the Resistant Subject." *U.C. Irvine Law Review* 1 (2011): 677–91.

———. "Impersonating Justice: Lynching, Dueling, and Wildcat Strikes in Nineteenth Century America." In *The Routledge Research Companion to Law and Humanities in the Nineteenth Century*, edited by Nan Goodman and Simon Stern, 163–87. Oxford: Routledge Press, 2017.

———. "The Luxury of the Law: The Codification Movement and the Right to Counsel." *Fordham Law Review* 73 (2004): 983–96.

Staiger, Janet. *Perverse Spectators: The Practices of Film Reception*. New York: New York University Press, 2000.

Stam, Robert. "Reflexivity in Film and Literature: From Don Quixote to Jean-Luc Godard." Ann Arbor, MI: UMI Research Press, 1985.

Sterne, Jonathan. *The Audible Past: Cultural Origins of Sound Reproduction*. Chapel Hill, NC: Duke University Press, 2003.

Streisand, Barbara, dir. *The Prince of Tides*. 1991; Culver City, CA: Columbia Pictures, 2002. DVD.

Stoloff, Benjamin, dir. *By Whose Hand?* Culver City, CA: Columbia Pictures, 1932.

Tagg, John. *The Burden of Representation: Essays on Photographies and Histories*. Minneapolis: University of Minnesota Press: 1993.

Taussig, Michael. *Defacement: Public Secrecy and the Labor of the Negative*. Stanford, CA: Stanford University Press, 1999.

Thurston, Thomas. "Hearsay of the Sun: Photography, Identity, and the Law of Evidence in the 19th Century." Hyptertext Scholarship in American Studies, *American Quarterly* (1998). http://chnm.gmu.edu/aq/photos/index.htm.

Tocqueville, Alexis de. *Democracy in America*. New York: Literary Classics, 2004.

———. *Democracy in America*, vol. 1 New York: Vintage, 1990.

———. *Democracy in America*. Edited by J. P. Mayer. Translated by George Lawrence. New York: Harper Collins, 1988.

Turow, Scott. *Presumed Innocent*. New York: Farrar, Straus, and Giroux, 1987.

Umphrey, Martha Merrill. "Dialogics of Legal Meaning: Spectacular Trials, the Unwritten Law, and Narratives of Criminal Responsibility." *Law and Society Review* 33, no. 2 (1999): 393–424.

———. "Law in Drag: Trials and Legal Performativity." *Columbia Journal of Gender and Law* 21, no. 2 (2011): 114–29.

Vardac, Nicholas. *Stage to Screen: Theatrical Origins of Early Film: David Garrick to D. W. Griffith*. Cambridge, MA: Harvard University Press, 1949.

Variety. January 25, 1956.

Verhoeven, Paul, dir. *Basic Instinct*. 1992; Santa Monica, CA: Lionsgate Entertainment, 2006. DVD. 2007. Blu-ray.

Viterbo, Heidi. "Seeing Torture Anew: A Transnational Reconceptualization of State Torture and Visual Evidence." *Stanford Journal of International Law* 281, issue 50 (2014): 281–317.

Wallace, Amy. "Courthouse Is Clubhouse for the Menendez Watchers." *Los Angeles Times*, June 15, 1994, A33.

Watt, Ian. *The Rise of the Novel: Studies in Defoe, Richardson and Fielding*. Berkeley: University of California Press, 1957.

Weisberg, Robert. "Proclaiming Trials as Narratives: Premises and Pretenses." In *Law's Stories*, edited by Peter Brooks and Paul Gewirtz, 61–83. New Haven, CT: Yale University Press, 1996.

White, Dennis L. "*Beyond a Reasonable Doubt*." In *Film Noir: An Encyclopedic Reference to the American Style*, edited by Alain Silver and Elizabeth Ward, 21–22. Woodstock, NY: Overlook Press, 1992.

Whyte, William H. *The Organisation Man*. New York: Simon and Schuster, 1956.

Wieviorka, Annette. *The Era of the Witness*. Translated by Jared Stark. Ithaca, NY: Cornell University Press, 2006.

Wilder, Billy, dir. *Witness for the Prosecution*. 1957; New York: Kino International, 2014. DVD.

Williams, Linda. "Mirrors without Memories: Truth, History, and the New Cinema." *Film Quarterly* 46, no 3 (1993): 9–21.

———. *Playing the Race Card: Melodramas of Black and White from Uncle Tom to O. J. Simpson*. Princeton, NJ: Princeton University Press, 2002.

Winston, Brian. *Claiming the Real: The Griersonian Documentary and Its Legitimations*. London: British Film Institute, 1995.

———. "The Tradition of the Victim in Griersonian Documentary." In *New Challenges for Documentary*, edited by Alan Rosenthal, 269–87. Berkeley: University of California Press, 1988.

———. "The Tradition of the Victim in Griersonian Documentary." In *New*

Challenges for Documentary, ed. Alan Rosenthal, 269–287. Berkeley: University of California Press, 1990.

Young, Alison. *The Scene of Violence: Cinema, Crime, Affect.* London: Routledge-Cavendish, 2009.

Zaillian, Steven, dir. *A Civil Action.* 1998; Burbank, CA: Touchstone Home Video, 1999. DVD.

Zangrando, Robert. *The NAACP Crusade against Lynching, 1909–1950.* Philadelphia: Temple University Press, 1980.

Zizek, Slavoj. *The Sublime Object of Ideology.* London: Verso, 1989.

Zola, Emile. *The Experimental Novel.* New York: Haskell House, 1964.

Contributors

Carol J. Clover is a professor emerita of film studies, rhetoric and Scandinavian mythology at the University of California, Berkeley.

Barry Langford is a professor of film studies and an associate dean in the graduate school at Royal Holloway, University of London.

Katie Model is a lecturer in film studies at the Ontario College of Art and Design University.

Jennifer Petersen is an associate professor in the Department of Media Studies at the University of Virginia.

Austin Sarat is the associate dean of the faculty, the William Nelson Cromwell Professor of Jurisprudence and Political Science, and professor of Law, Jurisprudence and Social Thought at Amherst College.

Ticien Marie Sassoubre is a lecturer in law at Stanford Law School.

Jessica Silbey is a professor of law and the codirector of the Center for Law, Innovation and Creativity (CLIC) at Northeastern University.

Norman W. Spaulding is the Nelson Bowman Sweitzer and Marie B. Sweitzer Professor of Law and the associate dean for curriculum at Stanford Law School.

Martha Merrill Umphrey is the director of the Center for Humanistic Inquiry and Bertrand H. Snell 1894 Professor in American Government in the Department of Law, Jurisprudence and Social Thought at Amherst College.

Index

Abu Ghraib prisoner abuse: civil suit, 201n67; investigations, 193–94; photographs of victims, 119, 178–79, 181, 182, 183, 185–86, 188–89, 191, 192–95; prosecutions, 192–93. See also *Standard Operating Procedure*

ACLU. *See* American Civil Liberties Union (ACLU)

The Act of Killing, 180, 197n28

Adams, Randall Dale, 5, 15nn22–23, 67n6. See also *The Thin Blue Line*

adversarial system: ambivalence toward, 132; in films, 1, 18–19, 115; narratives, 23; populist critiques, 132; presentation of evidence, 21, 22–24; roots of, 19–20, 22; unresolved issues, 88–89; vigilantism as alternative, 130, 131, 132. *See also* X-not-X narrative structure

African Americans: as actors, 78n167; antimiscegenation laws, 76n126; Central Park Five case, 60–63, 64, 67n6, 78n177, 79n179; Jim Crow and, 52; as judges, 95, 96; and juries, 60, 69n27; lynchings, 60, 122; racist depictions of in media, 52, 53, 56, 57–60, 77–78nn165–68; slavery, 8, 53, 54, 60, 76n131; as witnesses, 60

Agee, James, 32

AIDS. See *Philadelphia*

Algeria, footage of atrocities in, 147, 148, 149, 150

Alito, Samuel, 65–66

alternate trials, 39–40, 60, 62–63, 66, 67n8, 154–55

American Civil Liberties Union (ACLU), 193

Anatomy of a Murder, 32, 33n4, 36n20, 85, 100, 101; Biegler character, 3–4, 8, 82, 86, 91–94; judge character, 92, 94–95; jury perspective, 3–4; trial proceedings, 3–4, 14–15n14, 86, 90–95; visual style, 97–98

Anglo-American trials, 1, 2, 6–7, 11n1, 12n5, 17–20, 24, 32, 33, 34n6, 34n11, 39, 40, 42, 43, 64, 81, 142. *See also* adversarial system; juries; trials; X-not-X narrative structure

anti-Communism, 89, 96. *See also* McCarthy era

anti-Semitism, 154, 156, 160, 170, 171, 173n21

Arendt, Hannah, *Eichmann in Jerusalem*, 137n40, 145, 157, 158, 159, 162–64, 165, 167, 168, 175n55. See also *The Specialist*

Asimow, Michael, 82

attorneys. *See* lawyers, heroic

audiences: of documentary films, 4, 142, 179–80, 194–95; of early films, 68n17; of Eichmann trial, 163; juries as, 2, 20–21; of melodramas, 48. *See also* juries, audiences as

Basic Instinct, 31–32, 38n34; cinematography, 30–31, 175n68; genres, 26; opening and closing scenes, 26–28, 31, 37n25; suspects, 30, 37–38n30; trial structure, 7, 12n5, 28–30, 32, 37n26, 175n68

Bazin, André, 71n51, 170

Ben-Gurion, David, 154, 160, 161, 162–63, 164

Benjamin, Walter, 51, 64, 74n104, 166

Bentham, Jeremy, 161

Beyond a Reasonable Doubt, 8, 9, 85, 90, 99

The Big Sleep, 30

The Birth of a Nation, 15n16, 51–60; audiences, 6, 41, 68n17; blackface actors, 59, 78n167; book as basis, 76n129, 76n131; ending, 77nn165–66; historical "accuracy," 7–8, 49, 52, 54, 55–59, 64; influence, 41; melodrama, 41, 54–56, 59, 77–

78n166; plot, 52–59, 76n141, 77n160, 77n165; realism, 48, 53, 54–60, 78n168; red-tinted shots, 76n140, 77–78n166; similarities to *The Central Park Five*, 61, 62, 63, 64; trials, 4, 7–8, 40–41, 51–52, 54, 56, 57, 58, 59, 60, 63. *See also* African Americans: racist depictions of in media; Griffith, D. W.

Black, Angela, 63

blackface. See *The Birth of a Nation*: blackface actors

Body of Evidence, 32

Brecht, Bertolt, 100

Brooks, Peter, 33n5, 45, 71nn57–58, 72n66, 72n70, 129, 166–67

Burstyn v. Wilson, 90

Butler, Judith, 177, 191

By Whose Hand?, 25, 31, 36n20

Cambodia. *See* Khmer Rouge

cameras. *See* films; photography

Capital Cities Broadcasting Corporation, 161

Capra, Frank, 92

Cayrol, Jean, 148–49

Celan, Paul, 140–41

The Central Park Five, 39, 60–63, 64, 67n6, 79nn179–80

Central Park Five case, 60–63, 67n6, 78–79nn177–80, 79n183

Certeau, Michel de, 120

Chase, Anthony, 131

Chronicle of a Summer (*Chronique d'été*), 146, 161

cinema verité, 146, 161

A Civil Action, 64

Civil War, 43, 44, 52, 54, 55–56, 58

close-ups, 165–66, 167–68, 175n68

closing arguments, 24–25, 28

Clover, Carol J., 1, 3, 6–7, 12n5, 14n12, 15n15, 17–38, 40, 41, 49, 52, 54, 64, 74n92, 74n96, 79n184, 81–82, 84, 107n4, 126, 131, 136n24, 143, 144, 175n68, 177, 181, 195. *See also* trial structure in films; X-not-X narrative structure

Cold War, 8, 86, 89, 98

Communism. *See* anti-Communism

courtroom-drama-producing cultures, 6, 18

courtroom dramas. *See* trial films

Court TV, 25, 35n14, 36n21

court watchers, 25, 36–37n22

Cowie, Elizabeth, 143, 169

cross-examination, 21, 24

Crowther, Bosley, 100

Curtis, Edward, 44

Dargis, Manohla, 182

de Antonio, Emile, 142

defense attorneys. *See* adversarial system; lawyers, heroic

Delage, Christian, 151–52, 153, 155, 173–74n31

denial testimony: in documentaries, 140; in Eichmann trial, 169–70; by Nazis, 10, 140–151, 164–70, 176n75; in Nuremberg trials, 140, 141, 144, 146–47, 148–49, 151, 164

Denny, Reginald, 23

De-Nur, Yehiel, 137n40

Derrida, Jacques, 141, 146, 153–54, 156–57, 169, 171n1

Dershowitz, Alan M., 35n14, 35n17, 47

detective films, 26, 32, 34n10, 142, 179

detective novels, 24, 32, 35–36n19

Dickens, Charles, 46, 71n53, 75n112; *Oliver Twist*, 45

Dirty Harry, 104, 130, 131

disruptions and disorder: in *The Birth of a Nation*, 56; epistemological remainders, 116, 120–21; by jury members, 111–13, 133n6; melodrama and, 114–15, 128–30; in non-trial films, 128–29; in *Philadelphia*, 124–25, 126–27, 129, 137n36; in real trials, 113–14, 133n6, 134–35n10, 137n40; in trial films, 114–16, 119–20, 122, 126, 128, 129–30, 132; in *12 Angry Men*, 104, 120–21; in *The Verdict*, 116–19, 122, 130, 137n41; in *The Wrong Man*, 111–13, 115, 122; X-not-X structure and, 114–16, 118–19, 123, 125, 127; in *Young Mr. Lincoln*, 119, 122–24, 130, 137n41

Dixon, Thomas, *The Clansman*, 76n129, 76n131

documentary films: alternate trials, 39, 154–55; audience expectations, 179, 194–95; audiences as juries, 4, 142, 179–80, 194–95; critiques, 143; denial testimony, 140; expository, 180, 185, 198n34; haunting, 140, 141, 144–45, 170; identification with victim or perpetrator, 143–44, 184–85; interviews, 143–44, 155–57, 180; maps, 168–69; melodrama, 60–64; observational, 180, 185, 186, 198n34, 200n63; photography as evidence, 178–79, 181, 185–86, 189–91, 194–95, 198n34; poetic, 180, 200n55; reality and truth in, 4, 15n18, 158–59, 169, 180, 189–90; reflexive, 4–5, 195n4; scholarship on law and, 154–55; temporality and ontology of testimony, 141, 142–43; trial structure, 180; on war crimes, 141–44. See also *The Memory of Justice*; *The Specialist*; *Standard Operating Procedure*

Douglas, Lawrence, 154

due process, 90, 95, 100–101, 103, 114

Dwyer, Jim, 61, 62

Eastwood, Clint. See *Dirty Harry*

Eichmann, Adolf, 145, 157–58, 165–68

Eichmann trial: audiences, 163; courtroom design, 159, 169; denial testimony, 169–70; differences from Nuremberg trials, 160, 164; filming, 157, 158–60, 161–62, 163, 164–65, 166–67, 168–70; glass box for defendant, 159, 165, 168, 169; Holocaust narrative, 145–46, 160–61, 173n21; judges, 163, 169–70; particular and general in, 154; performative nature, 161–63, 164; plea, 168; prosecutor, 154, 159, 162, 163, 164; as show trial, 161, 162; testimony, 137n40, 145–46, 154, 158, 161, 164–65; witness selection, 163. See also Arendt, Hannah; *The Specialist*

Eisenhower, Dwight, 86, 89; Eisenhower era, 83–84, 94, 97, 101, 102, 106, 107

Eisenstein, Sergei, 51, 71n51, 71n53, 73n87, 75n112, 75n116, 166

Elfman, Danny, 182, 186

Elsaesser, Thomas, 46, 48, 72n70, 72–73n73

England, Lynndie, 178, 183, 184, 194

English justice system. See Anglo-American trials

Enoch Arden, 75n112

epistemological remainders, 116, 120–21, 132

epistemology: disruptions and, 114–15, 118; in documentaries, 4; of melodrama, 45–49; of trial structure in films, 39, 40

epistephilia, 2, 14n12, 143, 178

Epstein, Jean, 166

Erin Brockovich, 47

Eszterhas, Joe, 26, 31

Europe: Continental legal systems, 17, 18, 33–34n6, 38n36; literary realism, 43, 44–46; medieval trials, 19, 22, 33–34n6

evidence. See visual evidence

expert witnesses, 29

eyewitnesses, 176n75. See also witnesses

fairness, 5–6, 40, 49, 118

Fallon, Kris, 188

fantasy genre, 87–88

fascism, 168, 170. See also Nazis

Favreliere, Noel, 147, 150

Felman, Shoshana, 155, 160, 161, 163, 173n23, 176n75

Fenton, Roger, 44

Ferguson, Robert A., 43, 68n15, 70nn32–33

A Few Good Men, 12n6, 32, 114, 122, 137n34, 137n41

fiction: audiences, 41–42; detective novels, 24, 32, 35–36n19; nineteenth-century, 40–42, 43, 45, 71n51, 71–72n63; realism, 41–42, 43, 44–46, 68–69n22, 71n51, 71–72n63; *Uncle Tom's Cabin*, 59

Fiedler, Leslie, 71–72n63

Fifteenth Amendment, 52, 54

film criticism, 74n92, 81–82, 87–88

filmic denial testimony. See denial testimony

film metaphors in trials, 35n14

film noir, 26, 32, 97, 98, 99, 109n45

films: action in, 77n163; chase scenes, 66; early, 50, 75n111; as evidence, 37n27, 51–52, 151, 155, 156, 191, 192, 194; indexicality, 49–50, 141, 153; omniscient and omnipresent camera, 44–45, 50, 51, 74n104; science fiction, 98–99. See also audiences; documentary films; trial films

First Amendment, 90

Fisher, George, 60, 69n27

The Fog of War, 180, 183

Fonda, Henry, 105, 111. See also *12 Angry Men*; *Young Mr. Lincoln*

Ford, Glenn, 95–96. See also *Trial*

Ford, John: *The Man Who Shot Liberty Valance*, 94, 109n38; Nuremburg trial filming, 151. See also *Young Mr. Lincoln*

Foucault, Michel, 17, 32–33, 33n1, 108n28, 161, 200n52

Fourteenth Amendment, 52, 54

Fourth Amendment, 65

France: Algerian occupation, 147, 148, 149, 150; Nazi collaborators, 156; Revolution, 129; theater, 46

Frankenheimer, John, 85, 100, 101. See also *The Young Savages*

Frederick, Ivan, 193

French Revolution, 129

Freud, Sigmund, 31, 171n1, 176n75

Fury, 18, 114, 122, 137n37, 138n51

Gaines, Jane, 4
Garbo, Greta, 166
Gardner, Alexander, 44
genocide. *See* Holocaust; war crimes
genres: as socially symbolic acts, 86, 87; trial films as, 81–82
genre theory, 87–88
Germany. *See* Nazis; Nuremberg trials
Godard, Jean-Luc, 113, 170–71
Göring, Hermann, 146, 152–53
Gordon, Avery, 171n1
Graner, Charles, 178, 193, 195n1
Griffith, D. W., 40–41, 47, 49, 50–52, 68nn17–18, 75n110, 75n112, 75nn116–17. See also *The Birth of a Nation*

Harlan, Viet, *Le Juif Suss*, 156
Harmon, Sabrina, 183, 185, 186, 198n33
Harris, David, 5, 15n22
haunting: in documentaries, 140, 141, 144–45, 170; meanings, 171n1; in *Memory of Justice*, 144–45, 146, 150–51, 164; by Nuremberg trials, 140; in *The Specialist*, 145, 164
Hausner, Gideon, 154, 159, 162, 163, 164
Hebard, Andrew, 153
Herbert, Anthony, 148
heroes, 3, 4, 8–9, 12n3, 46, 47, 82–107, 116, 132
Hickman v. Taylor, 133n7
Himmler, Heinrich, 167
Hirsch, Foster, 97
Hitchcock, Alfred: *North by Northwest*, 12n6; *The Paradine Case*, 31–32; *Psycho*, 101; *Rear Window*, 14n12; *Vertigo*, 92; *The Wrong Man*, 111–13, 115, 122, 130, 135–36n21
Hoberman, J., 182
Holcomb, Mark, 105, 106
Hollywood blacklist, 89–90
Holmes, Oliver Wendell, Sr., 44
Holocaust: camp liberation films, 156, 173n21; documentaries on, 146, 147, 148–49; legal categories, 154; performative nature, 167; specificity, 154; survivor testimony, 145–46, 148, 160, 161, 164–65. See also Eichmann trial; *The Memory of Justice*; Nuremberg trials
homophobia. See *Philadelphia*
House Un-American Activities Committee (HUAC), 89–90
Hurwitz, Leo, 158, 159, 161–62, 163, 164, 165, 166. *See also* Eichmann trial

ideologemes, 87–88
Iraq war, 182. *See also* Abu Ghraib prisoner abuse
Israel. *See* Eichmann trial; Mossad
Ivins, William, Jr., 43–44, 70n42

Jackson, Robert, 151, 152–53
Jagged Edge, 31, 38n31, 38n34
Jameson, Fredric, 86, 87–88
Jim Crow, 52
Jordan, Steven, 193
Judgment at Nuremberg, 12n6, 14n14, 33n4, 82, 106, 147
Le Juif Suss, 156
juries: disruptions by members, 111–13, 133n6; historical origins, 19; lie detection by, 42–43, 44, 60, 69n27, 69–70n30; in nineteenth century, 42; not seen in trial films, 34n9; thought processes, 24; Tocqueville on, 2, 13–14n10, 20, 131–32; as trial audiences, 2, 20–21; in trial films, 5–6, 20–21; verdicts, 88, 89; violations of legal procedure, 120–21, 136n31. *See also* trials; *12 Angry Men*
juries, audiences as: of *Anatomy of a Murder*, 3–4; of *Basic Instinct*, 37n25; of documentaries, 4, 142, 179–80, 194–95; effects of montage, 51; of fiction, 41–42; juries not shown in films, 34n9; pleasures of watching, 3, 6, 11; of *Standard Operating Procedure*, 194–95; truth assessed by, 64–65; unresolved endings of trial films, 25; X-not-X structure and, 142, 179
justice: in films, 39–40, 96–97, 103, 105–7, 123–24; threats to, 5–6; vigilante, 130, 131, 132

Kahana, Jonathan, 182, 188, 197n24
Kamir, Orit, 93
Karpinski, Janis, 193
Keitel, Wilhelm, 146
Kennedy, John F., 101
Khmer Rouge, 144, 153, 155
KKK. *See* Ku Klux Klan (KKK)
Klarsfeld, Serge, 156
Koch, Ed, 61, 62
Kracauer, Siegfried, 168
Kramer, Stanley, *Judgment at Nuremberg*, 12n6, 82, 106, 147
Kramer vs. Kramer, 39
Ku Klux Klan (KKK), 49, 53, 56, 57, 58–59,

60, 77n152, 78n166. See also *The Birth of a Nation*

Lakoff, Robin Tolmach, 17
Lancaster, Burt, 100, 106. See also *The Young Savages*
Lang, Fritz, 99, 128. See also *Beyond a Reasonable Doubt*
Langford, Barry, 5, 8–9, 81–107, 107n10, 108n24, 196n16
Lanzmann, Claude, 146, 176n75
Laster, Kathy, 106
Latinos. *See* Central Park Five case
law films. *See* trial films
lawyers, heroic, 82, 85, 86, 91, 93–94, 99–103, 104–5. *See also* adversarial system; trials
Lee, Harper, 105. See also *To Kill a Mockingbird*
Levi, Ross D., 105
Levinas, Emmanuel, 168
lie detection: by camera, 28, 30–31, 37n27, 175n68; by juries, 42–43, 44, 60, 69n27, 69–70n30; polygraph, 24, 35n18; scientific, 23
lies, 23–24, 31. *See also* truth
Lincoln, Abraham, 54, 56, 57. See also *Young Mr. Lincoln*
Lippmann, Walter, 49
literature. *See* fiction
London, Lionel, 101
Lord, Arthur, 147, 150
Lumet, Sidney, 101. See also *12 Angry Men*; *The Verdict*
lynchings, 52, 58, 60, 61, 96, 105, 122, 124, 137n34, 137n37, 184

Macaulay, Thomas Babington, 22
Mann, Anthony, 92
Manovich, Lev, 79n187, 188
The Man Who Shot Liberty Valance, 94, 109n38
masculinity, 93–94
McCarthy era, 8, 85, 89, 94–95
McCray, Antron, 60–63
medieval trial procedures, 19, 22, 33–34n6
Meili, Trisha, 60–61, 79n179
melodrama: audiences, 48; in *The Birth of a Nation*, 41, 54–56, 59, 77–78n166; chase scenes, 66; conventions, 46; defining, 72nn65–66; disruptions and, 114–15, 128–30; in documentaries, 60–64; epistemology, 45–49; identification

with victim, 48; literary, 41; moral binary of good and evil, 46, 47, 48–49, 59, 63–64, 73n82, 128–29; in non-trial films, 47; origins, 129; realism and, 41, 45–49; resistance to law and, 129; as response to modernity, 46, 72n70, 129; social problems in, 48–49; in theater, 46–47; in trial films, 40, 49, 114–15, 128; in trials, 47
The Memory of Justice: Algeria and Vietnam footage, 147–48, 150–51, 155; cinematic techniques, 150; denial testimony, 146–47, 148–49, 151; films within film, 156, 157; haunting, 144–45, 146, 150–51, 164; interviews, 147, 148, 149–50, 155–57; *Night and Fog* references, 149–50, 151; Nuremberg trial footage, 146–47, 148, 149, 151, 152–53, 155, 156, 157; opening montage, 148–49, 151
Menuhin, Yehudi, 147, 149–50
Metropolis, 128–29, 138n45
Metz, Christian, 49, 67n12, 70n44, 74n97, 74n100, 165, 172n16
Miller, Ylana N., 163, 175n55
Mills, C. Wright, 84
Mnookin, Jennifer, 154, 162, 172n17, 199n47
Model, Katie, 9–10, 60, 140–71, 184
modernity, melodrama as response to, 46, 72n70, 129
Mograbi, Avi, 142
montage: audience reactions, 51; in Dickens, 71n53; in documentaries, 60, 61, 62; Eisenstein on, 51, 71n53, 75n116; Godard on, 170–71; Griffith's use of, 51, 58, 59
Montage Interdit (Forbidden Montage), 170–71
Moore, Michael, 142
Morin, Edgar, 146, 161
Morris, Errol, 142. See also *Standard Operating Procedure*; *The Thin Blue Line*
Mossad, 157–58
Mulligan, Robert. See *To Kill a Mockingbird*
Mutual v. Ohio, 90
Muybridge, Eadweard, 43, 50

NAACP (National Association for the Advancement of Colored People), 52
The Naked Spur, 92
narrative structure. *See* X-not-X narrative structure

Nazis: denial testimony, 10, 140–151, 164–70, 176n75; performances, 167–68; self-deception, 167–68. *See also* Eichmann, Adolf; Holocaust; Nuremberg trials
Nevins, Francis M., 82–83
New Deal, 85–86
Newman, Paul. See *The Verdict*
new media, 170
Nichols, Bill, 4–5, 143, 154, 179, 182, 188, 190
Night and Fog, 147, 148–50, 151, 153, 167, 173n28
novels. *See* fiction
Nuremberg: The Nazis Facing Their Crimes, 151–52
Nuremberg trials: courtroom design, 155; criminal charges, 154, 173n21; denial testimony, 140, 141, 144, 146–47, 148–49, 151, 164; differences from Eichmann trial, 160, 164; evidence, 160; filming of, 146–47, 148, 151–53, 155, 156, 157; film used as evidence, 151, 155, 156; haunting, 140; *Judgment at Nuremberg*, 82, 106, 147; newsreels, 140, 151; pleas, 146–47, 148, 151; prosecutors, 148, 149, 154; testimony, 146, 148. See also *The Memory of Justice*

opening statements, 21, 27
Ophüls, Marcel, 10, 141–42, 143, 144, 146, 148–51, 153, 155–57, 158, 165, 172n19, 174n31. See also *The Memory of Justice*
Ophüls, Regine, 157
Oppenheimer, Joshua, 142
outbursts. *See* disruptions and disorder

Pack, Brent, 183, 189, 191
Panh, Rithy, *S21*, 155
Papke, David Ray, 82, 89
Pappas, Thomas, 193
The Paradine Case, 31–32
perpetrators: interviews of, 62–63; testimony, 158; of war crimes, 142–44
Perry Mason, 25, 35–36n19
Petersen, Jennifer, 10–11, 60, 119, 142, 177–95
Philadelphia, 9, 32, 39, 124–27, 128–29, 137n36, 138n51
photography: compared to films, 49; digital, 79n187; as evidence in documentaries, 178–79, 181, 185–86, 189–91, 194–95, 198n34; as evidence in trials, 43–44, 191–93, 194, 195, 199n47, 201n75; of historical events, 51; indexicality, 4, 49, 65, 70n44, 185; lack of context, 194;

in nineteenth century, 43–44, 191–92, 199n47; realism, 43–45, 49, 50–51, 70n42, 191–92; staged, 44. *See also* Abu Ghraib prisoner abuse
Plessy v. Ferguson, 52
Plumhoff v. Rickard, 65–66
podcasts, 66
police, dashboard cameras, 65–66, 200n53
polygraph, 24, 35n18
popular culture. *See* fiction; films; television; trial films
populists, 132
power: address modes and, 169–70; photography and, 189–90
Preminger, Otto. See *Anatomy of a Murder*
The Prince of Tides, 128–29, 138n45
prosecutors. *See* adversarial system; trials
Psycho, 101
publicity, 161, 163

racial segregation, 52. See also *The Birth of a Nation*
Rafter, Nicole, 81, 82, 94, 97, 98
Raz, Gal, 164
realism: in *The Birth of a Nation*, 48, 53, 54–60, 78n168; cinematic, 41, 44–45, 49–51, 58–60, 67n12, 71n52, 75n117, 77n163; cultural influence, 42; legal, 41; literary, 41–42, 43, 44–46, 68–69n22, 71n51, 71–72n63; philosophical, 68–69nn22–23; photographic, 43–45, 49, 50–51, 70n42, 191–92; relationship to melodrama, 41, 45–49
Rear Window, 14n12
Reconstruction, 52, 53, 54, 56–59, 60. See also *The Birth of a Nation*
Red Scare, 89
remainders. *See* epistemological remainders
Renov, Michael, 4
resistance: to law, 129, 130, 131, 132; to trial structure, 123–24, 125; to X-not-X structure, 116, 120–21
Resnais, Alain, *Night and Fog*, 147, 148–50, 151, 167, 173n28
Reyes, Matias, 61, 62, 79n178
Richardson, Kevin, 60–63
Ricœur, Paul, 140, 156–57
Riesman, David, 84
Riis, Jacob, 44
Robson, Mark. See *Trial*
romance genre, 87–88
Rosen, Jeffrey, 66
Rosenberg, Alfred, 146

Rosenberg, Julius and Ethel, 89
Rosenberg, Norman, 33n5, 97
Rothberg, Michael, 146
Rouch, Jean, 146, 161
Rumsfeld, Donald, 193

S21, 155
Salaam, Yusef, 60–63
salvage ethnography, 190, 200n53
Sanchez, Ricardo, 193
Santana, Raymond, Jr., 60–63
Santana, Raymond, Sr., 62, 63, 79n179
Sarat, Austin, 1–11, 144, 172n17
Sassoubre, Ticien Marie, 4, 7–8, 39–66, 129,
    137n34, 138n51, 172n13, 183
Schroeder, Barbet, 142
science fiction films, 98–99
scopophilia, 2, 14nn11–12, 200n56
Scott v. Harris, 65, 200n60
Scott v. Sandford, 52, 76n126
sensationalism, 45, 77n163
Serial, 66
Servatius, Robert, 161
Shandler, Jeffrey, 146, 161, 162, 163, 166
Sherwin, Richard, 192
Shoah, 146, 176n75
Silbey, Jessica, 1–11, 15n18, 85, 154, 192
Simonett, John E., 25
Simpson, O. J., 22, 25, 66
Sivan, Eyal, 142, 170–71, 172n19. See also
    The Specialist
slavery, 54, 60, 76n131. See also *The Birth of
    a Nation*
Sobchack, Vivian, 16n28, 98
Sontag, Susan, 181, 184
The Sorrow and the Pity, 149, 151, 156
Spaulding, Norman W., 5, 9, 56, 104, 111–32,
    134n8, 138n56, 183, 197
The Specialist: cinematic techniques, 145,
    158–60, 164, 165, 167–69; focus on Eich-
    mann, 158, 164–66, 168; haunting, 145,
    164; "historical vertigo," 164; opening
    credits, 159–60; trial footage, 157, 158–
    60, 164–65, 168–70. See also Eichmann
    trial
spectacle lynching, 60
Speer, Albert, 152, 153, 156–57
Staiger, Janet, 74n92, 142, 179
Standard Operating Procedure: audience
    as jury, 194–95; cinematic techniques,
    186; costs, 187; critical reception, 177–78,
    180–82, 184, 185, 188, 191, 195n1, 197n24;
    failure, 179, 182; focus on characters,

183–85; interviews, 180, 183–86, 197n25;
    questions on photographic evidence,
    178–79, 180, 181, 185–86, 188–89, 190–
    91, 194–95; reenactments, 182, 183, 184,
    185, 186–88; score, 182, 186; structure,
    183, 188; trial form in, 177. See also Abu
    Ghraib prisoner abuse
state crimes. See war crimes
Stewart, James, 82, 91–93, 94. See also
    Anatomy of a Murder
Stewart, Potter, 67n11
Streisand, Barbara. See *The Prince of Tides*
Sumner, Charles, 54
Supreme Court: *Burstyn v. Wilson*, 90;
    Hickman v. Taylor, 133n7; *Mutual v.
    Ohio*, 90; *Paramount* decision, 90;
    Plumhoff v. Rickard, 65–66; *Scott v.
    Harris*, 65, 200n60; *Scott v. Sandford*, 52,
    76n126; Warren Court, 82–83, 85
surveillance, 161, 162, 189, 190
Syberberg, Hans-Jurgen, 142

Tagg, John, 189, 190, 191, 200n52
Taney, Roger, 52, 76n126
Taylor, Telford, 148, 149
television: Court TV, 25, 35n14, 36n21; trial
    dramas, 25, 35–36n19. See also trial films;
    video
testimony: in documentary films, 140, 141,
    142–43; haunted, 140, 141; of perpetra-
    tors, 158; of witnesses, 23–24, 42, 140–
    41, 145–46, 153–54, 156–57. See also denial
    testimony
theater: films based on plays, 40–41; Lin-
    coln's assassination, 56; melodrama, 46–
    47; nineteenth-century, 40–41; trials as
    dramas, 12n3
The Thin Blue Line: alternate trial, 5, 15n22,
    39; double narrative, 15n23; reenact-
    ments, 5, 183, 186, 187; trial structure, 5,
    180; verdict overturned after release,
    15n23, 25, 67n6, 154
Thirteenth Amendment, 60
thrillers, 26, 27, 31, 32, 34n10, 38n34
Tocqueville, Alexis de, 2, 13–14n10, 20, 25,
    34n7, 79n184, 81, 131–32
To Kill a Mockingbird, 8, 9, 12n6, 14n14, 18,
    82, 88, 90, 94, 96–97, 103, 104–6
torture. See Abu Ghraib prisoner abuse;
    war crimes
Tracy, Spencer. See *Judgment at Nuremberg*
transparency, 166–67
Trial, 85, 90, 95–97, 98

trial documentaries. *See* documentary films
trial films: based on real cases, 25–26,
37n23, 37n26; constitutive elements,
2–6; differences from real life, 2; double
voicedness, 5, 6; endings, 25, 31, 36n20,
88; as genre, 81–82; juror orientation,
20–21; of 1980s, 83; top-ten lists, 14n14.
See also documentary films; *individual
titles*
trial films of 1950s and 1960s: ambivalent
view of law, 85, 89–90, 106–7; as heroic
era, 82–85, 99–100, 103; heroic lawyers,
82, 85, 86, 91, 93–94, 99–103, 104–5; op-
timism, 82–83; social and political context, 82–86, 89–90, 101; visual styles,
97–98, 99, 101, 102. See also *Anatomy
of a Murder*; *12 Angry Men*; *The Young
Savages*
trials: artworks and, 176n75; convictions
of innocent, 112; declining number of,
13n8, 133–34n8; filmed, 141, 143, 145–46,
154–55, 161; film metaphors, 35n14; as
performances, 2, 12n3, 25, 161–63, 164;
power of judges, 130–31; public interest
in, 1–2, 17, 25, 36–37n22; similarities to
films, 18–19, 35–36n19, 179–80; televised,
25, 35n14, 36n21; verdicts, 25, 88, 89. *See
also* adversarial system; disruptions and
disorder; juries
trial structure: closing arguments, 24–25,
28; discovery procedures, 25, 113, 133n7;
examination phase, 21–24, 28–30; generativity, 1, 3, 18, 35n17, 81; opening
statements, 21, 27; in popular culture,
18–20, 32–33; resistance to, 123–24, 125.
See also adversarial system
trial structure in films, 11; alternate trials,
39–40, 60, 62–63, 67n8; in *Basic Instinct*,
12n5, 28–30, 32; in documentaries, 180;
endings, 25; epistemology, 39, 40; fairness, 40; narrative substructures, 19, 27,
40, 42; in non-trial films, 12n5, 26, 32,
40, 142; pervasiveness, 1, 18–19, 32; social questions, 39; in *Thin Blue Line*, 5,
180; in *12 Angry Men*, 34n9, 121. *See also*
adversarial system; X-not-X narrative
structure
truth: audience assessments, 64–65; in
documentaries, 60–63, 64, 162; in films,
39–40, 64–65; in melodrama, 46; of
photographs, 43–44; in trials, 22–23, 42,
88–89, 162; in X-not-X structure, 23–24,
42–43. *See also* lies; realism
Turow, Scott, 21

12 Angry Men, 18, 136n31; didacticism, 5, 88,
103–4; disorder, 104, 114; French film,
34n9; heroism, 9, 82, 103, 104; jurors,
5, 88; trial structure, 8, 14–15n14, 34n9,
36n20, 121; unresolved issues, 88; violations of legal procedure, 90, 104, 120–21

Umphrey, Martha Merrill, 1–11, 142–43,
144, 172n17
uncanniness, 89, 140, 143, 144, 145. *See also*
haunting
Uncle Tom's Cabin, 59
US Army. *See* Abu Ghraib prisoner abuse
US Army Signal Corps, 151

Vaillant-Couturier, Marie-Claude, 148, 150
The Verdict, 9, 33n4, 63–64, 91, 97, 114, 116–
19, 122, 130, 137n36, 137n41, 138n53
Verhoeven, Paul. See *Basic Instinct*
Vertigo, 92
victim impact statements, 172n13
victims: identification with, 48, 143–44,
184–85; interviews, 143
video: dashboard cameras, 65–66, 200n53;
of Eichmann trial, 157, 158–60, 161–
62, 163, 164–65, 166–67, 168–70. *See also*
television; visual evidence
Vietnam War, 10, 145, 147–48, 150, 151, 155,
157, 158
vigilantism, 130, 131, 132
violence: lynchings, 60, 122; vigilantism,
130, 131, 132
visual evidence: collection, 22; dashcam
video, 65–66, 200n53; in documentary
films, 178–79, 185–86, 188–91, 198n34;
films as, 37n27, 51–52, 151, 155, 156, 191,
192, 194; indexicality, 4; interviews, 62–
63; presentation in trials, 21, 22–24;
rules of, 21, 22, 42; truthfulness, 62–63.
See also photography
visual literacy, 66
Viterbo, Heidi, 194, 201n75
voting rights, 60

war crimes, 141–44. *See also* Eichmann
trial; Holocaust; Nuremberg trials
Warren Court, 82–83, 85
Watt, Ian, 32–33, 41–42, 68–69nn22–23,
70n34
Way Down East, 47
websites, *Montage Interdit* (*Forbidden
Montage*), 170–71
westerns, 93–94
West Side Story, 100

White, Dennis L., 99
white supremacy, 56, 59, 76n129, 96. See also *The Birth of a Nation*; Ku Klux Klan (KKK)
Whyte, William H., 84
Wiesel, Elie, 145, 166
Wieviorka, Annette, 145
Wilder, Craig Steven, 61, 62
Williams, Linda, 47, 59, 66, 73n82, 77n163, 79n179
Wilson, Woodrow, 52, 57, 77n152
Winston, Brian, 143, 190
Wise, Kharey, 60–63
witnesses: African Americans as, 60; disruptions by, 137n40; expert, 29; eye-, 176n75. *See also* testimony
The Wrong Man, 111–13, 115, 122, 130, 135–36n21

X-not-X narrative structure, 9; alternate trials, 63; in *Anatomy of a Murder*, 4; audiences, 142, 179–80; disruptions and disorder, 114–16, 118–19, 123, 125, 127; examination phase and, 24, 115, 142; multiple defense narratives, 23; in non-trial films, 4, 32, 142; resistance to, 116, 120–21; truth in, 23–24, 42–43; in *12 Angry Men*, 121; in "whodunit" films, 25, 135n16. *See also* adversarial system; trial structure

Young Mr. Lincoln: disruptions, 119, 122–24, 130, 137n41; idealism, 83, 106, 123, 137n35; trial proceedings, 86, 114
The Young Savages, 9, 85, 86, 88, 90, 100–103

Zola, Emile, 43, 45